DATE DUE

DEMCO 38-296

U.S. CONSUMER
INTEREST GROUPS

**Greenwood Reference Volumes on
American Public Policy Formation**

These Reference Books deal with the development of U.S. policy in various "single-issue" areas. Most policy areas are to be represented by three types of sourcebooks: (1) Institutional Profiles of Leading Organizations, (2) Collection of Documents and Policy Profiles, and (3) Bibliography.

Public Interest Law Groups: Institutional Profiles
Karen O'Connor and Lee Epstein

U.S. National Security Policy and Strategy: Documents and Policy Proposals
Sam C. Sarkesian with Robert A. Vitas

U.S. National Security Policy Groups: Institutional Profiles
Cynthia Watson

U.S. Agricultural Groups: Institutional Profiles
William P. Browne and Allan J. Cigler, editors

Military and Strategic Policy: An Annotated Bibliography
Benjamin R. Beede, compiler

U.S. Energy and Environmental Interest Groups: Institutional Profiles
Lettie McSpadden Wenner

Contemporary U.S. Foreign Policy: Documents and Commentary
Elmer Plischke

U.S. Aging Policy Interest Groups: Institutional Profiles
David D. Van Tassel and Jimmy Meyer, editors

U.S. Criminal Justice Interest Groups: Institutional Profiles
Michael A. Hallett and Dennis J. Palumbo

U.S. Educational Policy Interest Groups: Institutional Profiles
Gregory S. Butler and James D. Slack

U.S. Religious Interest Groups: Institutional Profiles
Paul J. Weber and W. Landis Jones

U.S. Health Policy Groups: Institutional Profiles
Craig Ramsay, editor

U.S. CONSUMER INTEREST GROUPS

/ / /

Institutional Profiles

Loree Bykerk and Ardith Maney

GREENWOOD PRESS
WESTPORT, CONNECTICUT • LONDON

Library of Congress Cataloging-in-Publication Data

Bykerk, Loree Gerdes.
U.S. consumer interest groups : institutional profiles / Loree
Bykerk and Ardith Maney.
p. cm.
Includes bibliographical references and index.
ISBN 0–313–26429–5 (alk. paper)
1. Consumer protection—United States—Societies, etc.—
Directories. 2. Consumer education—United States—Societies,
etc.—Directories. I. Maney, Ardith. II. Title.
HC110.C63B95 1995
381.3'4'02573—dc20 94–27949

British Library Cataloguing in Publication Data is available.

Library of Congress Catalog Card Number: 94–27949
ISBN: 0–313–26429–5

First published in 1995

Greenwood Press, 88 Post Road West, Westport, CT 06881
An imprint of Greenwood Publishing Group, Inc.

Printed in the United States of America

The paper used in this book complies with the
Permanent Paper Standard issued by the National
Information Standards Organization (Z39.48–1984).

10 9 8 7 6 5 4 3 2 1

CONTENTS

———————— / ————————

PREFACE

/

This volume profiles organized interest groups that have had an impact on consumer protection policy in the United States since 1960. Public interest groups, associations of state officials, trade associations, professional associations, general business associations, unions, think tanks, and policy research centers are included. The organizations are presented in alphabetical order, which makes them easy to find but does not reflect significance, longevity, or other characteristics. Some interrelationships can be seen by the cross-references among the groups: where a profiled organization is mentioned in another's profile, it is marked with an asterisk. More complex interrelationships and categories are discussed in the introduction.

Each profile includes the address or addresses and phone number or numbers for the group, followed by sections headed "Organization and Resources," "Policy Concerns," and "Tactics." The section on organization and resources includes information about the group's founding, whom it represents, basic goals, leadership structure, organization, staff size, budget and its sources where available, publications, and membership benefits such as educational programs. Policy concerns include the issue positions the group has taken, with particular emphasis on those which have been visible, politically important, and more recent in time. In some cases it also describes what major issues the group is anticipating on the political agenda. The tactics section describes group activities intended to influence public policy decisions. These range from monitoring Washington officials to suing opponents in court and include media relationships; grass-roots lobbying; meeting with legislative and executive staff; meeting with members of Congress, executive departments, and the White House; presenting testimony at congressional hearings; commenting on proposed regulations; serving on advisory committees; coalescing with other groups; producing television and radio shows; and electoral activity.

Groups have been selected for inclusion by consulting *Washington Information Directory, Encyclopedia of Associations, Public Interest Profiles, Washington Representatives, Consumers Resource Handbook,* and *Congressional Information Service Index.* Appearances at congressional hearings, with particular attention to House of Representatives hearings from 1977 through 1987, indexed by Congressional Information Service under "Consumer Protection," were systematically tabulated. Groups more active in presenting testimony at consumer protection hearings were more likely to be included than others.

Primary sources of information for most of the profiles were publications supplied by the organizations themselves. Most responded to written requests by sending recent annual reports, newsletters, and other publications. However, the materials varied widely in detail, quality, and sophistication, a variance that is reflected in the profiles. Frequently consulted supplementary secondary sources include *Congressional Quarterly Weekly Report, National Journal,* the *Washington Post* national weekly edition, and the *New York Times.* Efforts to keep the material up to date included ongoing attention to these sources as well as consultation of references such as Lexis, Public Affairs Information Service International Index, and Congressional Masterfile. In only a few cases are substantial scholarly publications available on these organizations; those which exist were consulted and noted in the "Further Reading" section. In a few cases, data were augmented by telephone or personal interviews, or by a questionnaire that a few organizations were willing to complete. The profiles have not been endorsed or approved by the organizations; any errors or omissions are the responsibility of the authors. The information about groups is as up-to-date as possible and reflects a continuing search for resource material through 1994.

INTRODUCTION
/

SCOPE AND HISTORY

Consumer protection policy in the United States addresses issues of availability, price, quality, and efficacy of goods and services and the conditions under which they are offered to the public for purchase. Ordinarily, consumers are considered to be acting on their own in coping with producer practices that may have economic, health, or safety consequences for those who use their products or services. However, abused or dissatisfied consumers or their survivors have a range of options to use for protection. These include asking the producer for more information, sharing information with other potential consumers, complaining directly to the provider, boycotting individually or with others, taking the producer to court, and trying to bring government officials into the conflict. The attention of political science is engaged when the scope of conflict is expanded beyond the individual consumer and individual producer, particularly if the issue is brought to government officials from whom authoritative action is sought. Government's response may be to strengthen existing laws or enact new ones regulating aspects of business activity, to reinvigorate existing administrative agencies, or to create additional agencies.

Consumers and their advocates have brought a wide range of issues to the public agenda. Among these are auto safety, food and drug safety, labeling and product content disclosure, banking and credit, deceptive sales practices, energy costs, housing availability, and health care, to name just a few. Consumer concerns also extend to the processes by which producers act in the public arena, such as accountability to stockholders, openness to consumer inquiries, and disclosure of investments.

Waves of consumer activism can be charted during the major reform periods of the past century. As the following profiles demonstrate, this does not mean there is not considerable activity in the periods between reform eras, but that it is more successful and salient at some times than at others. Several explanations may be offered as to why these cycles occur—that abuses build up to an intolerable level so as to cause a backlash, that economic crises create the need and opportunity for government activism, and that leaders capitalize on widespread dissatisfaction to take government in directions that will be popular with large segments of the electorate.

During the Progressive era, the administrations of Theodore Roosevelt and Woodrow Wilson developed new instruments for regulating financial institutions, the Federal Reserve Board and the Federal Trade Commission. Health and safety issues were addressed with pure food and drug legislation. Activism at the national level was echoed at state and local levels with laws regulating transportation, insurance, workers' wages and hours, and working conditions. Although most of the attempts to protect workers were struck down by the courts, Progressives succeeded in arguing that some industries are public utilities and that the public has an ongoing interest in their operation.

Consumers were also part of the broad New Deal coalition created by President Franklin Delano Roosevelt in response to the Great Depression. One strategy of the New Deal that would prove to be influential in the long run was to support various industries, such as agriculture and housing, to help them get back on their feet. New techniques of government interaction with the private sector were designed, and new agencies were created to carry them out. Some, like the Agricultural Adjustment Administration, were dissolved as the crisis eased; others, such as the Federal Deposit Insurance Corporation and the Securities and Exchange Commission, continue to this day. Consumer representatives or offices were required to be part of some of these agencies by law or executive action; in some cases consumer activists had to be satisfied with regular appointees who could be encouraged to include consumer concerns in their definition of the public interest.

The most recent reform wave, which began in the early 1960s and continued until the mid to late 1970s, suffers an identity problem because scholars are still competing to label it. It is called the Great Society, the public lobby regime, and perhaps most commonly, the 60's. Auto safety, deceptive credit practices, and laxity on the part of regulatory agencies were part of a long agenda of issues including urban decay, poverty, malnutrition, civil rights, and the environment. New laws were enacted and new agencies created to enforce them, including the National Transportation Safety Board and the Consumer Product Safety Commission. New consumer groups were founded, and old ones rejuvenated, and prominent politicians capitalized on the wave of interest. By most accounts, this was the "golden age" of consumer protection policy in the United States. Although President Jimmy Carter appointed numerous public interest activists to prominent positions in his administration, he was not able to persuade Congress to create the Agency for Consumer Advocacy, which had long been sought by consumer activists. The failure of the consumer agency bill in 1978 is an important landmark in consumer protection policy.

By the late 1970s, business entered the national political environment with significant efforts to cultivate self-protection. Trade, professional, and general business associations were refurbished, and numerous individual corporations established their own Washington presence. Public opinion lobbying, grass-roots lobbying, and direct lobbying of Congress, staff, the White House, administrative agencies, and the courts became the order of business. Other, more subtle efforts to turn the tide included contribution of corporate funds to think tanks, university centers and professorships for the study of American business, and publication of periodicals to disseminate free-market ideas (Vogel 1989).

Ronald Reagan the candidate and the president pledged to reduce the scope and cost of government, to rely more heavily on the private sector and the free market, and to deregulate business in general. Private-sector decisions would be unshackled to allow progress, and producers would be trusted to do best without interference by government or so-called public interest advocates. Although "revolution" is too strong a term to describe the Reagan era, it did significantly counter the reforms of the previous wave. Its messages that business should proceed without scrutiny and that profits are more important than any negative side effects struck powerful blows against consumer protection. The administration's efforts to abolish or gut the Consumer Product Safety Commission, the Federal Trade Commission, the National Highway Traffic Safety Administration, the Environmental Protection Agency, the Occupational Safety and Health Administration, the Legal Services Corporation, and the Freedom of Information Act took their toll. The Reagan counterreform accomplished as much as zealous appointees, budget and personnel cuts, and a choke hold on the regulatory process could be expected to do.

In this environment, consumer advocates and their allies resorted to traditional protest tactics like boycotts as a means to get the attention and cooperation of producers. Allies drawn from environmental, civil rights, women's and religious groups, and sympathetic media helped in boycotts of McDonald's, Nestlé, 7-11 stores, and others. In comparison with the chilly reception from the White House, congressional committees continued to provide a forum for consumer grievances. Some state and local governments also moved ahead on consumer issues, at times spurred by ballot initiatives, constituent complaints, or media attention.

SIGNIFICANCE

Although scholars are still debating the significance of the Progressive and New Deal reforms, the focus here is on appraising the impact of the public interest reform wave, particularly in light of the counterreforms of the 1980s. For discussion purposes, it is reasonable to focus on two leading schools of thought regarding the significance of the public interest era. One school describes the demands and accomplishments of public interest reformers—including the organized groups, mobilized public, Congress, the White House, and the courts—as a unique phenomenon in American history, bringing a new level of regulation and intervention to bear on American business (Weidenbaum 1975; Lilley and Miller 1977; Vogel 1981). In this view, the impact of the reform wave was so powerful as to pose a real threat to business decision making in fundamentals not previously constrained by outsiders. At a very minimum, the threat was taken seriously enough to stimulate business's political awareness, causing it to rally its resources to compete in Washington to defend and restore its position in the American political economy. The fruit of this backlash is popularly referred to as the Reagan Revolution.

A second school of thought is more critical of the values, intent, and impact of the public interest reformers and argues that intrinsic weaknesses facilitated the backlash associated with President Ronald Reagan. Richard Harris and Sidney Milkis (1989b) describe what they label the public lobby regime as pursuing fundamental change in the outcomes of a market society by institutionalizing permanent watchdogs made up of organized citizen groups and citizens participating directly. They claim that these opportunities are likely to be limited to a small circle of professional advocates. This point of view charges the failure of the reform movement to its implicit critique of materialism and consumer preferences, and to a strategy that effectively enlarged the powers of administrative and judicial institutions at the expense of institutions of republican governance, particularly Congress. The reform movement stalled because leaders such as Ralph Nader turned their backs on materialism, overemphasized quality of life issues, exaggerated the threats of resource limitations, and thus directly challenged the principles and achievements of an advanced capitalist economy.

Other prominent scholars of contemporary liberalism also find the recent public interest reform era wanting in comparison to the New Deal (McCann 1986; Katznelson 1989; Lichtenstein 1989; Galambos and Pratt 1988). Harris and Milkis (1989b) attribute this to the movement's choice of administrative and judicial strategies, a choice determined by flawed philosophical foundations. Elected representatives and democratic processes were not trusted to rise above the material interests embedded in the American electorate. At its very roots, citizen advocacy as envisioned by the reformers was in tension with representative government, a flaw attributed to the influence of the New Left's distrust of big government and big business. By contrast, the New Deal was willing to rely on government programs for solutions, placed faith in the presidency to lead change, and emphasized the need for economic security.

The larger debate that frames this significant question is that of the influence of private interests on American public policy. At least since Thomas Jefferson warned that banks are more dangerous than standing armies, scholars have asked how a market economy and popular sovereignty can coexist. In current scholarship, the debate is defined on one side by Charles Lindblom's arguments that the market is a prison (1982), or at least that producers use the political system more successfully for their own interests than do any other contestants, and are able to keep fundamental questions off the agenda entirely (1977). Neopluralists such as Andrew McFarland (1988), Jeffrey Berry (1989), and David Vogel (1989) take the other side of the debate. They acknowledge that producer interests are powerful but argue that countervailing influences in government, among producers themselves, and exerted by organized public interest groups keep the system balanced.

Within the interest group literature that a student might explore to become better informed about this great debate, consumer groups are difficult to trace. Earlier scholarship on the consumer movement and consumer groups explored events through the end of the 1960s (Nadel 1971), but since then the subject has been neglected until very recently. Most recent accounts of public interest group activity mention consumers but tend to focus on governmental reform groups (McFarland 1984) or environmental organizations (McCann 1986; Vogel 1989). The lapse of attention together with the varying assessments of significance outlined above invite a refocusing of attention and further exploration.

THE SCORECARD—YOU CAN'T TELL THE PLAYERS WITHOUT ONE

All of the organizations in the following profiles have been active in trying to influence public policy as it impacts consumers. This means we have captured not just what are conventionally called "consumer groups" but rather groups that are actively interested in the consumer policy domain. Within this domain one might first distinguish those organizations which have a private or special interest in the policy, such as the U.S. Chamber of Commerce,* from those which profess to advocate unselfishly for the public, such as the Consumer Federation of America,* rather than just the narrow economic advantage of their members. This is a meaningful distinction and a significant one, in that it allows many of the public interest groups to undergird their arguments by claiming a higher moral ground than their producer opponents, and to be more persuasive than one might estimate from looking at their membership numbers in comparison with all the American consumers for whom they purportedly speak. On the other hand, one must also note that producers often defend their actions by arguing that what is good for them is good for those who consume their products. This argument was given more credence in the 1980s with the prominence of supply side economics and its claim that prosperity would "trickle down" to consumers.

Although the private–public distinction is useful, it is not complex enough to categorize all of the groups who speak out on consumer policy. The American federal system contributes officials from state and local levels of government whose legal responsibilities include various aspects of consumer protection. Organizations of these officials, such as the National Association of Regulatory Utility Commissioners* and the National Association of Attorneys General,* add their voices to national policy considerations when proposals have the potential to alter state or local responsibilities or resources. Also prominent in the consumer policy domain are think tanks, organizations of scholars such as the Brookings Institution* and the American Enterprise Institute for Public Policy Research,* who study the issues and produce reports intended to elevate the intellectual level of policy decisions.

Among the private interest producer groups it is useful to distinguish among general or "peak" business associations such as the U.S. Chamber of Commerce* and the Business Roundtable,* and trade and professional associations such as the American Bankers Association* and the American Medical Association,* respectively. It is expected that the general associations will become active on those issues which impact businesses across the board rather than differentially among sectors or sizes. The trade and professional associations are active on those issues which may impact their sector.

In many business sectors there are a number of groups that speak for different subsectors and sometimes compete against each other, at least on the fine-tuning of policy. For example, the American Bankers Association,* the Savings & Community Bankers of America,* the Independent Bankers Association of America,* and the Consumer Bankers Association* are concerned with how the savings and loans are rescued but have different specific interests in how the burdens and regulations are crafted. In addition to these group representatives, spokespersons for numerous individual corporations are found lobbying decision makers. Thus a hearing on health care reform will be attended by representatives of the U.S. Chamber of Commerce,* the Health Insurance Association of America, Prudential, Blue Cross/Blue Shield, and Mutual of Omaha, among others.

Groups that are usually thought of as consumer groups may be categorized as generalists and specialists as well. The generalists include the Consumer Federation of America,* Consumers Union,* and Public Citizen.* Over time, these organizations have carried the main burden of representing the consumer voice on consumer protection issues before congressional committee and subcommittee hearings (Bykerk and Maney 1991). But since the late 1970s, specialized organizations have carried out an important role as well. Bankcard Holders of America,* the Center for Auto Safety,* the Center for Science in the Public Interest,* and the National Insurance Consumer Organization* exemplify the specialized organizations that bring their expertise forward when proposals impacting their particular niche appear on the policy agenda.

A large number of organizations whose principal focus is a segment of consumers such as the elderly, or is concerned with health or the environment as it relates to consumer protection, supply allies to the core consumer groups. Most prominent among these allies is the American Association of Retired Persons;* the National Women's Health Network* is representative of the health groups that also include the American Cancer Society.* The Environmental Defense Fund,* the National Audubon Society,* and Greenpeace* are included among the environmental allies on consumer protection issues. Organized labor frequently is a part of the coalitions active on consumer issues; the American Federation of Labor–Congress of Industrial Organizations is most often the labor voice, but individual unions such as the United Auto Workers are also active on consumer issues.

Having a scorecard for these players, unlike in sports, does not include having comparable means of scoring. In looking at the resources that the various organizations have, it may be tempting to compare their budgets or staff sizes. That may be easy (and even yield computer-manipulable formulas), but it is not a measure by which to understand or predict policy outcomes. There are various reasons that budgets and staffs are not comparable measures. Some organizations include in their budget and staff numbers outside contracts for performing specific research or outreach functions; while these may help to build the organization in the long run, they are not flexible to use for other purposes, and hence not equivalent to unrestricted resources. It is particularly risky to make comparisons between core consumer groups and producers' trade or professional associations. The Washington offices of the latter sometimes act as the main lobbying arm but often are more the coordinators of member experts who are brought in to write legislative or regulatory language, or to meet with members of Congress or executive branch officials. All the expertise and contacts these organizations can draw upon go unreported in budget and staff figures.

There is no equivalent for the stature that state and local officials have when they come to Washington; a state governor or attorney general is in a wholly different category than other interest representatives. The access and respect accorded state and local officials puts them in a category not directly comparable with ordinary lobbyists. Neither is there any certain scale for comparing the letters from genuinely aggrieved consumers, the heartrending testimony of senior citizens defrauded of their life savings, and the pleas of a manufacturer for relief from liability suits that have brought him to the brink of bankruptcy.

WHAT DO THE PLAYERS WANT?

Each category of players usually comes to the political arena with a basic set of preferences that underlies the positions it advocates. Although these are not always predictable or consistent, they generally help an observer understand who is likely to want what when they come to bargain. (General preferences are described here; more specifics are in the individual profiles.) The core consumer groups, both generalists and specialists, tend to begin with a preference for informed individual consumer action; they want consumers and citizens to seek information, participate, and demand remedies from producers, regulators, and elected officials (Nader 1973). Businesses and government should be organized on a scale and in a manner that are open, clear, and understandable to the ordinary person. Producers are asked to observe elementary standards of honesty, safety, and utility in producing and selling goods and services, and to refrain from corrupting politicians with money, monopolizing, deceiving, exposing workers to hazards, and tyrannizing people of conscience within their companies (Nader 1983).

Government is asked to require that honest information be available to consumers, that producer behavior be policed, and that remedies be available for redress—including mediation, rights to sue for damages, and criminal penalties for white-collar crime. More open processes in both business and government are believed to lead to fairer distributions of burdens and benefits among both generations and categories of wealth (Nader 1984). Notable by contrast are the few consumer groups, such as Consumer Alert,* that begin with a posture of trusting the free market behavior of producers and advocate that they be more unfettered, and that government be run more like business rather than vice versa.

Allies such as senior citizens and health groups advocate for consumers with special needs or vulnerabilities. Representatives of the elderly want protection against fraudulent sales schemes; funeral, credit, and insurance sales abuses; and attention to health care problems. Health groups tend to weigh in on behalf of those particularly at risk of disease made more likely by poor nutrition, dangerous additives in food and medicine, and untested products. Environmental allies come forth on issues like agricultural chemical residues in food and seek incentives for both producers and consumers to move toward more sustainable food and product preferences. Relationships on energy issues are more strained because consumer groups prefer cheap energy while environmentalists advocate conservation, which is facilitated by higher energy prices.

Organized labor speaks out for both moderate- and low-income consumers and for workers. As workers, labor brings inside knowledge of producer operations but also seeks protection for whistle-blowing and for keeping jobs rather than shifting them to cheaper, younger, or foreign workers. Labor is in the position of being sought as an ally by both consumer groups and those producers who employ them; the latter sometimes succeed if workers can be convinced that consumer protection measures will cost them their jobs. This tension was exemplified by the position of organized labor on raising the collision impact standards for automobile bumpers. The unions expressed support for the consumer preference for enhanced safety and lower repair costs but also concern over the potential for higher production costs to reduce sales and employment.

Think tanks and organizations of state officials are somewhat less predictable sets of actors in consumer policy. Think tanks provide intellectual stimulation that connects with prominent policymakers on salient issues, a combination that sometimes leads in new directions, as it did with the wave of deregulation that began in the late 1970s. These organizations tend to be regarded as either liberal (Brookings*) or conservative (American Enterprise Institute,* Heritage Foundation*), with the latter enjoying dramatic growth in resources and prominence since the late 1970s. State officials generally seek to protect their roles within the federal system. They frequently are able to provide data on the extent of problem behaviors and usually want to protect their flexibility to act independently without federal interference. However, they may also seek support in stronger federal standards that they will have a role in creating and enforcing. In some cases, they try to fend off federal preemption when some of their members are moving their states ahead more rapidly than the federal government is willing or able to move. Even though the states change very unevenly, some being more progressive than others, associations of the intergovernmental lobby tend to point with pride to the "experimental laboratory" advantage of federalism.

"Peak" business associations want to remind observers and policymakers of the significance of material wealth to the American dream. They advocate recognition of the role of productivity, competition, self-help, and individualism, which they take to be the foundation of American political economy. Trade and professional associations claim credit for the contributions of their members to consumer well-being. If problems or complaints are raised, they seek to handle them with voluntary standards, training, or education programs. Sectors of the economy such as food producers, manufacturing, or insurance may come to government seeking protection from competition or unfair practices on the part of foreign producers or other sectors of the domestic economy. In these cases, the trade or professional associations may compete with each other, some taking the position of consumers and even allying with consumer groups. Additional complexity may develop when individual corporations become directly involved to protect their interests apart from the positions advocated by the association or associations to which they belong (Bykerk 1992).

PATTERNS OF INTERACTION

If one considers a constellation of consumer groups and their allies, producers, and state officials and then adds to it federal legislative and executive decision makers, it is obvious that multiple complex patterns of interaction on issues are possible. The current trend in interest group scholarship is to analyze the coalitions and issue networks or policy communities that have replaced subgovernments or "iron triangles" (an interest group, a congressional committee, and an executive agency exercising stable, closed, self-serving control) in many policy arenas. Interaction on consumer protection issues is an exception to the direction characteristic of agriculture, transportation, health, education, and other areas. Consumer interests have not enjoyed an "iron triangle" relationship with a congressional committee and an executive branch agency for a variety of reasons. The effort to create what would have been "their" executive agency failed in the face of strong business opposition; although a number of executive agencies have jurisdiction over programs of interest to consumers, none is available for consumers to dominate. On the legislative side, issues impacting consumer interests may, and do, come out of a wide array of committees from agriculture to trade, banking to telecommunications. They do not have even their own watchdog committee to ask for sequential referral in order to throw up a roadblock. Finally, Congress and the executive branch are more nearly organized around producing functions rather than around consumption. This means that consumer advocates are always playing on someone else's "home court" with all the attendant disadvantages of unfamiliarity and having to work harder to do as well.

Consumer organizations do form coalitions to monitor and try to influence policy-making, but not because their political environment is deteriorating from subsystem to policy network. Consumer groups coalesce because their resources are spread so thinly over everything they have to cover. They are careful not to waste themselves in overlapping of multiple groups on most issues; one group takes the lead, and others support it as they can but also count the issue as covered unless there is an unexpected crisis. When consumer groups find themselves courted for a coalition by producer organizations, they sometimes link up because it gives them temporary, indirect access to policymakers that they would be unlikely to access on their own. However, it does not augment their resources in a direct fashion or over the longer run except that it supports a reputation of being a "player" rather than an outsider.

Some scholarship (Loomis 1986) suggests that alliances are increasingly likely to be put together or brokered by consultants. While this is a supportable observation among producer associations (Bykerk 1992), consumer groups are much less likely to use consultants. And when they do use consultants, they are not apt to be the same ones used by trade or professional associations. Thus, they may be sought out by these brokers but are less likely to be paying the consultant who is creating the coalition. Coalitions of their own creation are much more likely to be arranged informally on the basis of long-run knowledge of the focus and expertise available in the relatively small circle of consumer organizations (Bykerk and Maney 1994).

In contrast with subgovernments, networks like the consumer policy network are larger, more permeable, more inclusive, and bounded by expertise, but they are also less stable and result in less predictable outcomes. The greater complexity of actors and interrelationships accounts for the unusual alliances that occur more frequently than in the past, and also for the greater difficulty in coming to decisions, forging change short of consensus and without formal authoritative leadership. This is the political environment in which consumer groups have functioned since the 1960s, the period in which most of them were founded. From a traditional vantage point, one might say that consumer groups, like other public interest groups, are relative newcomers and have helped destabilize old subgovernments in the direction of policy networks or communities. But looking at the consumer policy arena in itself, this is the norm rather than a new development.

THE QUESTION OF MEASURING INFLUENCE

The question most often asked about interest group involvement in politics is "How much influence do they really have?" Sometimes the question is "an-

swered'' by describing the resources that the various parties bring to the competition and concluding that the party with more resources got what it wanted.
Thus, two warnings are in order here. First, resources are not equivalent to
influence; the two are related but distinct. Second, the question is not whether
an interest got what it wanted, because that rarely occurs in our political system,
but whether the processes or outcomes were different because of their involvement.

If one asks whether the American political process is different than it would
have been if organized consumer groups had not been active, the answer is
clearly yes. The groups grew in number, flourished, became sufficiently well
established to withstand the battering of the conservative backlash, and have
continued to be an audible voice in the consumer policy network. They have
contributed to making the consumer protection agenda more complex, more
responsive to consumer grievances, better researched, and better publicized than
had they not been involved.

When we turn to assessing their influence on the outcomes, the answer is less
clear. As we turn back to the larger questions with which we began and project
on that backdrop the goals of the consumer movement, it appears that few gains
remain. The public interest reform movement posed a powerful if not unique
reform threat to American business for a time; the movement did not collapse
of its own weaknesses but encountered the intrinsic bias of a market society.
The critics' charge that the reform movement inadvertently weakened Congress
is unsupported; it was Congress and existing statutory provisions that enabled
any of the reforms to withstand the counterreform wave. And certainly the belief
that watchful citizens are necessary even with representative government institutions has deep and honorable roots in Western liberalism.

However, on the larger question of influence, our assessment is that the political economy is still largely moved by producer innovations motivated by
short-run profit; consumers are not sovereign but must beware to protect
themselves after the fact. Resource disparity is part of the explanation; producer
voices seriously outnumber consumer voices by a ratio of 2 or 3 to 1 (Bykerk
and Maney 1991). Producer resources outweigh those available to consumer
groups by even wider margins; only in media relationships and reputation do
the consumer groups pose a serious challenge. To even begin to compete, consumers must capitalize on crises or scares, and find advocates in Congress or
the executive branch, or ad hoc allies from among producers. While their opponents may be able to engage in pressure politics, consumer groups must engage in the politics of ideas because they rarely have the resources to wield
pressure.

Although it is generally the case that producer interests continue to be ad-
vantaged in the American political system, one ought at least to note those issues
for which consumer advocates currently are able to gain attention. Health care
reform, nutrition labeling, meat and poultry safety, fish and seafood inspection,
product safety such as that of silicone gel breast implants, interest calculations

on adjustable rate mortgages, home equity loan abuses, discrimination in mortgage lending, executive compensation, and campaign finance reform are salient issues at present because consumer groups and their allies make them visible. Consumer stakes in the federal budget deficit and in international trade policy also cannot be ignored because of the organized voices for consumers. Persistence in promoting concerns like these does make a difference.

SPECULATING ABOUT THE FUTURE

One issue for the consumer protection optimist to observe in the near-term future is health care reform. Consumer groups are forming extensive coalitions, impressive data are forthcoming at a steady pace, there is strong potential to play producers against each other, widespread public concern is evident, and elected officials seek to lead toward reform. A second trend with potential impact on consumer protection is the growing appeal for environmentally sensitive choices in the marketplace. "Buying green" may prove to be a powerful vehicle for both consumer and environmental causes. The other theme that seems to promise forward-looking responses to change is the willingness of some states to move ahead on issues left unresolved by the federal government, such as campaign finance reform. State action, as uneven and ill-informed as it sometimes proves to be, may be the means by which health care reform occurs.

Less promising are the indications that the American public is unreceptive to the admonitions to be watchful and participatory consumers and citizens. Young adults show little interest in direct individual or collective activity, and no readiness to use political groups or parties to wield government tools to remedy problems. It is difficult to imagine what will occur when the Nader generation of activists and group members is no longer on the scene. Are Americans coming to expect inferior goods and services, misleading information, complaint procedures that wear down the complainant, overpaid but underskilled corporate leaders, and unresponsive systems of production and politics? Will a new paradigm intervene to protect them from getting what they expect?

U.S. CONSUMER
INTEREST GROUPS

A
——————————— / ———————————

ACCURACY IN MEDIA (AIM)
1275 K Street N.W.
Washington, DC 20005
(202) 371–6710

ORGANIZATION AND RESOURCES

Accuracy in Media was founded in 1969 in response to the media's coverage of the Vietnam War. Its organizers believed that the war's coverage showed bias on the part of the national media in the United States. A watchdog of the national media, its goal is to ensure fair and unbiased coverage of issues and events in the media. The group is conservative in nature, and it has often attacked what it perceives as the media's liberal bias.

Accuracy in Media publishes *AIM Report,* a biweekly newsletter discussing instances where AIM officials believe the media did not provide fair and unbiased coverage of issues and events. It also publishes *How to Write Letters to the Media,* a guide to getting letters to the editor published in newspapers.

POLICY CONCERNS

Since its founding, AIM has concerned itself with the issue of bias in the media, particularly liberal bias. Besides criticizing media coverage during the Vietnam War, AIM has criticized the media for exaggerating the dangers of asbestos and global warming, downplaying the Bill Clinton/Gennifer Flowers affair, failing to investigate Social Security fraud, and depicting Native American activist Leonard Peltier as a political prisoner, not a murderer. AIM also criticizes newspapers such as the *Washington Post* for not publishing letters to the editor that disagree with the paper's views.

TACTICS

In their campaign to curb journalistic bias, AIM members make personal contact with editors, publishers, and producers in the various national media and write letters to the editor criticizing the media. Members are encouraged to buy a copy of *How to Write Letters to the Media,* and other publications such as *Silent Coup* and *Communists in the Democratic Party,* to gain an understanding of the issues behind AIM's campaigns. Names and addresses of media executives are given in the newsletter so that members may write to them and voice their concerns.

Naturally, AIM President Reed Irvine and his group have made some enemies within the media industry. The *Washington Post,* the *New York Times,* ABC, NBC, and CBS are constant targets of the group's attacks.

FURTHER READING

AIM Report. Biweekly. Washington, DC: Accuracy in Media.
Colodny, Len, and Robert Gettlin. 1991. *Silent Coup.* Washington, DC: Accuracy in Media.
How to Write Letters to the Media. n.d. Washington, DC: Accuracy in Media.
Lucolm, Wilson C. n.d. *Communists in the Democratic Party.* Washington, DC: Accuracy in Media.
Mathews, Jay. 1992. "To Yank or Not to Yank." *Newsweek,* April 13, p. 24.
"Redbaiting Still." 1992. *Washington Post,* August 15, p. A18.

ACTION FOR CHILDREN'S TELEVISION (ACT)
20 University Road
Cambridge, MA 02138
(617) 876–6620

ORGANIZATION AND RESOURCES

Action for Children's Television was a nonprofit child advocacy organization working to encourage diversity in children's television offerings, to discourage overcommercialization of children's programming, and to eliminate deceptive advertising aimed at young viewers. ACT's approach was to encourage broadcasters to offer a greater variety of programs rather than to remove programs from the air, and to suggest ways for families to help children choose programs more carefully and to limit their viewing time.

ACT was founded in 1968 by Peggy Charren and a small number of other young mothers from her Boston-area neighborhood. It grew to an organization with a budget of $225,000 in the mid-1980s but declined financially in the early 1990s. Over 20,000 members contributed, providing about 70 percent of the funds available to the group; foundation grants and fees from lectures, films, and book sales also supported ACT. A thirteen-member board of directors was formally responsible for governance, but ACT was always identified with Ms. Charren, who was president and spokesperson. ACT had as many as eight staff members in the mid-1980s but only four in the early 1990s when it disbanded.

POLICY CONCERNS

ACT proceeded on the understanding that American children are exposed to so many hours of television that it is a major influence in their lives, an influence that can be made to work for their betterment if properly regulated by government, broadcasters, and parents. The proportion of children's television time devoted to advertising, program-length commercials targeted at children, news and science programming for children, and 976 and 900 telephone services were ACT's main targets. Program-length commercials are programs, often cartoon-like, designed around toys such as Teenage Mutant Ninja Turtles in order to increase sales of the products.

Soon after ACT was founded, the Federal Communications Commission (FCC) accepted its petition to study and formulate rules for children's television. In response to more than 100,000 letters, the FCC in 1974 adopted a Children's Television Report and Policy Statement that required children's programming and limited the amount of advertising during those programs to 9.5 minutes per hour on weekends and 12 minutes on weekdays. The National Association of Broadcasters (NAB) adopted a voluntary code that created the evening "family hour" and an era of science specials, historic and literary dramas, and news shows for children. These standards were challenged by writers and directors in the entertainment industry and by the Department of Justice, and in 1984 the FCC rescinded the 1974 guidelines in favor of free market principles.

ACT collected data on increases in advertising time and declining program quality, and revived the issue. It filed suit against the FCC, and in 1987, the U.S. Court of Appeals for the District of Columbia ruled that the FCC had failed to justify its 1984 decision to eliminate advertising limits. While the FCC slowly moved to reconsider, Congress debated more stringent requirements on advertising time, educational programming, and elimination of program-length commercials. ACT and Ms. Charren were credited with leading the coalition advocating the changes. In 1988, over the opposition of the White House, the FCC, and the Department of Justice, Congress passed compromise legislation acceptable to ACT and the NAB that restricted commercial time to 10.5 minutes per hour on weekends and 12 minutes per hour on weekdays, and required the FCC to consider in license renewal proceedings whether a station had served the educational and informational needs of children in its overall programming. The Children's Television Act was pocket vetoed by President Reagan after the adjournment of the 100th Congress on the grounds that it violated the First Amendment protections of broadcasters' programming decisions. Identical legislation was passed by Congress and allowed to become law without the signature of President Bush in October 1990.

TACTICS

ACT's tactics included petitioning the FCC and the Federal Trade Commission (FTC), filing suit against the FCC, assembling data for policymakers including the FCC and congressional committees, and presenting testimony at congressional hearings. Coalitions with allies including the American Academy of Pediatrics,* the American Psychological Association, the National Education Association, the Consumer Federation of America,* and others extended its expertise and its communication networks. ACT, Ms. Charren in particular, enjoyed superlative relations with representatives of the mass media that reported its statements, research, and positions frequently and faithfully.

ACT publications included booklets for parents and children to help them be more critical consumers of television programming with tools such as a TV report card for children to fill out. Other publications advised parents about how to incorporate art, reading, and other activities into viewing, to utilize community cable resources, and to publicize quality videos.

Annual Achievement in Children's Television Awards were conferred on people, stations, and institutions for contributing to quality children's television. ACT's twentieth anniversary celebration in 1988 included conferring Hall of Fame Awards on the Children's Television Workshop, the John and Mary R. Markle Foundation, and Fred Rogers and his Family Communications company. Prominent members of the House and Senate, such as Representative Edward Markey, network executives, and entertainment figures such as Jay Leno and Jane Pauley participated in the celebration.

FURTHER READING

Action for Children's Television. 1991. Information packet. Cambridge, MA: Action for Children's Television.

Cannon, Carl. 1989. "Parents, Congress Upset by Children's Television." *Omaha World-Herald,* May 30, pp. 1, 11.

"Children's TV Advocacy Group Celebrates 20th Year." *Omaha World-Herald,* May 17, p. 3.

Fessler, Pamela. 1988. "Limit on Kids' Television Ads Gets Strong Backing in House." *Congressional Quarterly Weekly Report,* June 11, p. 1600.

"Final Children's Television Bill Seems Likely to Get by Bush." 1990. *Congressional Quarterly Weekly Report,* October 6, p. 3215.

Kunkel, Dale. 1991. "Crafting Media Policy: The Genesis and Implications of the Children's Television Act of 1990." *American Behavioral Scientist,* November/December, pp. 181–202.

Pertschuk, Michael. 1982. *Revolt Against Regulation: The Rise and Pause of the Consumer Movement.* Berkeley: University of California Press.

Public Interest Profiles 1988–1989 and *1986–1987.* 1988, 1986. Washington, DC: Congressional Quarterly, Foundation for Public Affairs.

Pytte, Alyson. 1989. "Congress Ready Once Again to Curb Children's TV." *Congressional Quarterly Weekly Report,* July 15, pp. 1764–1765.

Starobin, Paul. 1988a. "Bill to Boost Quality of Kids' TV Clears Despite Veto Possibility." *Congressional Quarterly Weekly Report,* October 22, p. 3065.

———. 1988b. "Fewer Ads, More Quality Shows Demanded for Kids' Television." *Congressional Quarterly Weekly Report,* May 21, pp. 1405–1406.

ACTION ON SMOKING AND HEALTH (ASH)
2013 H Street N.W.
Washington, DC 20006
Tel (202) 659–4310
Fax 202–833–3921

ORGANIZATION AND RESOURCES

Founded by John F. Banzhaf III, who is still its executive director and chief counsel as well as a law professor, Action on Smoking and Health has been involved in the growing anti-smoking community since 1967, three years after the first surgeon general's report linking smoking and health. ASH is a 501(c)(3) organization that had a budget of about $900,000 in the 1990s. The organization has a staff of nine and publishes *ASH Smoking and Health Review* monthly, which is available for $15 a year and is mailed to about 30,000 people.

POLICY CONCERNS

The first results of ASH's policy advocacy were decisions by the Federal Communications Commission to allow anti-smoking messages to be broadcast on television under the agency's fairness doctrine. ASH was also involved in the activities leading up to the 1971 law banning cigarette advertisements on television. Recently ASH has been trying to protect children from tobacco advertising and marketing, and to initiate workplace limits and bans on smoking in public places.

TACTICS

Anti-smoking policy efforts demonstrate the complexity of consumer protection because work must be done with a multitude of governmental agencies including the U.S. Department of Agriculture, the Federal Communications Commission, airline regulators, health research agencies, and Congress. Other advocacy organizations involved in smoking policy include the Coalition on Smoking and Health, the American Cancer Society,* the American Heart Association, the American Lung Association, and organizations representing medical professionals. The anti-smoking forces have been fought at every turn for over thirty years by a determined tobacco industry.

ASH's piece of this larger picture very much reflects Banzhaf's personality and interests. The organization's targets include business, government, and the media. Besides the tobacco industry and its lobbyists in Washington, that means television, advertising, and related industries. Government targets have included the Federal Communications Commission and other agencies, the courts, and of

course Congress. Tactics include conferences, testimony, litigation, and participation in legislative and regulatory decision making and monitoring.

FURTHER READING

Hilts, Philip J. 1994. "Way to Make Safer Cigarette Was Found in 60s, but Idea Was
    Shelved." *New York Times,* May 13, p. A10.
Pertschuk, Michael. 1982. *Revolt Against Regulation: The Rise and Pause of the Con-
    sumer Movement.* Berkeley: University of California Press.
————. 1986. *Giant Killers.* New York: W. W. Norton.
Schwartz, John. 1994. "Smoking Under Siege." *Washington Post,* national weekly edi-
    tion, June 27–July 3, pp. 6–7.

AIDS COALITION TO UNLEASH POWER (ACT-UP)
135 West 29th Street, 10th floor
New York, NY 10001
Tel (212) 564–2437
Fax 212–989–1797

ORGANIZATION AND RESOURCES

Act-Up was founded in 1987 by the playwright Larry Kramer and remains
among the most militant organizations whose objective is to end the AIDS crisis.
It seeks to help AIDS patients who are consumers of health care and science
whose advances have managed to prolong the lives of many AIDS patients but
have not yet made much progress toward curing the disease or preventing it
from taking the lives of most AIDS sufferers.

Organizationally, Act-Up is a 501(c)(4) organization headquartered in New
York City. Its budget as of the early 1990s was $1.2 million, almost half of
which came in response to direct mail appeals. Approximately half of the remainder came from money raised by special events and the other half from the
sale of group-sponsored merchandise. The organization publishes a quarterly
newsletter, *Act Up Rights,* and has expanded outside the United States to include
some eighty chapters worldwide.

POLICY CONCERNS

Substantively, Act-Up has been interested in speeding up the pace of govern-
ment-sponsored research, overcoming bureaucratic caution, speeding new drugs
onto the market, and broadening the availability to health care consumers of
existing drugs such as Ganciclovir and AZT.

TACTICS

Act-Up is controversial because of its operational style and its willingness to
pressure government officials charged with fighting the disease by disrupting
meetings and organizing other types of direct actions. Among its targets are
officials at the Department of Health and Human Services, including those in

the National Institutes of Health, and special blue-ribbon citizens' groups charged with formulating governmental AIDS policy.

Other targets include judges, pharmaceutical companies, and the Roman Catholic Church hierarchy. Act-Up deploys a panoply of techniques including coalition formation, demonstrations, grass-roots organizing, participating in regulatory proceedings, and monitoring legislation. Like radical environmental organizations, Act-Up does not mind being out in front on an issue even if it means antagonizing some who are sympathetic to its goals.

FURTHER READING

Dawson, Robert. 1990. "ACT-UP Acts Out." *Commonweal,* 117:476–477 (September 14).

Handelman, David. 1990. "ACT UP in Anger." *Rolling Stone,* March 8, pp. 80–82.

Leo, John. 1990. "The AIDS Activist with Blurry Vision." *U.S. News and World Report,* July 9, p. 16.

Rosenthal, Andrew. 1991. "PBS Cancels Film about ACT-UP Protest." *New York Times,* August 13, p. B1.

Salholz, Eloise. 1988. "Acting Up to Fight AIDS." *Newsweek,* June 6, p. 42.

Taylor, Paul. 1990. "AIDS Guerrillas." *New York,* November 12, pp. 62–63.

AMERICAN ACADEMY OF PEDIATRICS (AAP)
1331 Pennsylvania Avenue
Suite 721 North
Washington, DC 20004–1703
Toll-free (800) 336–5475
Tel (202) 662–7460

ORGANIZATION AND RESOURCES

The American Academy of Pediatrics was founded in 1930 by thirty-five pediatricians with the mission of improving the health and welfare of the nation's children. It is a nonprofit Illinois corporation organized for scientific and educational purposes and is exempt from income tax under Section 501(c) (3) of the U.S. Internal Revenue Code. AAP receives the bulk of its total operating revenues of over $22 million from membership dues. Other funding sources include subscription and meeting fees, initiation and project enrollment fees, contracts, grants, investment income, commissions, and advertising revenues. AAP publishes an annual report; a monthly newsletter, *AAP Washington Report;* and numerous specialized medical materials (e.g., *Pediatrics, Pediatrics in Review, AAP Red Book, Policy Reference Guide, Sports Medicine, Management of Pediatric Practice, Guidelines for Perinatal Care*).

POLICY CONCERNS

Since its founding, AAP has concerned itself with issues that affect the status of health care for American children, such as immunization for all children, universal health coverage for children, and warning labels on broadcast and print advertisements for alcohol. The latter issue puts it on the same side as the National PTA and the Parents' Music Resource Center,* although AAP did not endorse a specific labeling proposal. Other issues, such as AAP's support for reproductive rights (including a woman's right to an abortion), put the organization into the middle of one of the nation's most divisive social issues. On other issues, such as AAP's support for deferred repayment of medical student loans, the organization supports concerns of importance to medical education.

TACTICS

AAP's action on issues such as the government's ban on fetal tissue research shows that its focus is on executive branch as well as congressional decision making. Based upon members' belief that fetal tissue research is necessary for medical advances, AAP has worked to overturn the ban. AAP uses legislation alerts to disseminate information to its members before crucial votes. Information on other issues before Congress is conveyed in newsletters and magazines. AAP seeks to shape the public debate about emerging legislative issues, and arranges for members and officials to testify in Congress on pending legislation.

FURTHER READING

Sandow, Gregory. 1990. "Doctors Deny PMRC Alliance." *Rolling Stone,* February 22, p. 34.

AMERICAN ASSOCIATION OF RETIRED PERSONS (AARP)
601 E Street N.W.
Washington, DC 20049
(202) 434–2560

ORGANIZATION AND RESOURCES

The American Association of Retired Persons is a nonprofit membership organization of persons fifty and older dedicated to helping older Americans achieve lives of independence, dignity, and purpose. It was founded in 1958 by Dr. Ethel Percy Andrus, a retired high school principal. The organization evolved out of the National Retired Teachers Association (NRTA), which Andrus established in 1947 to deal with pension, tax, and health insurance issues. In 1982 the NRTA merged into AARP and became a special membership division within the newer but larger organization. AARP is now the largest organization of older Americans, with membership of more than 34 million. All persons age fifty or over are eligible, whether they are working or retired; membership dues are $5 annually for an individual or a couple; and approximately half of all eligible Americans are members. Income from dues comprises the largest share of AARP's revenues, followed by royalty fees and administrative allowances from the companies that provide services for members, advertising revenues from periodical publications, and interest income. The organization's annual operating expenses total approximately $310 million.

Horace B. Deets is executive director of a paid staff numbering over 1,500 persons in the Washington office, a western office in California, and ten area offices covering the fifty states, the territories, and the District of Columbia. A national volunteer network mobilizing over 350,000 members assists with activities in 4,000 local AARP chapters and 2,500 NRTA units. The Association's national board of directors is made of up of twenty-one members, who are elected every two years; a national legislative council develops federal and state legislative priorities for consideration and adoption by the board.

AARP engages in education and community service programs, provides services to members, and advocates for policy at the national, state, and local levels. Among its education efforts are the publication of periodicals, newsletters, and research reports. *Modern Maturity* is the bimonthly magazine that goes to all members, giving it the largest circulation of any American magazine; *AARP Bulletin* is a monthly newspaper of current events affecting older persons. *AARP Highlights* is a monthly newspaper for AARP volunteers; *Working Age* is a bimonthly newsletter about changes in the older work force that is distributed to employers and policymakers. AARP also researches, produces, and makes available more than 140 titles on topics such as retirement planning, consumer affairs, and legal issues. Slide-tape and video cassette program kits on a wide range of topics are available to members and other nonprofit organizations.

The AARP also has become a recognized source for broadcast information on aging with its "Mature Focus" radio program and its Spanish-language counterpart. "Maturity Broadcast News," AARP's video news release service, reaches more than 18 million television viewers weekly. AARP also produces publications for the education of attorneys specializing in aging issues, holds annual conferences on aging and the law, and has set up statewide toll-free hotlines in six states that are staffed by attorneys to provide legal advice and referrals to persons needing help. Other programs included in the organization's extensive community service efforts are a consumer affairs program, driver retraining for motorists over fifty-five, an intergenerational program for youth and educators, an employment program to train economically disadvantaged older persons and place them in permanent jobs, and a tax aide program in cooperation with the Internal Revenue Service.

Besides the publications, information services, and volunteer opportunities provided to members, AARP makes available an extraordinary array of direct member services. Group health, auto, homeowners, and mobile home insurance are available to members from insurers. An investment program includes seven mutual funds managed for AARP by an investment firm. A travel service and special motor club plans are available to members, as are other travel and recreation privileges and discounts. AARP's pharmacy service provides prescription medicines and other health care items to members by mail or through direct purchase at pharmacies in thirteen cities around the nation. AARP does not try to duplicate existing services but provides services for members that otherwise might not exist at all or might not be conveniently available with comparable quality, service, and value. When members voice a need not being met in private-sector services, the Association conducts feasibility studies and examines whether the service fits with the organization's goals. If the decision is to proceed, AARP develops performance specifications including cost, quality, and continuity parameters; takes proposals from providers; and enters into contracts that are subject to periodic review and renewal.

POLICY CONCERNS

One of AARP's main goals is to advocate for the interests of older Americans; its membership includes workers and retirees, healthy and frail, rich and poor. The issues it addresses go well beyond Social Security and Medicare out of recognition that transportation, education, financial services, the workplace, the budget deficit, civil rights, and other issues are of concern to older Americans. AARP advocates reducing the federal budget deficit in a fair and effective manner, not singling out entitlements for spending cuts but rather using both spending cuts and tax increases. It argues for raising revenue by increasing compliance, broadening the income tax base, taxing the highest-income taxpayers more heavily, broadening and expanding the estate tax, and increasing excise taxes.

The AARP seeks improvement in transportation services for rural residents, the handicapped, and frail elderly persons. It works for housing and energy assistance programs that help older low-income persons to continue living in their homes and advocates for more action on the problems of the homeless.

AARP takes the position that regulatory agencies need to enforce consumer laws more vigorously, improve food safety and labeling, and strengthen protections in financial services, communications, and insurance. It supports regulatory oversight of cable television rates and service quality, and nondiscriminatory carriage and provision of programming. A broad range of consumer banking safeguards is supported by AARP, including requiring financial institutions to offer accounts with small minimum balances and reasonable charges, cash checks for their own customers, and provide comparable information on interest rates, account benefits and requirements, and other products and services using standard terminology. With respect to insurance, AARP supports a hybrid of federal and state regulation and is concerned about insurers' use of age to determine rates and availability of coverage. The Association urges Congress to reduce motor vehicle hazards through stricter safety standards, such as the five-mile-per-hour bumper standard, in order to reduce insurance costs. It seeks broader regulation of the telemarketing industry so that individuals buying in response to telephone solicitations receive the same protections afforded to mail-order or door-to-door purchasers. It also supports providing state attorneys general with the authority to act against fradulent telemarketers who victimize customers in their jurisdictions.

The Association seeks strengthened government integrity and ethics standards, focusing particularly on comprehensive campaign finance reforms, improved voter education efforts, and simplified voter registration procedures. Their position is that campaign finance reform should include limits on independent expenditures, time limits for fund-raising, limits on political action committee contributions, and elimination of "bundling" and "soft money." Environmental protection, particularly the health aspects of indoor air pollution, is an issue for AARP as well.

Education, health care, and workplace issues relate to AARP's intergenerational concerns. It advocates continued support for and improvement in the public school systems, increased teachers' salaries, and more equitable funding of school districts. It seeks access to health care for pregnant women and children, and priority attention for immunizations against childhood diseases. AARP supports family leave provisions for care of children and other family members.

AARP supports strengthening programs for the poor, including food stamps, increased benefits and asset limits for Supplemental Security Income, extension of Medicaid to all eligibles, and effective outreach programs to bring benefits to those who live in poverty. The Association also supports the streamlining and coordination of application procedures among the various federal assistance programs.

Simplification of pension laws is supported by AARP as long as such changes do not erode the protections already in place, particularly for low- and middle-income persons. It also favors incentives for expanding private pension plan participation and improving the portability of pension contributions. AARP is concerned that Social Security be prudently managed to ensure current and future benefits; it opposes redirecting trust fund reserves to other investments or reducing the Social Security tax rate. Concerns about the adequacy of the support provided to low-income Social Security recipients leads AARP to oppose reductions in benefits or in cost-of-living adjustments; it also opposes increasing the portion of benefits subject to taxation.

AARP supports expanding health care to those Americans who are uninsured or underinsured. It argues for controlling the growth in health care costs through a comprehensive restructuring of reimbursement without increasing out-of-pocket costs to patients. Its position is that reform of the health care system should provide both acute and long-term care for persons of all ages, regardless of income. The long-term care program sought by AARP would include a comprehensive range of services from in-home assistance to institutional care; the program would be funded as social insurance, with the cost spread across the entire population via tax revenues earmarked for a trust fund. Private insurance could supplement the public system by covering copayments, deductibles, and extra services.

TACTICS

AARP reviews existing data, conducts its own research, and surveys its members and the general population to gather information on their views. The Association's affiliated Andrus Foundation supports university research projects on aging and demonstration projects to illustrate the outcomes of research. Staff and volunteers work at national, state, and local levels to recommend policy and monitor the implementation of existing laws. Through its members and its publications, AARP encourages people to make lawmakers aware of their views; the Association informs its activists about how to communicate their views effectively and conducts special issue briefings on salient topics such as health care reform.

Association members and staff often appear before congressional committees and subcommittees to testify on a wide range of issues. They also testify before regulatory agencies and serve on advisory committees in both policy and technical capacities. For example, AARP staff serve on the Department of Energy's Task Force on Home Energy Rating Systems, working to assure that programs to promote home energy efficiency do not discriminate against the owners of older, less energy-efficient homes. Staff members also advise the Department of Health and Human Services in its review of the quality of board and care homes. AARP forms coalitions with other groups to support or oppose specific legislation; allies include other consumer organizations as well as business and provider groups such as the American Medical Association* and the Health Insurance Association of America.*

In every state AARP is represented by a state legislative committee of ten or more volunteer members who have been trained in dealing with lawmakers and government officials on state and local issues. They work on drafting and promoting legislation, appear before regulatory commissions, and foster grass-roots support through the media and in letter-writing and telephone campaigns. AARP's stature and resources allow it to present its case with organizations of state officials such as the National Governors' Association and the National Conference of State Legislatures. Utility and telephone rate regulation, living wills, and right-to-die issues are among those recently prominent for AARP at the state level.

AARP's Citizen Representation Program encourages individuals to seek positions on public boards and commissions that make decisions on issues of concern to older people, such as housing commissions and hospital and medical boards. AARP helps recruit, train, place, and support citizen representatives on governing bodies, licensing boards, peer review organizations, and other commissions at national, state, and local levels.

Increasing voter and candidate awareness of issues important to older persons is the aim of AARP/VOTE. This program solicits and publicizes candidates' views on specific issues but does not endorse candidates. Volunteers are trained in effective techniques for contacting and being interviewed by the media as well as on the substance of issues. AARP volunteers arrange public forums where older voters can question candidates, raising their awareness of issues as well as informing the public. Volunteers and consultants staff state offices in Iowa and New Hampshire in preparation for the presidential caucus and primary activities in those two states.

AARP engages in litigation by filing friend-of-the-court briefs and test cases before federal and state courts. Litigation in age discrimination and pension-related cases on behalf of older Americans has gained favorable court interpretations of legislation such as the Age Discrimination in Employment Act.

AARP's successful provision of extensive member services also serves as a policy tactic in that it has initiated services not available in the private sector that in turn have stimulated both government and industry to be more responsive to the needs of older consumers. For example, the success of its group health insurance program encouraged the passage of Medicare and prompted commercial insurers to offer supplemental health policies to older Americans.

FURTHER READING

AARP News: Fact Sheet. Monthly. Washington, DC: American Association of Retired Persons.

The AARP Public Policy Agenda. Annual. Washington, DC: American Association of Retired Persons.

Accomplishments: Division of Legislation and Public Policy. Annual. Washington, DC: American Association of Retired Persons.

All About AARP. 1992. Washington, DC: American Association of Retired Persons.

American Association of Retired Persons: Report and Financial Statements. Annual. Washington, DC: American Association of Retired Persons.

Introducing AARP. 1991. Washington, DC: American Association of Retired Persons.

Kosterlitz, Julie. 1993. "Golden Silence?" *National Journal,* April 3, p. 800.

Report to the Board of Directors by the Executive Director. Annual. Washington, DC: American Association of Retired Persons.

Weisskopf, Michael. 1994. "Health Care Forums Leave Public Aside." *Washington Post,* March 7, p. A6.

AMERICAN AUTOMOBILE ASSOCIATION (AAA)
1000 AAA Drive
Heathrow, FL 32746–5063
(407) 444–7000

ORGANIZATION AND RESOURCES

The American Automobile Association was established in 1902 by nine motor clubs with fewer than 1,000 members and has grown to a federation of 145 affiliated motor clubs with more than 1,000 offices and over 33 million members in the United States and Canada. Eighteen percent of the U.S. driving population are AAA members, and 21 percent of all cars registered in the United States belong to AAA members. The organization is a not-for-profit, taxpaying corporation; its purpose is to provide specialized services and facilities for members and to protect the rights, safety, comfort, and economic well-being of car owners and other travelers. Annual dues vary from club to club but range from $10 to $35 for associate membership and $21 to $68 for master membership. With sales, services, and dues, it generates over $10 billion in annual income—over $13 billion if credit card volume is included. AAA employs more than 35,000 persons; James B. Creal, president for twenty years, retired in December 1991; he was replaced by Paul R. Verkuil, former president of the College of William and Mary.

AAA is organized in four main service lines: motoring services, travel agency services, insurance and financial services, and public and government services. Motoring services includes AAA club responses to emergency road service calls, more than 21 million of them a year; a toll-free number allows members to obtain service and information when away from their home club area. AAA is the world's largest travel publisher, distributing TourBooks, Triptiks (individually tailored routings), a road atlas, and maps that are researched and produced by the organizations's own cartographic department. TourBooks include ratings based on AAA inspection of 28,000 lodgings and restaurants; some lodgings, restaurants, and other attractions offer discounts to AAA members. An Approved Auto Repair service identifies repair facilities that meet customer satisfaction, equipment, and competency standards; the AAA-approved sign guarantees work and assures members that any disputes will be arbitrated by AAA. *AAA AutoTest,* an annual review of 112 new vehicles, is available through AAA clubs and in bookstores.

With more than 950 full-service travel agencies, AAA is the largest travel agency organization in North America. It offers members negotiated discounts on car rentals and cruises and provides international driving permits, passport photos, and assistance in applying for passports and visas. TripAssist helps members resolve medical or legal problems, and find or replace lost luggage, documents, or travel tickets worldwide.

AAA insurance and financial services include making American Express Travelers Cheques available free to members. Many clubs offer their members home, auto, accident, auto repair, and breakdown insurance and car buying, leasing, and financing services. AAA/Visa was the first ''affinity group'' credit card, in 1979; more than 2 million AAA members now use AAA/Visa or AAA/ MasterCard at a lower annual fee than banks charge and account for over $3 billion in annual transactions.

Public and government services range from supporting school safety patrols to lobbying Congress. AAA originated the national school safety patrol movement in 1920; now more than 500,000 children serve as patrol members. AAA recognizes youngsters who save lives while on duty by awarding them medals and honoring them at a national ceremony that includes a trip to the White House to meet the president or first lady. Other school programs include alcohol education for all ages and an annual traffic safety poster program. Formal driver education was pioneered by AAA in 1936, and it continues to publish a widely used text for high-school driver education courses, *Responsible Driving*. Its instructional materials are also used in commercial driving schools, fleet driver training, and driver education courses for the physically handicapped. Handicapped drivers are further served by AAA research to test and develop standards for adaptive equipment, instructor-training classes, and *Handicapped Driver's Mobility Guide,* an annual publication.

AAA clubs provide monthly, bimonthly, and/or quarterly magazines or newsletters. Publications include a wide range of automotive, energy, environmental, travel, and legislative topics. AAA also produces brochures and pamphlets aimed at informing the public about driving costs, and providing tips for older drivers, on gasoline conservation, and on buying cars.

POLICY CONCERNS

AAA focuses on highway facilities, safety, energy policy, and taxation. It has consistently advocated an expanded and enhanced system of highways in the United States and was a major player in making the federal interstate highway program a reality. It has helped persuade Congress to increase highway funds, draw down the balance in the Highway Trust Fund, and expand the national highway system.

In addition to the many safety-related services noted above, AAA promotes the use of safety belts, child safety seats, and air bags; members and the general public are served through programs, texts, and promotional materials. AAA has helped achieve federal incentives for states that enact safety belt and mortorcycle helmet laws, laws requiring administrative suspension of driver's licenses for drinking and driving, and laws lowering legal blood alcohol levels to .08. AAA was also instrumental in encouraging Congress to limit use of longer combination vehicles to those areas where they now legally operate. It opposes the use of radar detectors in commercial motor vehicles, especially large trucks. Along with other safety groups, the organization supports extending car safety standards on side-impact protection, center high-mounted stop lamps, and roof-crush resistance to light trucks and vans. It also advocates improvement in overall safety belt design and design improvements to reduce rollover risks in passenger cars, light trucks, and vans.

Perhaps most controversial of all AAA positions is its opposition to increases in gasoline taxes by federal or state governments, particularly to raise revenue for deficit reduction. Member survey responses, showing a commitment to automobile use and a strong preference for lower rather than higher gasoline prices, are used by AAA leaders to defend this anti-tax position against charges that it is not environmentally sensitive. On the other hand, AAA does promote energy-efficient driving skills and supports switching to at least 25 percent nonpetroleum fuels by 2010.

AAA has been a leading advocate of federal funding for intelligent vehicle/ highway systems (IVHS) and has helped form IVHS America, a nonprofit corporation of private and public groups involved in researching IVHS. TravTek, a project for testing IVHS, is a joint venture of AAA, General Motors, the Federal Highway Administration, the Florida Department of Transportation, and the city of Orlando, Florida. TravTek provides in-vehicle navigation with address-to-address driving directions, travel information, and up-to-the-minute traffic data. AAA is providing the navigable map database, local tourist information, and a twenty-four-hour "help desk" to answer driver questions and provide road service if needed. It is also recruiting and training over 5,000 members to take part in the yearlong test in the Orlando area.

TACTICS

AAA is positioned as the organization speaking for the American driver, giving it a strong, "apple pie" image in national policy. Its publications inform and urge action by more than 33 million consuming members, without doubt making AAA a powerful grass-roots lobbying group. Data, research, and expertise provided by AAA make it a necessary player in highway transportation, safety, and energy issues; its spokespersons testify before congressional committees, serve on numerous executive branch advisory panels, and participate in both long-standing and temporary coalitions.

AAA serves as a consumer voice on issues such as gasoline price, availability, and quality. It provides a weekly nationwide survey of gasoline prices that is often reported by the media. Motorists are advised by AAA about availability and hours of station operation during periods of gasoline shortages. Its quality data formed the basis for urging a congressional investigation into incorrect octane postings on gasoline pumps nationwide. Results of the investigation generated extensive news coverage about the need for better gaoline quality inspections and helped AAA clubs gain passage of state octane-posting programs in Washington and Indiana.

FUEL, a nationwide coalition of more than 1,000 organizations led by AAA, opposes congressional proposals to increase the federal gasoline excise tax to reduce the deficit. The coalition joined White House efforts to defeat a 5-cent-per-gallon increase that was to be attached to the Intermodal Surface Transportation Efficiency Act of 1991.

Among the advisory roles played by AAA is its membership on the U.S. Alternative Fuels Council, which advises the Department of Energy and Congress on establishing a national alternative fuels policy. AAA also lobbies executive branch agencies by use of petitions, as it did to urge the Federal Highway Administration to ban radar detectors in commercial motor vehicles. It participates in rulemaking proceedings, for example, persuading the National Highway Traffic Safety Administration to include pedestrian safety in its program priority list in order to increase resources for states and communities working to improve pedestrian safety. AAA and other groups convinced the National Park Service to mandate use of safety belts by all drivers and front-seat passengers visiting national parks.

AUTOSOLVE involves AAA directly in consumer arbitration. A relatively new endeavor, it is certified by consumer affairs bureaus in ten states. It handled approximately 4,000 cases in 1991 for aggrieved consumers and Toyota, Hyundai, Lexus, Subaru, and Porsche. Government agencies as well as public and private groups use AAA's driver improvement programs designed for minor and repeat traffic offenders, and for volunteers like fleet drivers and operators over age fifty-five. Thirty-six states recognize driver improvement programs for reduction of traffic violation points or insurance premium discounts.

FURTHER READING

AAA at a Glance. Annual. Heathrow, FL: American Automobile Association.
AAA Facts. Annual. Heathrow, FL: American Automobile Association.
AAA Operations Report. Annual. Heathrow, FL: American Automobile Association.
Cook, James. 1991. "Heading for the 21st Century." *Forbes,* June 24, pp. 17–18.
A History of Service. 1992. Heathrow, FL: American Automobile Association.
McKnight, A. Scott and A. James McKnight. 1992. *The Effect of In-vehicle Navigation Information Systems Upon Driver Attention.* Washington, DC: AAA Foundation for Traffic Safety.

AMERICAN BANKERS ASSOCIATION (ABA)
1120 Connecticut Avenue N.W.
Washington, DC 20036
(202) 663–5000

ORGANIZATION AND RESOURCES

The American Bankers Association's mission is to enhance the role of America's commercial banks as the preeminent providers of financial services. It claims to be the voice of the American banking industry, and works through councils of members to determine commercial banking's positions on proposed federal legislation and regulations. The Association began in 1875 and now has over 10,000 member banks representing approximately 95 percent of the assets of the banking industry. Members include the full range of size, but two-thirds of member banks are small, having less than $100 million in assets. Each member institution has one vote in the General Convention, the annual membership meeting that has the power to set policy for the ABA. The Association supports a staff of 400 persons under the leadership of Don Ogilvie, executive vice president of the Association. Its annual budget is approximately $62 million.

Members may avail themselves of a wide range of services offered by the ABA. It maintains a library of over 60,000 volumes and 1,000 serial titles, reference to which is provided by toll-free telephone. ABA publishes a weekly newspaper that circulates to its members and members of Congress. The Washington Wire is a toll-free telephone news service on federal legislative and regulatory actions affecting banking.

The American Institute of Banking, the largest industry-sponsored adult education program in the world, is managed by the ABA. More than 350,000 students take courses each year through 600 local chapters and study groups. Education programs for senior bank executives, the Stonier Graduate School of Banking, and twenty-four other specialized banking schools are managed by the ABA. It has been a leader in introducing new educational technologies, such as computer-based simulation and tutorial programs, in bank management.

POLICY CONCERNS

The ABA consistently has been able to unite in opposition to federal regulations that impose costs on banks. It opposes low-cost bank accounts and basic services for the low-income or elderly; expedited funds availability requirements; additional or revised disclosure requirements on home mortgages, home equity loans, mortgage applications, community reinvestment, credit card charges, and truth-in-savings proposals. ABA takes the position that these individual laws snowball into a crushing regulatory burden on banks, which must compete with other financial service enterprises that are not subject to the same rules. Ogilvie characterized the 1991 Truth in Savings Act as demonstrating Congress's penchant for swatting flies with sledgehammers. The legislation requires banks to disclose rates, fees, and charges to consumers. For example, if a bank advertises free checking, the legislation forbids it to impose monthly maintenance fees, per-check charges, or other costs. It also forbids banks to calculate interest only on the "investable balance" (that share beyond what they are required to keep on reserve) or on the lowest balance of a customer's account.

Interest in reducing the regulatory burden on banks has led the ABA to support several initiatives offered by the Clinton administration. These have included efforts to streamline and coordinate bank examinations when more than one agency has responsibility for examining a bank, providing an easier process to allow banks to appeal fines and other enforcement actions by regulators, to lighten the appraisal requirements on real estate used as collateral for loans, and to give banks greater flexibility to make "character" loans.

TACTICS

Representing the ABA before Congress and the regulatory agencies is the Government Relations Group, directed by Edward L. Yingling. Extensive consultation among the diverse interests of members precedes policy development and lobbying. During the 1991 effort to overhaul banking legislation, the ABA was able to give general support to Bush administration proposals but unable to take a stand on such key issues as interstate branching because of division among its members. When it is able to forge a position, its staff and members have frequent contact with members of Congress and their staffs. They are often asked to testify before congressional committees and subcommittees on banking. On the executive side, the ABA serves on advisory committees, and regularly reviews and comments on proposed regulations from the Treasury Department, particularly the comptroller of the currency; the Federal Reserve; the Federal Deposit Insurance Corporation; and the Office of Thrift Supervision.

The ABA aids its members directly and indirectly in their relations with the mass media. Its national staff selects and trains individual bankers to do media tours of the country. The Association conducts national advertising programs and provides support for other special ad programs. Although it is a powerful organization on its own, the ABA enters into alliances with other trade and professional associations in related areas. Although independent of state bankers associations, the ABA does work with the state associations on government relations, education, and communication.

In addition to lobbying Congress and the executive branch, the ABA conducts litigation on behalf of the commercial banking industry. It acts as a plaintiff directly and also as a friend of the court on a wide range of issues. For example, ABA and four North Carolina banks sued the National Credit Union Administration for its decision to allow nonaffiliated employee groups to join the AT&T credit union. ABA also sponsors BankPac, the industry's largest political action committee; state bankers association donors are pictured in the *Bankers Weekly* centerfold feature presenting their contribution checks. BankPac's 1992 fund-raising goal was $2 million.

FURTHER READING

ABA Bankers Weekly. Weekly. Washington, DC: American Bankers Association.

Alston, Chuck. 1991. "Lobbyists Storm Capitol Hill, Clash over Banking Bill." *Congressional Quarterly Weekly Report,* August 24, pp. 2313–2318.

Ballen, Robert G. and Joseph P. Savage, 1994. "Interstate Bank Branching: Are the Walls Starting to Crumble?" *Banking Law Journal,* March/April, pp. 149–72.

Campagna, Anthony S. 1994. *The Economy in the Reagan Years: The Economic Consequences of the Reagan Administrations.* Westport, CT: Greenwood Press.

Crenshaw, Albert B. 1993. "The Truth Hangs in the Balance." *Washington Post,* national weekly edition, June 28–July 4, p. 18.

Jordan, Steve. 1990. "York Banker Soon to Leave Fast Lane After Year in the National Spotlight." *Omaha World-Herald,* October 14, p. M-1.

Meier, Kenneth J. 1985. *Regulation: Politics, Bureaucracy, and Economics.* New York: St. Martin's Press.

Taylor, Andrew. 1993. "Clinton Plan Aims to Ease Bank Loan Restrictions." *Congressional Quarterly Weekly Report,* March 13, p. 588.

This Is the ABA. 1989. Washington, DC: American Bankers Association.

AMERICAN CANCER SOCIETY (ACS)
316 Pennsylvania Avenue S.E.
Suite 200
Washington, DC 20003–1146
(202) 546–4011

ORGANIZATION AND RESOURCES

The American Cancer Society is a voluntary, nonprofit health organization exempt from income tax via section 501(c)(3) of the Internal Revenue Code. Information provided by the ACS showed that in the early 1990s, total revenue was close to 400 million. The majority of the revenue came from public contributions; the organization had just over 2 million volunteers and 4,300 staff. The ACS has as its main objective eliminating cancer as a major health problem through prevention. Until that goal is reached, the organization is committed to saving lives of people already stricken with the disease in its many forms and diminishing suffering from cancer through research, education, and service.

The ACS has its national office in Atlanta. Besides a Washington office, there are some 57 chartered divisions and 3,143 local units. A national board of directors is composed of volunteers representing each division. Half of all the voting members come from medical or scientific professions, and the rest from the lay public. Volunteer boards of directors from the medical/scientific professions and the lay public govern each division and unit. ACS publishes an annual report, a public affairs newsletter, a year-end legislative scorecard, and numerous other educational materials.

POLICY CONCERNS

The American Cancer Society is best known nationally for its involvement in tobacco policy. Recent initiatives on this front have included a bill introduced by Senator Edward Kennedy (D–MA) to further restrict tobacco marketing. On these issues the ACS and other anti-smoking advocacy groups have been staunchly opposed by the tobacco industry and its supporters in Washington. ACS also supports the work of the National Cancer Institute and the surgeon general's efforts. Increasingly, however, ACS has broadened its focus from tobacco to work on public policy in nutrition and health issues.

TACTICS

ACS officials in Washington disseminate information to membership groups through newsletters, legislative reviews, and so on. The purpose is to develop grass-roots support for legislation, instigate letter-writing campaigns (e.g., the organization's "Do the Write Thing"), and build public awareness and participation in ACS activities like the Great American Food Fight and Great American Smokeout. ACS has also developed public service advertisements against tobacco use for television broadcast.

Besides this public policy agenda, ACS funds research and cancer detection programs and operates education centers. Increasingly such activities also focus on nutrition, and the organization is trying to develop targeted public information campaigns for low-income and minority communities. Considerable organizational resources are devoted to fund-raising.

FURTHER READING

Byal, Nancy. 1989. "Good Food, Good Health: Project LEAN." *Better Homes and Gardens,* September, p. 46.

Day, Kelly A. and George B. Frisvold, 1993. "Medical Research and Genetic Resources Management: The Case of Taxol." *Contemporary Policy Issues,* July, pp. 1–11.

Facione, Noreen C. 1993. "Delay Versus Help Seeking for Breast Cancer Symptoms: A Critical Review of the Literature on Patient and Provider Delay." *Social Science and Medicine,* 36:12, pp. 1521–34.

AMERICAN COUNCIL FOR SCIENCE AND HEALTH (ACSH)

1995 Broadway, 16th floor
New York, NY 10023
Tel (212) 362–7044
Fax 212–362–4919

ORGANIZATION AND RESOURCES

Founded in 1978 to seek scientific evaluations of chemicals and human health to balance those offered by most liberal public interest consumer, health, and environmental organizations, the American Council for Science and Health has been led by Elizabeth Whelan since its inception. It has the status of a 501(c)(3) organization under U.S. tax laws. At the beginning of the 1990s, it operated on a budget slightly over $1.2 million. ACSH publishes *Inside ACSH* twice a year.

POLICY CONCERNS

ACSH is a reliable proponent of a conservative consumer point of view on scientific and technical issues associated with safety and health issues posed by today's consumer marketplace. It has weighed in on such issues as baby foods, the animal growth hormone BST used to increase milk production, safety issues posed by the presence of natural and man-made carcinogens in food, and others.

TACTICS

The organization often works with other conservative groups, holds periodic seminars on public health issues, and offers scientific studies supporting its views to the media, decision makers, and other interested parties.

FURTHER READING

Kurtz, Howard. 1990. "Dr. Whelan's Media Operation." *Columbia Journalism Review,* March/April, pp. 43–47.

Lamb, Lynette. 1991. "Beware of Medical Quackbusters." *Utne Reader,* November/December, pp. 36–38.
Politzer, Brianna. 1991. "Sweet Talk." *American Health,* September, pp. 40–42.
"Public-Interest Pretenders." 1994. *Consumer Reports,* May, pp. 316–320.
Whelan, Elizabeth. 1987. "Health Hoax and a Health Scare." *Vital Speeches of the Day,* 54:57–61 (November 1).
"Women and Alcohol." 1992. *Mademoiselle,* April, pp. 112ff.

AMERICAN ENTERPRISE INSTITUTE FOR PUBLIC POLICY RESEARCH (AEI)
1150 17th Street N.W.
Washington, DC 20036
(202) 862–5800

ORGANIZATION AND RESOURCES

The American Enterprise Institute was founded in 1943 as the American Enterprise Association. It is an independent, nonpartisan organization that sponsors original research on government policy, the American economy, and American politics. Its research aims to preserve and strengthen competitive private enterprise, traditional cultural and political values, limited government, and a vigilant defense through inquiry, debate, and writing. With a staff of 125 and a budget of $12 million, the Institute supports prominent economists, legal scholars, political scientists, and foreign policy specialists. Its board of trustees has included such prominent figures as Malcolm Forbes, David Packard, and the presidents of Dow Chemical, Morgan Stanley, and Amoco. Its Council of Academic Advisers includes James Q. Wilson, Samuel P. Huntington, Sam Peltzman, Nelson Polsby, and Murray Weidenbaum. Approximately half of its revenue comes from corporate contributions, one-third from foundations, and the remainder from individuals and revenues from conferences and other sales. Christopher C. DeMuth, AEI president since 1986, a University of Chicago-trained lawyer, was head of the White House Regulatory Office during Ronald Reagan's first term.

AEI's research is organized under three general topics—domestic and international economic policy, foreign and defense policy, and social and political studies. Faculty includes distinguished and well-known persons such as Jeane J. Kirkpatrick, Norman J. Ornstein, Michael Novak, Robert H. Bork, and Herbert Stein. AEI is able to draw prominent and powerful political figures, such as former President George Bush; Michael J. Boskin, former chairman of the Council of Economic Advisers; and Alan Greenspan, Federal Reserve Board chairman, to its various events. AEI publishes a monthly newsletter as well as *The American Enterprise,* a bimonthly magazine that presents articles, conference papers, and lectures delivered at AEI. Each issue includes regular columns on economics and public opinion.

POLICY CONCERNS

AEI's economic policy study topics include fiscal and monetary policy, regulation, international trade and finance, and the labor market and retirement.

AEI, along with the Chicago school of economists, is regarded as having been a significant contributor to the intellectual groundwork for the deregulation movement of the Ford, Carter, and Reagan administrations. Its current concern is that deregulation has lagged, state and federal regulation is growing again, and deregulation must be revived. AEI's work argues that the problems of the savings and loan industry and of banking were the result not of deregulation but of too little deregulation.

AEI research focuses on deregulation in broadcasting and communications, financial markets, food and pharmaceuticals, and the environment. AEI seeks environmental deregulation through the use of markets and economic incentives for more reasonable risk-reduction goals. Activities of the Food and Drug Administration are described by AEI as an inexplicable "crusade to suppress the dissemination of truthful information about foods and pharmaceuticals, based on the pernicious idea that consumers and physicians cannot assess information that is partial or that comes from an interested source."

The work of the Bush administration's Council on Competitiveness was applauded, although DeMuth lamented that the Office of Management and Budget's cost-benefit standard and review process had not been codified in statute and applied to the independent regulatory agencies. AEI scholars are also working on proposals for reform of health care financing, medical research, and private-sector initiatives. In the area of labor and retirement studies, AEI is concerned about the future of Social Security and Medicare and the provision of retiree health benefits by employers, and has published a study criticizing the Americans with Disabilities Act. AEI as an organization is attentive to the status of organized labor in that it attributes some of its own increased influence in the late 1970s to the decline in the influence of unionized labor.

Foreign and defense policy studies at AEI include U.S.–post Soviet relations, defense and arms control, China studies, and regional and development issues. AEI claims to have played a critical role in sustaining the anticommunist consensus in the United States throughout the Cold War. The growth of military expenditures in the 1980s is described by AEI as a "spectacularly productive investment" even in light of the associated budget deficits. The Institute's chief priority is to help define a new set of principles for American policy in the post–Cold War era, characterized by threats that are more subtle than they used to be and in which traditional notions of national sovereignty are losing ground to ideals of democratic self-government. In defense policy, the focus is on the tension between superpower disarmament and proliferation of weapons and technology among other powers. Its studies of China have led AEI to forecast that China is becoming an economic superpower and will be a superpower in other respects early in the twenty-first century.

AEI's social and political studies include legal and constitutional studies, political studies, social and individual responsibility, and religion and philosophy. Its concern is to support traditional cultural, educational, and social institutions. Particular attention here is on the challenges posed to traditional values by "radical" ideas about race, gender, and family; Robert H. Bork is devoting research to this theme. Political reform proposals, such as term limitations and campaign finance changes, are also under scrutiny.

Looking ahead, AEI research is under way on regulation and federalism, tort liability, arms control, and constitutional protections of economic liberty. New research focuses on congressional reform, income distribution, middle-class entitlement spending, technology policy and international trade, communications and broadcasting deregulation, and defense priorities for the post–Cold War era.

TACTICS

AEI's core tactic is to do intellectual battle on behalf of the free economic and political system. By adopting a longer time horizon than elected officials or journalists, but staying closer to practical policy issues than do pure academic research institutions, it prepares useful research to make policy debates more informed. AEI is closer to top corporate leaders than are other public policy research organizations and regards business corporations as the single most important positive force in American politics.

AEI's research is disseminated to a wide audience of businesspeople, academics, policymakers, and journalists. AEI publishes books and magazines, and sponsors frequent conferences, seminars, and lectures. AEI Press has more than 250 books in print, with new titles appearing on a regular basis; AEI scholars also write for major trade and university presses. Conferences include those focused on specific research, an annual policy conference addressed by prominent persons such as President George Bush, an annual world forum, and Election Watch, in which business executives meet monthly during national election years. Some AEI conferences are broadcast to nationwide audiences over C-SPAN.

AEI scholars appear frequently on television and radio, are cited in the nation's leading newspapers, and write regular newspaper and magazine columns. They are also invited to testify before congressional committees and other governmental bodies and to serve on study groups. Hundreds of articles are published annually by AEI scholars in newspapers, opinion magazines, and professional journals. Conference papers, book summaries, article reprints, and audiotapes and videotapes based on their research are also distributed in vast numbers by AEI.

AEI maintains relations with academia through fellowships allowing scholars to do research at AEI, lecture series, and monthly roundtables on regulation and on religion and economics. The Institute works cooperatively with other interested organizations, such as the Brookings Institution,* with which they sponsor the Renewing Congress Project, bringing together scholars and members of Congress and state legislatures. The Working Seminar on Integrated Services for Children and Families is sponsored in cooperation with the White House and Congress.

FURTHER READING

Annual Report. Annual. Washington, DC: American Enterprise Institute for Public Policy Research.

Beales, J. Howard and Timothy J. Muris. 1993. *State and Federal Regulation of National Advertising.* Lanham, MD: University Press of America for American Enterprise Institute.

Meyerson, Adam. 1992. "Captain of Enterprise: Christopher C. DeMuth on the Business of Liberty." *Policy Review,* Spring, pp. 10–19.

Newsletter. Monthly. Washington, DC: American Enterprise Institute for Public Policy Research.

Viscusi, W. Kip. 1993. *Product-Risk Labeling: A Federal Responsibility.* Lanham, MD: University Press of American for American Enterprise Institute.

AMERICAN FAMILY ASSOCIATION (AFA)
P.O. Drawer 2440
Tupelo, MS 38803
Tel (601) 844–5036
Fax 601–844–9176

ORGANIZATION AND RESOURCES

The American Family Association took its current name in 1988 but traces its activities back to 1977, when Reverend Donald E. Wildmon, a Methodist minister, formed the National Federation for Decency. With a 501(c)(3) tax designation, Reverend Wildmon's organization has made itself felt nationally from its base in Mississippi, especially in the worlds of television production and advertising in Los Angeles and Hollywood. By the early 1990s, it claimed 25 staff, 560 branches, and over 400,000 members nationwide. Information about AFA's activities and those of its affiliate, the AFA Law Center, is reported eleven times a year in the *AFA Journal.*

POLICY CONCERNS

The Association's purpose is to promote decency and Christian values in American society through the activities of a media watchdog group of concerned television viewers. This means bringing pressure on corporations that sponsor television shows AFA believes use excessive violence or sexually explicit images and/or messages.

TACTICS

Targets have included companies such as Chrysler, which pulled its advertisements from *Playboy* after receiving letters written by AFA members and sympathizers. The PepsiCo Company distanced itself from an ad campaign that had been scheduled to feature the singer Madonna after the AFA and other organizations drew attention to the arrangement. In these and other cases, AFA has proven adept at using grass-roots organizing, direct action, media outreach, threats of boycotts, and related techniques.

In some ways, this is an example of the old-fashioned fundamentalist Christian crusade against the evils of the big city adapted to the media age with corporations as diverse as Clorox, Noxell, Ralston Purina, General Mills, Southland (7–11), and Domino's Pizza feeling the heat. It also shows that conservative as well as liberal consumer watchdog groups can use these techniques. Government arts agencies also have felt AFA's ire. Specifically, AFA joined the organizations critical of the National Endowment for the Arts when conservatives drew attention to what they saw as government subsidization of pornographic art in 1989.

FURTHER READING

Dedman, Bill. 1992. "Bible Belt Blowhard." *Mother Jones,* November/December, pp. 40–43.
Dreifus, Claudia. 1992. "TV's Watchdog from Tupelo." *TV Guide,* September 5–11, p. 11.
Giles, Jeff. 1992. "The Wild Men on Prime Time." *Newsweek,* June 28, p. 66.
Klawans, Stuart. 1992. "Damned Ban." *The Nation,* December 7, pp. 688–689.
"Wildmon vs. Brown." 1992. *The Christian Century,* 109:707 (July 29–August 4).

AMERICAN FEDERATION OF LABOR AND CONGRESS OF INDUSTRIAL ORGANIZATIONS (AFL–CIO)
815 16th Street N.W.
Washington, DC 20006
(202) 637–5000

ORGANIZATION AND RESOURCES

The AFL–CIO is a voluntary federation of eighty-six national and international unions that have more than 45,000 local unions with combined membership of approximately 14 million. Its members are in occupations as diverse as actors, steelworkers, bus drivers, engineers, teachers, cannery workers, and letter carriers. This union of unions was established in 1955 when the American Federation of Labor and the Congress of Industrial Organizations merged into a single organization, ending a twenty-year division in the ranks of American labor. The merger recognized the principle that both craft and industrial unions are appropriate methods of organization.

Each member union is autonomous in deciding its own policies, negotiating contracts, setting dues, and providing member services. Each has its own headquarters, officers, and staff but cedes to the Federation a degree of authority to decide disputes and guide organizing drives. In turn, the Federation serves its members by speaking for the whole labor movement in national affairs, representing American labor in world affairs, helping organize unorganized workers, and coordinating activities such as community services, political education, and voter registration.

Member unions may affiliate with a variety of trade and industrial departments that promote common interests within the AFL–CIO. These include building and construction trades, food and allied service trades, industrial unions, maritime trades, metal trades, professional employees, public employees, transportation trades, and union label and service trades. The AFL–CIO is organized into state and local federations in each of the 50 states and Puerto Rico, and in 615 communities.

The highest governing body of the AFL–CIO is its convention, which meets every two years. Each national and international union is entitled to send delegates to the convention based on the size of its membership. Between conventions an executive council elected by the convention, made up of thirty-three vice presidents, a secretary-treasurer, and the president govern the organization. Lane Kirkland as president, and Thomas Donahue as secretary-treasurer, are responsible for operations of a staff of 400. In addition to staff departments in areas such as job safety and occupational health, civil rights, and health and employee benefits, institutes in television, labor education, and group purchasing of consumer benefits have been developed in recent years.

The chief internal communication vehicle is *AFL–CIO News,* a biweekly newspaper distributed to members through locals and state- and city-level affiliates. Courses and workshops on organizing, negotiating, arbitration, labor law, and media relations are offered through the George Meany Center for Labor Studies.

POLICY CONCERNS

The AFL–CIO's constitution spells out the organization's broad and ambitious policy aspirations. It seeks to improve wages, hours, and working conditions and to bring the benefits of collective bargaining to all workers. It aspires to equality of opportunity for all workers regardless of race, creed, color, sex, or national origin. It aims to protect and strengthen democratic institutions, to preserve America's democratic traditions, and to aid in promoting peace and freedom in the world. Supporting legislation helpful to workers, and protecting the labor movement against corruption and totalitarian influences are also among its goals. Finally, it pledges to encourage workers to register to vote and fully exercise their responsibilities as citizens and to encourage the sale of union-made goods.

Thus the policy agenda pursued by the AFL–CIO includes taxes, civil rights, Social Security, international trade, economic policy, education, jobs legislation, consumer protection, and the environment. Because of this wide scope, most major legislation is of concern to the organization. It claims partial credit for building and protecting the foundation for Social Security for elderly Americans, and it advocates progressive revenue measures and quality education for all children.

Organized labor has long recognized that workers have interests as consumers as well as producers. Unions have played an active role in the formation of consumer cooperatives and worked at national and state levels for consumer protection legislation. At the same time, they have expressed concern about goods imported from low-wage countries, arguing that they are not bargains in the long run. They have led the call for revitalizing American manufacturing industries and protecting American jobs in trade negotiations. Recent policy victories include legislation requiring employers to notify workers when a plant is going to close and the Family and Medical Leave Act. They support more rigorous meat, poultry, and seafood safety inspection, and truth-in-savings and truth-in-lending legislation. National health care reform is also of keen interest to the organization.

TACTICS

More than 130,000 collective bargaining contracts have been negotiated by the local unions affiliated with the AFL–CIO, and 98 percent of these run their course without a strike or other work interruption. These contracts cover rates of pay, hours of work, overtime, hospitalization and medical benefits, vacations, holidays, seniority, the handling of grievances, pensions, and other provisions. Beyond winning gains at the bargaining table, the AFL–CIO sees itself as the voice of social and economic justice for all citizens, and it serves as a legislative advocate for all working people. President Lyndon Johnson called it "the People's Lobby," and its members wear the label with pride.

The AFL–CIO is the voice of labor in Congress as its state federations are the labor voice in state legislatures, each backing up the other when needed. At the grass-roots level, its Committee on Political Education (COPE) provides programs of political education and conducts voter registration and get-out-the-vote campaigns. Its literature includes extensive analyses of candidates' voting records on key issues. State COPEs endorse candidates for governor, other state-level candidates, and U.S. senators and representatives with two-thirds approval of its delegates; national COPE may endorse presidential candidates by decision of the AFL–CIO general board. Some areas also have panels of individuals who make direct lobbying contacts with members of Congress in their districts.

AFL–CIO staff members monitor each stage of legislation, frequently testify before congressional committees and subcommittees, and monitor the implementation of legislation. Labor representatives, often AFL–CIO staff, serve on government advisory panels for the Occupational Safety and Health Administration, the Bureau of Labor Statistics, the Department of Health and Human Services, and the Toxic Substances Control Administration, to name just a few. The organization also acts as an administrative watchdog, as it did after the 1991 fatal fire at the Imperial Food Products plant in Hamlet, North Carolina. Pointing out that inspection of the poultry was more careful than enforcement of worker safety provisions, the AFL–CIO petitioned the U.S. Department of Labor to return North Carolina OSHA inspections to federal jurisdiction.

The AFL–CIO works cooperatively with other organizations that share its concerns, as it does with the U.S. Conference of Mayors* and the National

Housing Conference on housing issues. Direct action tactics may be seen in the work of the AFL–CIO Housing Trust, an investment vehicle for unions and qualified pension funds that finances construction and rehabilitation of housing and medical facilities.

More recently the organization has focused on expanding communications technology. With the founding of the Labor Institute of Public Affairs it has begun to develop programming for commercial, public, and cable television to present labor's view on salient issues. The Institute also has developed electronic internal communication capabilities for the AFL–CIO and its affiliates.

Labor's tactical heritage is on display in its Solidarity Day parades, held each Labor Day since 1981 in Washington, D.C. These marches attract several hundred thousand participants from all over the nation who rally to reaffirm their commitment to the cause.

FURTHER READING

AFL–CIO News. Biweekly. Washington, DC: AFL–CIO.
Hurd, Richard and Jeffrey Sohl. 1992. "Strategic Diversity in Labor PAC Contribution Patterns." *Social Science Journal,* 29:1, pp. 65–86.
Pearlstein, Steven and Dana Priest. 1994. "Touching the Untouchable for Health Reform." *Washington Post,* national weekly edition, May 2–8, p. 18.
Proceedings of the Convention. Biannual. Washington, DC: AFL–CIO.
A Short History of American Labor. 1981. Washington, DC: AFL–CIO.
Starobin, Paul. 1989. "Unions Turn to Grass Roots to Rebuild Hill Clout." *Congressional Quarterly Weekly Report,* September 2, pp. 2249–2254.
This Is the AFL–CIO. n.d. Washington, DC: AFL–CIO.

AMERICAN HOSPITAL ASSOCIATION (AHA)
840 North Lake Shore Drive
Chicago, IL 60611
(312) 280–6000

ORGANIZATION AND RESOURCES

The American Hospital Association is an organization of health care institutions including hospitals, other health care systems, and individuals. Its mission is to promote high-quality health care and services through leadership in the development of public policy, representation and advocacy of hospital and health care organization interests, and provision of services to assist hospitals and health care organizations in meeting the needs of their communities. Founded in 1898, and until 1906 called the Association of Hospital Superintendents of the U.S. and Canada, the AHA now has 54,500 members. Its annual budget is approximately $80 million; its staff numbers about 900 persons under the direction of Richard J. Davidson.

AHA conducts research and provides education for members in the areas of hospital economics, health care administration, and community relations. In-service education of hospital personnel and multimedia educational materials for member use also are available. Services such as institutional effectiveness review programs, technology assessment, and administrative support are made available to members. Members also may use AHA's substantial library on health care administration. The organization's periodical publications include *AHANews,* a weekly newsletter, and *Hospitals,* a biweekly. Annual statistical publications include *Guide to the Health Care Field* and *Hospital Statistics.*

POLICY CONCERNS

AHA becomes involved in a wide range of issues that impact the role of its members in health care. It is among the many organizations actively concerned with national health care reform, advocating universal, basic health care coverage for all individuals through employer-sponsored programs and a consolidated public program combining and expanding Medicare and Medicaid. AHA advocates restructuring the delivery system by developing community care networks that would receive predominantly per capita payments and negotiate provider payments within the network; this, AHA argues, would help impose economic discipline. AHA also supports private insurance reform to improve availability and affordability of private insurance, including coverage for small groups; it also supports precluding underwriting practices such as preexisting conditions clauses but favors reinsurance mechanisms and state-level insurance pools.

AHA's national health care strategy calls for reform of the tort system to decrease the practice of defensive medicine and avoid periodic liability insurance crises. AHA seeks changes in antitrust law and other barriers to mergers, advocating greater consideration of potential efficiencies, the financial condition of hospitals, and competition from nonhospital providers. In the same vein, the Association has supported efforts to provide alternative dispute resolution systems and improve state-level monitoring of health care professionals. While it supports widely available consumer information on individual practitioner and provider cost and quality outcomes, it argues that the information must be useful, be suitable to its purpose, and be prepared and released in a fashion that enables the public to make valid observations. AHA argues that those releasing data should take steps to assure that subjects of disclosure have adequate opportunity to review and respond to proposed disclosures, that providers be equitably selected so that no class of providers is held to a higher standard or disproportionately burdened, and that data be released only if their value to the public outweighs their potential for harm.

On the volatile issue of AIDS, AHA recommends universal precautions to minimize the risk of transmission but is against mandatory testing and routine notification of patients when it becomes known that a health care worker is infected. Instead, determination of an HIV-infected worker's fitness for duty should be made on a case-by-case basis with regard to the risk of transmission.

In the area of indigent care, AHA favors a Medicaid minimum payment that would ensure that payments to hospitals equal the full financial costs of providing services; it is also concerned that hospitals providing a disproportionate share of Medicaid services not be disadvantaged in reimbursement formulas. Proposals for a Medicaid buy-in for pregnant women and children, expanded Medicaid and Medicare eligibility for disabled children, special grants for maternal and child health care, and requiring maternity coverage for dependent children under family insurance plans are supported by AHA as responses to maternal and child health concerns.

Controversy over emergency care has led AHA to support safeguards against inappropriate transfers but to insist that hospitals should not be liable for acts and omissions that are not within their control. AHA is actively concerned with the prospective pricing policies under Medicare and seeks periodic recalculation of prices as well as refinements reflecting variations in costs such as those based on labor, provision of medical education, and the special needs of rural hospitals. Recognizing that there is a legitimate oversight role for external review under Medicare prospective pricing, AHA has urged that any oversight system be built on hospitals' existing internal quality controls.

The AHA strongly supports current tax exemption policies for not-for-profit hospitals and the tax-favored status of not-for-profit foundations sponsored by investor-owned hospitals. The organization backs current requirements that tax exemption be based on community benefit standards rather than on charity care requirements. Federal assistance to states for the development of local, regional, or statewide trauma systems is welcomed by AHA. However, it seeks flexibility within those programs to allow states and localities to develop their own standards and criteria. It also believes that hospitals should receive assistance for their uncompensated costs associated with trauma services.

Interest in the future supply of health care professionals leads AHA to advocate greater provider involvement in addressing basic skill and education deficiencies, more flexibility in staffing (including using cross-trained and multiskilled practitioners), and the use of alternative competency measures such as proficiency tests. Graduate medical education should, in AHA's view, continue to be financed primarily through patient care revenues.

On the sensitive and highly visible issue of living wills, AHA calls for widespread use of advance directives to improve patient self-determination and limit nonbeneficial final care. AHA strives to foster individual, family, and surrogate decision making within the framework of the physician–patient relationship and standards of informed consent.

TACTICS

AHA pursues its policy interests with a range of tactics from providing research and testimony to grass-roots advocacy through its members. Data collected from members, such as the current effort to analyze the impact of probable changes in Medicaid regulations on state programs, are a significant and unique resource for the organization. This type of information is useful in helping shape regulations, negotiating with federal agencies such as the Health Care Financing Administration, and presenting testimony to Congress. Such data are also distributed through publications produced and sent to AHA members. AHA surveys have documented the overcrowding problems facing hospital emergency departments, particularly acute for those with trauma centers; they accompanied a call for full funding for the 1990 Trauma Care Systems Act. Advocating for the special needs of rural hospitals resulted in the publication of five monographs in 1992.

Efforts devoted to maternal and child health resulted in the distribution of *Health Care Reform—a Must for Women and Children,* which illustrates the effect of today's financing and delivery system flaws on women and children. In this work, as on other issues, AHA coalesces with trade and professional associations having similar views; here the coalition includes insurers, health care providers, other businesses, and child advocates. The coalition has urged more rapid implementation of Medicaid eligibility for poor children and has tried to persuade Congress to oppose the Clinton administration's proposed cap on federal Medicaid matching funds for acute care services for the nonelderly. AHA staff members also work across federal agency boundaries to remedy inconsistent standards; for example, they work with the departments of Justice and Health and Human Services, and the Federal Trade Commission to develop guidance on antitrust standards and collaborative endeavors by providers. AHA also assists its members in coping with federal regulations once they are finalized; for example, the organization sends members a guide on the methodology to use in responding to Health Care Financing Administration requests for mortality data. Judicial strategies used by AHA include filing amicus curiae briefs in support of state hospital associations or individual hospitals litigating such issues as Medicaid payments or liability judgments.

FURTHER READING

Kosterlitz, Julie. 1992. "Survival Tactics: Once Seen as Stubborn Naysayers, the American Medical Association and the American Hospital Association Are Trying a Kinder, Gentler Approach to the Health Care Reform Debate." *National Journal,* October 24, pp. 2428–32.
Public Policy Priority Summary. Annual. Chicago: American Hospital Association.

AMERICAN MEAT INSTITUTE (AMI)
P.O. Box 3556
Washington, DC 20007
Tel (703) 841–2400
Fax 703–527–0938

ORGANIZATION AND RESOURCES

Formed in 1906 by the journal *National Provisioner,* in response to a call for an organization to deal with concerns felt by the meat industry, the American Meat Institute has operated under several different names (e.g., the Association of American Meat Packers, and the American Meat Packing Association) before acquiring its present name in 1940. It operates with a staff of 18, publishes a newsletter, and is supported by about 300 members. Most are meat-processing and -packaging companies; others, such as those making machinery and supplies used in the industry, can be affiliate members.

POLICY CONCERNS

Established to help the meat packing industry adjust to the federal health and safety inspection standards that followed in the wake of public disgust at the unsanitary conditions reported by investigative journalists like Upton Sinclair at the turn of the century, the AMI represents an early example of how trade associations gear up to deal with governmental regulation. In addition to meat inspection, government programs and policies in which AMI and its member companies take an active interest today include livestock production and feeding, animal diseases, food additives and labeling, and environmental requirements that the industry must meet.

Although they did not get as much attention after 1906, food safety concerns have resurfaced periodically. In the face of consumer activism since the mid-1960s, a period that saw new legislative interest in pure and wholesome meat, we are most interested in AMI's involvement with food safety issues, regulatory reform, and international trade. On the latter issue, the industry wants to get the U.S. government to pressure the Common Market to reverse a ban on imports of American meat treated with hormones. In the 1970s, AMI was involved in the beginning of a new round of concern about food safety and health in reaction to proposals to ban nitrite from meat processing and curing.

TACTICS

Like other trade associations, AMI lobbies Congress, monitors regulatory decision making, organizes and participates in coalitions, develops information for its members and interested publics, and operates a speakers' bureau.

FURTHER READING

"The Enlightened Burger." 1991. *Prevention,* November, p. 78.

AMERICAN MEDICAL ASSOCIATION (AMA)

515 North State Street
Chicago, IL 60610
(312) 464–5000

1101 Vermont Avenue N.W.
Washington, DC 20005
(202) 789–7400

600 Third Avenue
New York, NY 10016
(212) 867–6640

ORGANIZATION AND RESOURCES

The American Medical Association is the nation's largest medical organization, providing a voice for physicians in shaping health care policy. The AMA's objective is to promote the science and art of medicine and the betterment of public health. More than 290,000 physicians are members. It employs a staff of 1,100 in offices in Chicago, New York, and Washington, D.C.; 50 staff members work in the Washington, D.C. office. The AMA's annual budget is approximately $200 million, about 40 percent of which comes from membership dues, 25 percent from advertising and subscriptions, over 10 percent from investment income, and the remainder from other sources.

A 19-person board of directors governs the AMA, but its policy positions are adopted by the AMA House of Delegates, comprised of over 400 physician delegates representing every state, more than 80 national medical specialty societies (such as the American College of Obstetricians and Gynecologists), 5 federal service groups (including the U.S. surgeon general and the Veterans Administration), and 5 sections representing hospital medical staffs, resident physicians, medical students, young physicians, and medical schools. State medical associations are entitled to one voting delegate and one alternate in the House of Delegates for each 1,000 members or fraction thereof; other organizations are entitled to one delegate and one alternate each. The AMA describes itself as the unified voice of medicine because it represents over 90 percent of physicians who belong to a county medical society, a state association, a specialty society, or some combination of these. The House of Delegates meets twice a year, preceded by meetings of individual committees that consider resolutions and reports and make recommendations for adoption by the House of Delegates.

In the early 1800's, medicine was not regarded as a profession; anyone could be called a doctor. Some were trained, others were not, and some sold miracle cures and potions. The AMA was founded in 1847 by representatives of twenty-eight medical schools and forty medical societies to professionalize medicine by raising medical education standards and establishing a code of ethics. Today's medical education and state licensing structure is the product of AMA influence; its Council on Medical Education maintains accreditation standards for undergraduate, graduate, and continuing education. The AMA Council on Ethical and Judicial Affairs maintains the Principles of Medical Ethics, recognized as the code for the profession; it interprets the principles by offering opinions on controversial subjects, and can rule to censure, suspend, or expel a member who does not comply. Incompetent or unethical practitioners can be identified and disciplined or reported to other authorities.

The AMA has published the *Journal of the American Medical Association* (*JAMA*) since 1883; it is now published in eleven languages and is the world's most widely read medical journal. *JAMA* and the AMA's ten medical specialty journals, such as *Archives of General Psychiatry* and *Archives of Internal Medicine,* have a worldwide circulation of more than one million; their features are reported regularly in the mass media as well. *American Medical News* is a weekly paper covering news and opinion on issues of political, social, and economic significance, such as legislation, regulations, and court decisions.

The AMA is the authoritative source on the practice of medicine. Physician Data Services and the AMA Center for Health Policy Research regularly collect information, including the number of physicians, their specialties, types of practice, income, and expenses; the data are reported to AMA members and the public. AMA also polls physicians and the public for their opinions on health care issues. It publishes a series of consumer books such as the *American Medical Association Encyclopedia of Medicine,* which provides accessible health information.

POLICY CONCERNS

The AMA has a long history of activism not only in professionalizing the practice of medicine but also in supporting public health initiatives. As early as 1860 it supported the labeling of packages containing poison; early in the twentieth century it endorsed testing children's vision and hearing in schools and supported quality standards for milk. In 1954 it endorsed requiring auto manufacturers to equip all vehicles with seat belts. More recently it has supported state drunk driving laws setting the illegal blood alcohol level at .05 percent and banning all advertising and promotion of tobacco products.

Concern over upgrading and protecting the practice of medicine brings the AMA into state and federal policy forums on a wide range of topics including research funds, medical education standards and financial support, the parameters under which other health professionals such as nurses or physician assistants may practice, regulation of advertising, and liability insurance for malpractice. Another recurring issue that has brought the AMA into the policy limelight periodically over the twentieth century is how health care is to be financed and delivered. During the first serious debate in the United States over national health insurance, the AMA was among those who argued in favor; the 1917 House of Delegates voted for a government health insurance program. But by the time of the Great Depression, when the issue arose again, the AMA was firmly in opposition; and in more recent times, the AMA's commitment has been to preserve independent, fee-for-service practice of medicine. Its dire warnings that proposals being heard in the 1950s amounted to "socialized medicine" reverberated across America. Significantly scaled back from earlier models, Medicare and Medicaid were enacted in 1965 in spite of the AMA's opposition. However, the AMA more recently has found itself busy defending Medicare and Medicaid payment systems against cuts or changes. It has opposed recent efforts to alter the Medicare reimbursement system in the direction of greater support for basic care and equity for rural and other underserved areas; its opposition is directed at the threat posed to physician income expectations insofar as the reform intends to dampen the rate at which health care costs are increasing.

In the 1990s debate over medical care, the AMA launched a massive public campaign to discredit the Canadian health care program, which is often taken as a model for potential U.S. reforms. The AMA points out the delays and shortages experienced by Canadian patients and physicians, and emphasizes that Americans enjoy more advanced medical technology and greater freedom of choice. The Association advocates strengthening the public–private partnership already in place in the United States. Health Access America, its sixteen-point plan competing for the attention of policymakers, would require employers to provide health insurance for full-time workers and their families, allow tax incentives to make such coverage more affordable, and create state risk pools for those who cannot afford private insurance or who have illnesses that make them uninsurable. It also would expand Medicaid to provide nationally uniform coverage of persons below the poverty line and would contain costs by reforming the medical malpractice system and capping damage awards. Health Access America includes neither cost estimates nor financing mechanisms.

TACTICS

The AMA Washington staff monitors legislative and regulatory activities. The AMA's expertise is sought by both legislative and executive decision makers; spokespersons for the AMA testify regularly before Congress, as often as several times each month. AMA data and experts are frequently cited when issues are debated in Congress. The AMA has a reputation for a "hard-hitting" lobbying style in both direct and grass-roots approaches; it pursues its interests whether such action puts it among usual allies or not. Among the techniques used by the AMA to inform members for grass-roots lobbying and to influence voting behavior is analysis of congressional votes on issues related to health care. It also undertakes massive advertising campaigns on proposals such as the effort to revise the way Medicare pays physicians. Such campaigns include bumper stickers, full-page newspaper ads, television time, barrages of telephone calls, and direct visits to members of Congress by their personal physicians.

AMPAC, the American Medical Political Action Committee, is consistently one of the major contributors to federal election campaigns. It also engages in high-conflict tactics, for example, spending more than $250,000 in a vain 1986 effort to unseat Congressman Pete Stark (D-CA), chairman of the House Ways and Means health subcommittee. The organization also monitors the impact of the judiciary on the practice of medicine and engages in litigation on behalf of the profession, including arguing cases before the Supreme Court.

The AMA's expertise makes it a respected source of information for the news media. AMA public information officers answer 15,000 phone calls a year, helping reporters with background information and arranging interviews with physician spokespersons. In addition, AMA officers and trustees visit more than forty cities each year to discuss health policy issues with reporters, editors, and talk show hosts. Medical and science reporters receive a weekly packet of news releases covering articles from *JAMA;* the most significant story in each packet is also distributed via satellite as a video news release and is used by over 300 stations in the United States and Canada. American Medical Radio News produces daily health news reports used by more than 700 stations in the United

States; American Medical Television provides 10 hours of medical programming on CNBC aimed at the public and physicians. The AMA also provides public service announcements on topics ranging from AIDS to child abuse that are aired by over 1,000 local, network, and cable stations each year.

FURTHER READING

American Medical Association: Physicians Dedicated to the Health of America. 1992. Chicago: American Medical Association.

Johnson, James A. and Walter J. Jones. 1993. *The American Medical Association and Organized Medicine.* Hamden, CT: Garland.

Rovner, Julie. 1989a. "Members May Target Referrals to Doctor-Owned Facilities." *Congressional Quarterly Weekly Report,* March 4, pp. 458–460.

———. 1989b. "Ways and Means OKs Overhaul of Medicare Payment Plan." *Congressional Quarterly Weekly Report,* July 1, pp. 1626–1628.

———. 1991a. "Congress Feels the Pressure of Health-Care Squeeze." *Congressional Quarterly Weekly Report,* February 16, pp. 414–421.

———. 1991b. "Growing Health-Care Debate Widens Partisan Divisions." *Congressional Quarterly Weekly Report,* November 16, pp. 3377–3382.

Specter, Michael. 1989. "Searching for the Best Medical Care Money Can't Buy." *Washington Post,* national weekly edition, December 25–31, pp. 31–32.

Sullivan, Louis W. 1989. "How to Curb Physician Payments." *Washington Post,* national weekly edition, July 17–23, p. 34.

AMERICAN PUBLIC POWER ASSOCIATION (APPA)
2301 M Street N.W.
Washington, DC 20037–1484
(202) 467–2959

ORGANIZATION AND RESOURCES

Established in 1940, the American Public Power Association has as members over 1,750 municipal and other local, publicly owned electric utilities. The organization's objectives are to provide services to members concerning power supply, communications, energy management, training, engineering and operations, financial management, publications, and customer service.

Among the organization's publications are periodicals including *Public Power Weekly, Public Power,* and management and technical information in various forms, including material that member organizations can use as bill stuffers and other kinds of consumer information. This is the equivalent organization to the Edison Electric Institute* for public-sector electrical utilities.

POLICY CONCERNS

Current issues of concern to the organization include private use limitations on tax-exempt bonds issued for output facilities, tax simplification, tax exemptions, state authority over energy and environmental regulations, Clean Water

Act issues, and Occupational Safety and Health Administration reform. Some of these are similar to issues faced by investor-owned utilities.

TACTICS

Like their private-sector colleagues, APPA officials are concerned about regulations placed on them by the national government, as well as consumer and environmental group critics. Among APPA's activities are utility education programs, legislative scorecards, and legislative status reports. The organization also has an information center library and offers award programs and other recognitions.

FURTHER READING

Brown, Ashley C. 1993. "Electricity After the Energy Policy Act of 1992: The Regulatory Agenda." *Electricity Journal,* January/February, pp. 33–50.
Crawford, Mark. 1985. "The Electricity Industry's Dilemma." *Science,* July 19, pp. 248–250.

AMERICAN SOCIETY OF TRAVEL AGENTS (ASTA)
1101 King Street
Alexandria, VA 22314
(703) 739–2782

ORGANIZATION AND RESOURCES

Formed in 1931, ASTA has 22,000 members, a budget of $11 million, and a staff of eighty. The organization sponsors ASTAPAC, conducts training for travel agency staff (e.g., ASTA School at Sea for cruise sales), and publishes *ASTA Agency Management.* ASTA's purpose is to promote travel and encourage people to use the services of its members, who own and operate travel agencies. Affiliate membership is open to major transportation carriers such as AMTRAK, the airlines, and the cruise industry as well as hotels, resorts, and important corporations in the entertainment, vacation, and leisure industries.

POLICY CONCERNS

ASTA has been involved in many of the major controversies involving airline deregulation since the mid-1970s. Like the airlines and the other lobbyists involved, ASTA claims to speak for passengers on issues like air travel delays, discount airfares, and the effect of city taxes on rental car rates. Such a view leads ASTA and other sectors of the travel industry to be concerned about the effects of new taxes on travel (e.g., proposals to raise recreational users' fees on commercial tour owners operating in national parks). The travel agency industry also sought a rollback of the national airline ticket taxes added by Congress in the early 1990s. These concerns have parallels on the state level, where ASTA has sought repeal of a New York tax on hotel rooms, arguing that it was too high.

American industry's increasing concerns about international trade issues have taken form in efforts to make government understand the effects that globalization of industry is having on their business. Along with American air carriers and aircraft manufacturers, ASTA wants government's help in attaining fair access for U.S. airlines abroad. However, the travel industry believes that it is regarded by government policymakers as a luxury sector rather than as a major sector of the U.S. economy.

Air travel still had not stabilized in the early 1990s after the turbulence created by deregulation. Since ASTA represents thousands of small businesses, its members want the organization to monitor and weigh in from that perspective on issues such as government's interest in employer mandates included in the Family and Medical Leave Act of 1993 and the proposed universal coverage feature of the Clinton health care plan.

TACTICS

The players in Washington public policy debates affecting the travel industry in recent years have been many and varied. On issues concerning air travel, which received much media coverage during the 1980s, consumer and safety groups and unions (e.g., pilots, flight attendants, machinists, and air traffic controllers) were prominently involved, as were federal government agencies charged with regulating air fares and safety. Other government targets include the departments of Commerce, Treasury, State (on the subject of international travel and terrorism against tourists), and Transportation. Independent federal agencies like the Federal Trade Commission are also important, as are state attorneys general, who investigate and prosecute travel scams. State and federal officials are also involved when ASTA and its affiliates complain about unfair competition from nonprofit groups that organize travel programs.

Consider also the role played in Washington politics by organizations such as the American Association of Airport Executives. Also important are manufacturers (e.g., major companies such as Boeing, United Technologies, Cessna); the second generation of no-frills carriers, like Southwest Airlines, which have taken advantage of airline deregulation and the mistakes made by the major passenger carriers; and freight carriers like Federal Express.

Many issues of concern to ASTA in Congress come before the transportation committee in each house. Issues under the House Public Works and Transportation Committee's responsibility, profiled in ASTA's *Government Affairs Issue Brief,* have included bills improving airline service (e.g., to small communities, enhancing competition among airlines, and protecting consumer rights in airline bankruptcy proceedings), tax rules governing business meals and entertainment, cruise ship legislation, and bills seeking to curb travel scams. The fortunes of the travel industry can also be affected by the tax-writing committees of each chamber, which decide matters such as whether frequent flyer bonuses should be subject to tax and how travel and entertainment expenses will be treated for tax purposes.

Besides monitoring and seeking to shape legislation and regulatory decision making, ASTA has been active in coalitions with other industry representatives in Washington. For example, ASTA was a founding member of the Business Coalition for Fair Competition (BCFC), organized to convince Congress to include nonprofit organizations in the tax code's provisions for unrelated business tax. This alliance included a number of trade and professional associations seeking to educate Congress and the public on the importance of "fair" taxation to the operation of a free enterprise system.

FURTHER READING

Peterson, Barbara S. 1993. "Commission Impossible." *ASTA Agency Management,* August, pp. 34–36.

AMERICANS FOR SAFE FOOD (ASF)
1501 Sixteenth Street N.W.
Washington, DC 20036
(202) 222–9110

ORGANIZATION AND RESOURCES

Americans for Safe Food is a project of the Center for Science in the Public Interest.* Its particular goal is to improve the quality of the U.S. food supply.

POLICY CONCERNS

In its focus on the safety of the food supply, ASF gives particular attention to promoting organic food.

TACTICS

ASF tactics include negotiating with local supermarkets to promote organic food, networking with environmental groups, publicizing health food and diets in the media, encouraging letters to the editor, and publishing sources of organically grown food. It also relies on pamphlets, fliers, posters, and "safe food" fairs.

ASF finds allies among environmental groups, local food cooperatives, animal rights groups, health food stores, medical and health professionals, consumer groups, civic organizations, some farmers' organizations, and religious groups.

FURTHER READING

Anderson, Emily. 1988. "The Natural Foods Labeling Controversy." *Utne Reader,* January/February, pp. 25–27.
Durner, Pat. 1987. "How Safe Are the Pesticides on Food?" *Rodale's Organic Gardening,* June, pp. 69–76.
Katz, Mira. 1987. "Pasta al Pesticidio, with a Side of Salmonella." *Sierra,* September/ October, pp. 16–17.

U.S. Congress. House Committee on Agriculture Subcommittee on Department Operations and Nutrition. 1994. *Hearing on Food Quality Protection Act of 1993.* Washington, DC: Government Printing Office.

U.S. Congress. House Committee on Agriculture Subcommittee on Department Operations and Nutrition. 1993. *Hearing to Review Nutrition Research and Education Activities.* Washington, DC: Government Printing Office.

ASSOCIATION OF BIOTECHNOLOGY COMPANIES (ABC)

1666 Connecticut Avenue N.W.
Washington, DC 20009
Tel (202) 234–3330
Fax 202–234–3565

ORGANIZATION AND RESOURCES

The Association of Biotechnology Companies, founded in 1983, is a relatively new trade association on the Washington scene. This organization represents some 320 member firms seeking to market health care products, drugs used in animal husbandry, and specialty products used in industrial processes. Member firms argue that the results of the biotechnological revolution will bring myriad benefits to consumers, but some organizations representing the interests of consumers, family farmers, and others disagree.

The organization publishes *ABC Alerts* on a periodic basis and *Details,* a newsletter on legislative and regulatory developments, six times a year.

POLICY CONCERNS

One of the main issues tackled by ABC has been securing agreement from national government regulatory agencies, chiefly the Food and Drug Administration, for the use of the growth hormone BST in milk production. Meanwhile, at the behest of farm groups in at least two dairy states, milk from cows treated with BST has been banned from the retail market.

TACTICS

ABC, working with individual companies involved in the field of biotechnology, has sought to convince regulatory officials that its products are safe. Besides the FDA, governmental agencies involved in these issues have included the National Institutes of Health, the Department of Agriculture, the Environmental Protection Agency, the Office of Science and Technology, and the Office of Technology Assessment. At the same time ABC is working with health and science agencies, the industry has sought to influence public opinion and ward off legislative curbs. Allies in these efforts include the Center for Scientific Information, a biotechnology advocacy group; the Council for Responsible Genetics, a group of scientists and academics headquartered in Cambridge, Massachusetts; and conservative and industry-oriented research organizations such as the Hudson Institute and the American Council for Science and Health.*

Among the industry's critics are family farm groups, environmentalists such as Friends of the Earth's* Jack Doyle, and consumer activists such as Jeremy Rifkin, the chief spokesperson for the Foundation on Economic Trends.*

FURTHER READING

Beardsley, Tim. 1992. "Piecemeal Patents." *Scientific American,* July, pp. 106ff.
Browning, Graeme. 1992. "Biotech Politics." *National Journal,* February 29, pp. 511–514.
Doyle, Jack. 1985. *Altered Harvest.* New York: Viking Press.

ASSOCIATION OF COMMUNITY ORGANIZATIONS FOR REFORM NOW (ACORN)
739 8th Street S.E.
Washington, DC 20003
(202) 547–2500

ORGANIZATION AND RESOURCES

ACORN is a grass-roots, direct-action organization committed to winning economic power and improvement for low- and moderate-income people. It was founded in 1970 by a group of Arkansas welfare mothers dedicated to organizing the poor and powerless. Its membership numbers over 75,000 African American, white, and Latino families organized in more than 500 neighborhood chapters and 26 state groups with offices in Chicago, Brooklyn, New Orleans, and Little Rock in addition to the one in Washington. Chief organizer is Wade Rathke, who was previously with the Massachusetts branch of the Welfare Rights Organization.

The association has worked at reaching low-wage service workers by organizing them in the United Labor Unions, which it helped found in 1979. Now affiliated with the AFL–CIO,* it has over 20,000 members in schools, nursing homes, hospitals, and other services in Louisiana, Illinois, Arkansas, and Texas.

The principle of self-sufficiency guides the organization's budget philosophy; 80 percent of its funds come from member dues, raffles, ad sales, dinners, and other events. Its annual budget is approximately $10 million; most of its 200 staff members are assigned to organizing in low-income communities. ACORN prides itself on having its members, not staff or lawyers, speak for and lead the organization. In on-the-job and in formal training programs, members are taught the skills and confidence to chart the group's direction from the neighborhood level to the national board.

ACORN's Housing Corporations, operating in seven states and the District of Columbia, acquire and rehabilitate abandoned buildings. Low- and moderate-income families who contribute sweat equity buy the houses at below-market prices; the land remains in the ACORN Community Land Association to ensure its use for affordable housing over the long run.

POLICY CONCERNS

Access to mortgages for low-income home buyers is the issue most frequently associated with ACORN in national policy since the late 1970s. It has developed extensive expertise in getting lenders to invest in inner cities by challenging proposed bank mergers under the Community Reinvestment Act of 1977 and getting banks to revise discriminatory lending practices and criteria. Its work has brought federal secondary-mortgage buying support from Fannie Mae and Freddie Mac to support lending to low- and moderate-income families. Nonbank financial intermediaries are also targeted in this effort. Insurance company redlining practices have come under fire, and ACORN is among those seeking to prohibit redlining, to require insurers to report where they write policies by census tract, and to impose community reinvestment standards on insurers.

More general housing and financial reform are also of concern to ACORN. It advocates expansion of affordable housing opportunities for the poor and revitalization of deteriorating neighborhoods. Availability of general credit and banking services for low-income consumers are sought through incentives to keep banks in urban neighborhoods, to provide basic banking accounts, and to cash government checks for nondepositors at cost. As the savings and loan industry bailout has proceeded, ACORN has been among those asking that the industry increase lending for low-cost housing and make foreclosed properties available to low-income buyers.

Jobs, schools, and neighborhood safety are also on this group's agenda. It advocates requiring developers to hire low-income, unemployed residents and has secured such ordinances or agreements in a number of cities, including Miami, Pittsburgh, Dallas, and Des Moines. It has won establishment of alternative public schools in ACORN neighborhoods in Brooklyn and Queens, New York, improved school facilities and governance in Chicago and New York, and won free transportation to schools in Little Rock. City officials and police have been forced to respond more effectively to rapes and to establish rape prevention programs in a number of cities where ACORN is active, including Boston and St. Louis. Programs to fight drugs, including police foot patrols and improved recreation facilities, are also of concern to ACORN.

Toxic wastes and health care are part of this organization's agenda as well. It has worked to get companies to clean up, move, or cancel plans for toxic chemical plants, dumps, or discharges in a number of cities. Its efforts have led to expanded childhood immunization programs, improved lead screening and treatment, and better hospital care for low-income families.

TACTICS

ACORN's tactics range from demonstrations, such as occupying bank lobbies, to acquiring and rehabilitating abandoned housing. It is confrontational in its approach to both corporate and government decision makers and uses direct tactics such as picketing, marching, sit-ins, and even going to jail. It creates and helps to upgrade homesteading programs, and helped to win passage of a national homesteading bill. Election tactics are part of its repertoire, in that it conducts voter registration drives, educates voters, gets voters to the polls, and recruits and trains candidates from among its membership. Barriers to voter registration have been struck down in a number of cities because of ACORN's work, and it has helped to replace at-large city council elections with district elections.

ACORN works to influence legislators and staff by face-to-face work on legislative language as well as presenting formal testimony before congressional committees. Its efforts with executive branch agencies on the regulation and administration of programs sometimes include ACORN's own research on financial institutions' abuses, such as insurance redlining. It advocates that federal regulators use more techniques, such as test shoppers, to strengthen the enforcement of fair-lending laws.

ACORN has become skilled at finding and using opportunities to influence powerful institutions, as when it persuaded Congress to attach innovative provisions to the savings and loan bailout legistion that require the industry to increase lending for low- and moderate-income housing. Proposed bank mergers, subject to challenge under the Community Reinvestment Act, provide ACORN with opportunities to publicize banks' behaviors and persuade them to improve their lending and other services to low-income communities. It sometimes works in coalitions, as it did on the savings and loan effort with other community, farm labor, and church organizations.

The organization's direct tactics extend to its efforts to build a progressive radio and television network. It has FM radio stations in Dallas and Little Rock, a television station in Salinas, California, and other license applications pending. Good relations with the media are important for sympathetic coverage of ACORN's demonstrations.

FURTHER READING

Capital and Communities: A Progressive Financial Reform Agenda for the Clinton Administration and the 103rd Congress. 1992. Washington, D.C.: ACORN.

Cloud, Cathy and George Galster. 1993. "What Do We Know About Racial Discrimination in Mortgage Markets?" Review of Black Political Economy, Summer, pp. 101–120.

Leslie, Wayne. 1992. "New Hope in Inner Cities: Banks Offering Mortgages." New York Times, March 14, pp. 1, 29.

Who Is on the Streets, in the Neighborhoods, etc. n.d. Washington, DC: ACORN.

Young, Amy E. 1993. "Banking on the Inner City: Reverse Redlining Pays Off for a Network of Alternative Lenders." Common Cause Magazine, Winter, pp. 35–37.

AUTOMOTIVE CONSUMER ACTION PROGRAM (AUTOCAP)

National Automobile Dealers Association
8400 Westpark Drive
McLean, VA 22102
(703) 821–7144

ORGANIZATION AND RESOURCES

The Automotive Consumer Action Program is a third-party mediation program founded in 1973 by the National Automobile Dealers Association (NADA), the trade association of new car dealers and importers. NADA sets standards for the program and administers it, but it is voluntarily supported by state and metropolitan franchised auto dealer associations. Consumers may find AUTOCAP locations in twenty-five states and the District of Columbia; there are thirty-five offices besides the national office. New York State is most thoroughly served, with five metropolitan or regional association offices in addition to one sponsored by the New York State Automobile Dealers Association to serve the balance of the state. Forty-seven auto manufacturers and importers, from Acura to Yugo, participate in the program directly; Chrysler, General Motors, Ford, Nissan, and Toyota are among the manufacturer members.

In addition to the NADA-sponsored program, there are similar third-party arbitration services sponsored by the Council of Better Business Bureaus, the American Automobile Association,* and manufacturers. The Better Business Bureaus support AUTO LINE, which has a national toll-free number that routes calls to local Better Business Bureaus in forty-two states and the District of Columbia. Fifteen manufacturers participate directly in AUTO LINE for mediation and arbitration of warranty and reliability disputes. The American Automobile Association offers AUTOSOLVE from its national headquarters in Florida; this service uses technical evaluation and is designed to meet or exceed the guidelines set forth in Federal Trade Commission Rule 703. Only Hyundai, Lexus, Porsche, Subaru, and Toyota participate in AUTOSOLVE. Chrysler and Ford also have their own programs. Chrysler's Customer Arbitration Board, consisting of one consumer advocate, one technical representative, and one representative of the general public, reviews product and warranty disputes. Its decisions are binding on the manufacturer or dealer but not on consumers. The Ford Consumer Appeals Board, consisting of three independent consumer representatives and one Ford or Lincoln-Mercury dealer, reviews service, product, and warranty disputes and issues decisions that bind the manufacturer but not the vehicle owner.

POLICY CONCERNS

AUTOCAP and similar dispute resolution programs are designed to improve dealer–customer relations by reviewing and mediating disputes involving participating franchised new car and truck dealers. Manufacturers and importers use the program to assist in resolving their customers' warranty and product reliability disputes. Having such programs in place is the first line of defense for dealers, manufacturers, and importers who face public criticism for their treatment of consumers. Claims that such programs serve as self-correction or self-regulation sometimes allow producers to escape more stringent legislation or regulation by state or federal policymakers.

TACTICS

Informational brochures describing AUTOCAP are distributed through participating dealers. Consumers are advised that most automotive disputes are a result of a lack of communication, so their first step is to speak to someone in authority at the dealership, providing vehicle information, the nature of the problem, and the action they think is fair. If the customer relations manager, general manager, and dealership owner are not able to resolve the problem, consumers should contact the appropriate national, zone, or distributor customer relations office, using information found in the owner's manual or provided by the dealer. If they are not able to resolve the dispute, the consumer may contact AUTOCAP, which works in two ways. Its staff will first attempt to settle the dispute through informal mediation between the parties. This is usually successful in resolving the issue; in recent years only 14 percent of cases have gone to the next step.

If informal mediation is unsuccessful, disputes are mediated by a panel consisting of consumer representatives and auto dealers, with a minimum of half of the panelists representing consumers. The panel examines the facts of the case and recommends a solution that is not binding on the consumer. Unless the particular state or local program has obtained appropriate commitments from the participating manufacturer or dealer, the decision to accept an AUTOCAP recommendation is at the discretion of the manufacturer or dealer as well. Consumers who have hired an attorney or taken any legal action must agree to take no further action during AUTOCAP mediation. If the consumer's problem involves anything other than a participating new car dealer or manufacturer, such as an independent service shop, service station, or used car dealer, AUTOCAP is not an alternative. Because of its limitations, AUTOCAP does not comply with the requirements of the Federal Trade Commission's Rule 703, nor is it designed to meet the standards of state "lemon laws."

FURTHER READING

About AUTOCAP. n.d. McLean, VA: National Automobile Dealers Association.

Automotive Customer Relations Directory. Annual. McLean, VA: National Automobile Dealers Association.

Consumer's Resource Handbook. 1988. Washington, DC: United States Office of Consumer Affairs.

Fact Sheet. Annual. McLean, VA: National Automobile Dealers Association.

Nader, Ralph, and Clarence Ditlow. 1990. *The Lemon Book: Auto Rights.* 3rd ed. Mount Kisco, NY: Moyer Bell.

"On the Process of Dispute Settlement." 1993. *Negotiation Journal,* October, pp. 293–353.

AVIATION CONSUMER ACTION PROJECT (ACAP)
2000 P Street N.W., Suite 700
P.O. Box 19029
Washington, DC 20036
(202) 833–3000

ORGANIZATION AND RESOURCES

Aviation Consumer Action Project is a nonprofit consumer organization that works for improved safety and consumer rights for airline passengers. It was founded by Ralph Nader in 1971 to improve the lot of ordinary airline passengers by representing their point of view against the organized lobbyists for the airline industry.

ACAP depends on contributions, memberships, and publication sales for revenue; its annual budget is approximately $65,000. It has 501(c)(3) tax status and is part of the Combined Federal Campaign, which allows federal employees to donate tax-deductible dollars. Membership dues are $35 a year, and those who join receive a quarterly newsletter, *Problems and Solutions for Airline Passengers.* ACAP also publishes a booklet, *Facts and Advice for Airline Passengers,* which it sells for a small fee.

Most of the work to keep this small organization going is done by volunteers who have experienced personal tragedies related to airline safety. For example, the Washington office used by ACAP is the gift of a woman whose husband was killed in a terrorist attack at the Rome airport. The daughter of ACAP president and newsletter editor, Tom O'Mara, was killed in an airliner crash at Sioux City, Iowa. ACAP's advisory board, chaired by Ralph Nader, is made up of experts in aviation safety, security, and regulation; Christopher J. Witkowski is executive director.

POLICY CONCERNS

ACAP is concerned about passenger rights, ground and air safety, air fares, regulatory action, and accessible consumer complaint procedures. The organization advocates legislation requiring a boarding pass that would meet product labeling guidelines. It would inform the passenger of the aircraft's age, the crew's years of experience, any security threat against the flight, and any unfinished airworthiness work on the aircraft. Passengers would be allowed to cancel a reservation without penalty if an airline failed to meet the conditions promised with the reservation.

Specific issues on which the group collects and disseminates data include the age of the aircraft fleet, and how that benefits airlines but poses dangers to passengers. Protection for child passengers is also of concern to the organization; it advocates more stringent Federal Aviation Administration (FAA) standards, such as requiring special seats and reduced fares for infants. On the grounds of cost-benefit analysis, the FAA has continued to allow children under the age of two to fly seated on a parent's lap. ACAP points out the risks to children thus seated, including the availability of sufficient oxygen masks.

Air traffic control personnel and standards are another of ACAP's issues. It cites data on the reduced number of experienced air traffic controllers to handle increased flights since 1981, when President Reagan fired striking controllers. It advocates rehiring fired controllers and requiring that at least two controllers be on duty while an airport is in operation. ACAP members are advised to insist on flying only into airports that have more than one controller on duty.

TACTICS

ACAP's tactics range from presenting testimony at congressional hearings and petitioning the FAA to advising members to take direct action to protect themselves during air travel. Representatives of ACAP serve on FAA committees on air traffic, general aviation, and security, and ACAP petitions the FAA on specific issues. An example of the latter was its effort to have the FAA require airlines to provide smoke hoods for passengers on commercial flights. After the petition was rejected, ACAP sought out suppliers and advised their members how to purchase, test, and use their own smoke hoods in the event of an airliner crash and fire.

The organization helped form an international coalition that brought together survivors and next of kin from six nations to share their experiences and make suggestions for aviation safety. The group has also worked directly with the Air Transport Association, the airline trade association, in a task force on the quality of parts used to repair aircraft. ACAP's newsletter advises members on writing to their senators and representatives on safety issues that are under consideration. It also suggests how members can work through travel agents and make safer travel choices on their own; for example, it provides members a list of airports that pilots do not like to fly into because of air traffic control problems.

FURTHER READING

Problems and Solutions for Airline Passengers. 1993. Washington, DC: Aviation Consumer Action Project.

Phillips, Richard A. and Wayne K. Talley. 1992. "Airline Safety Investments and Operating Conditions." *Southern Economic Journal,* October, pp. 157–64.

Worsnop, Richard L. 1993. "Airline Safety: Are Financial Problems Causing U.S. Airlines to Cut Corners?" *CQ Researcher,* October 8, pp. 867–87.

B
/

BANKCARD HOLDERS OF AMERICA (BHA)
560 Herndon Parkway, Suite 120
Herndon, VA 22070
(703) 481–1110

ORGANIZATION AND RESOURCES

Bankcard Holders of America was founded in 1980 to help bankcard holders become better-informed consumers. The group is unique, being the first and (thus far) only organization dealing exclusively with issues of importance to holders of credit cards. It is a private, nonprofit group with 501(c)(3) tax status and is dedicated to consumer credit education and advocacy. It is not a lobbying organization as defined by federal law, but is involved in credit policy at national and state levels. It receives no government, foundation, or corporate support, nor does it have any connection with any bank, credit card company, or financial institution. Ninety-five percent of its annual budget of approximately $1.5 million is received in dues from about 100,000 members. Elgie Holstein is president of a staff of eleven; consultants and additional staff often are hired for special research projects. Holstein has experience as a legislative staff person, in political campaigns, and with the National Conference of State Legislators.

Bankcard Consumer News is BHA's bimonthly newsletter designed to inform members about credit and personal finance issues. Members have access to a toll-free consumer dispute hotline. BHA compiles and publishes lists of banks that offer credit cards with no or very low annual fees, those that offer gold cards at low cost, and those that offer secured bankcards designed for persons who find it difficult to obtain credit because of a poor credit history or lack of previous credit. The *Nationwide Credit Bureau Directory* is published to assist members in contacting credit bureaus. *Money Management Guide* is a workbook to assist members in setting up a budget. Among BHA's pamphlets is *Consumer Rights at the Cash Register,* which includes a consumer action wallet card (to go with one's credit cards) detailing specific privacy and purchasing rights when buying at retail stores. Other pamphlet topics include women's credit rights, senior citizens' credit rights, college students and credit, credit card fraud, understanding credit bureaus, establishing credit, and resolving billing questions.

POLICY CONCERNS

BHA is concerned about the entire range of issues affecting consumers' use of credit cards. It was a prime mover behind the Fair Credit and Charge Card Disclosure Act, effective in 1989, which requires lenders to reveal more clearly the terms of card contracts in mailed solicitations. BHA continues to advocate better disclosure of rates and fees in advertising and other types of solicitations. Sophisticated marketing practices of those offering credit cards, particularly to susceptible populations, is a matter BHA continues to follow. Discrimination against applicants for credit is an ongoing issue for BHA.

The group has taken on retailers who demand credit card numbers to accept checks and then charge an insufficient-funds check against the credit card, a practice prohibited by Visa and MasterCard. Other billing practices, such as how a lender follows procedures to allow a consumer to correct errors, continue to be followed by BHA. How credit bureaus deal with the information they gather and the rights of consumers in accessing and correcting credit files are a major ongoing topic. BHA advocates making files more accessible for consumers to dispute and easier to correct, and holding credit bureaus liable for damages because of inaccurate credit information. Debt collection practice guidelines and abuses are ongoing matters of concern for BHA.

Rising consumer debt levels in general, and of credit cards in particular, is a topic of BHA research and policy education. The group contends that credit cards disguise debt problems both for the individual borrower and at the public policy level. Credit card interest rates that are noncompetitive, and have not decreased along with other interest rates, are a major concern. BHA supports lenders' reducing these rates, if not under legal requirements then with borrowers protesting the high rates and shifting their business to more competitive lenders. It advocates allowing cardholders to pay off and close their credit card accounts under previous terms when a lender raises its interest rates or other charges. It also supports Congress's closing the loophole that prevents states from limiting charges on cards sent to residents from outside the state where they live.

TACTICS

BHA's primary tactic is direct education of bankcard users, particularly its members. It also offers free speakers who present seminars, workshops, and lectures to civic, volunteer, and community organizations. The group monitors current economic trends and developments in the banking industry, and is an expert source on how such changes impact consumers of bankcard credit. BHA has established and cultivates a good relationship with the mass media, providing useful information that appears in a wide variety of print media. Being cited in news columns generates inquiries to the organization about its pamphlets and other services.

The group and its members have assisted in gathering information on telemarketing offers of credit products using false and deceptive claims. Members have collected and turned in samples of postcards sent by telemarketing companies, thus aiding the Federal Trade Commission in halting the operations.

The organization's reputation as a source of expertise in a well-defined niche brings it invitations to testify before legislative committees at national and state levels. While Holstein is usually the spokesperson in these settings, organization members who have experience with the lender practice in question sometimes help convey the message.

FURTHER READING

Bankcard Consumer News. Bimonthly. Herndon, VA: Bankcard Holders of America.
BHA Fact Sheet. Annual. Herndon, VA: Bankcard Holders of America.
BHA Publications List. Annual. Herndon, VA: Bankcard Holders of America.
Cantrell, Wanda. 1990. "Where Bankcard Holders of America Will Strike Next." *Credit Card Management,* February, pp. 15–17, 22.
Consumer Credit Rights. 1990. Herndon, VA: Bankcard Holders of America.
Holland, Kelley. 1994a. "Plastic Talks: Credit and Debit-Card Use Is Growing and That's Fine with Banks." *Business Week,* February 14, pp. 105–107.
———. 1994b. "Stalking the Credit-Card Scamsters." *Business Week,* January 17, pp. 68–69.
Holstein, Elgie. 1991. "Bring Down Credit Card Interest Rates." *USA Today,* May 28, p. 7.
Kehrer, Daniel. 1988. "How to Cut out Debt." *Changing Times,* April, pp. 23–27.
Public Interest Profiles 1992–1993. 1992. Washington, DC: Congressional Quarterly, Foundation for Public Affairs.
Quinn, Jane Bryant. 1991. "Addressing Credit Report Errors." *Washington Post,* August 25, p. H3.

THE BROOKINGS INSTITUTION
1775 Massachusetts Avenue N.W.
Washington, DC 20036
(202) 797–6000

ORGANIZATION AND RESOURCES

The Brookings Institution is a private, nonprofit organization devoted to research, education, and publication in economics, government, foreign policy, and the social sciences. Its principal purpose is to bring knowledge to bear on the current and emerging policy problems facing the American people. The

Institution traces its beginnings to 1916 with the founding of the Institute for Government Research, the first private organization devoted to public policy issues at the national level. In 1922 and 1924, the Institute was joined by two supporting organizations, the Institute of Economics and the Robert Brookings Graduate School. In 1927 these three organizations were consolidated into one and named in honor of Robert Somers Brookings, a St. Louis businessman whose leadership shaped the earlier organizations.

A thirty-two-member board of trustees is responsible for general supervision of the Institution, approval of fields of investigation, and safeguarding the independence of its work. Such notables as David Rockefeller, Jr., Louis W. Cabot, Pamela C. Harriman, Donna E. Shalala, and Nannerl O. Keohane serve as trustees. The president, Bruce K. MacLaury, is chief administrative officer, responsible for formulating and coordinating policies, recommending projects, approving publications, and selecting staff. Approximately 250 persons work as staff and scholars of the Institution. Its activities are carried out through research programs in economics, foreign policy, and government; a center for public policy education; a publications program; and a social science computation program.

Brookings's $18 million annual budget is financed largely by endowment and by the support of philanthropic foundations, corporations, and private individuals. Its own funds are devoted to carrying out its research and educational activities. It also undertakes some unclassified government contract studies, reserving the right to publish its findings.

The Institution maintains a specialized library of books and periodicals designed to support its research programs; holdings include 80,000 volumes, 700 periodical titles, pamphlets, U.S. government documents, and United Nations documents. The library is automated and serves the staff both directly and through cooperative arrangements with other libraries. Brookings's social science computation center provides computing and related services for its scholars, other organizations engaged in social science research and public administration, and the federal government.

The Institution publishes books that result from its research and conferences and books of a similar nature by outside authors. It also publishes *Brookings Papers on Economic Activity* and *The Brookings Review,* a quarterly journal designed to make its research and public policy proposals accessible to a wide audience.

POLICY CONCERNS

Brookings research in economics attends to improving the performance and efficiency of the U.S. economy, making social programs more effective in an era of constrained resources, and improving international economic relations in an increasingly interdependent world. The slowdown in the growth of productivity and wages, and the rise in wage and income inequality in the 1980s, prompted Brookings to establish the Center for Economic Progress and Employment in 1987. Its recommendations focus on specific steps that federal and state governments can take to accelerate economic growth and achieve a more equitable distribution of jobs and wages; among these are improved education, reformed research and development policies, and higher national savings rates. Companion research has questioned the effects of the financial restructuring of American business in the 1980s and raises questions about the management of public corporations and their relationships to financial markets.

Brookings scholars' work in social economics focuses on policies to improve the efficiency and quality of health care by building upon current employer-sponsored health insurance along with a public backup plan and rigorous cost controls. A study focusing on Great Britain, Canada, Germany, Japan, France, and Australia will assess how these nations deliver medical services and the differences among them in access, quality of care, and degree of freedom for patients and physicians. Other studies address the need to expand educational opportunities, promote mobility in labor markets, reduce the number of people living in poverty, and improve the urban environment. A recent Brookings publication advocates expanding drug treatment programs for prisoners, greater reliance on community policing, and temporary sheltering of the homeless. Strategies to enhance cooperation among different levels of government and across jurisdictional boundaries are suggested to ameliorate the political isolation of urban governments.

For two decades, Brookings has studied the interrelationships of law, economics, and politics. Its studies on the regulation of economic activities provided the major intellectual underpinning for the movement to deregulate beginning in the late 1970s. The Center for Law, Economics, and Politics has been established to continue to support this line of study in cooperation with other think tanks, advocacy groups, and professional organizations. Upcoming issues for study include the civil jury system and financing for cleaning up toxic waste sites by Superfund.

The concerns of scholars working on Brookings's governmental studies include the challenges posed to governmental legitimacy by low voter turnout, public anger, and institutional ineffectiveness. Brookings is engaged in a comprehensive examination of the effectiveness and organization of the Congress at the request of a bipartisan group of members of Congress. A wide range of topics is under examination—from the jurisdictions and assignments of congressional committees and the roles of party leadership to the budget process and the relationship between Congress and the executive branch. A study completed by Alice Rivlin, former director of the Congressional Budget Office, recommends that the federal government devolve to the states most domestic responsibilities, such as education and housing, thereby becoming responsible for the public investment that supports productivity. Under this scenario, the federal government would take responsibility for health care along with entitlement programs, environmental protection, and defense.

In foreign policy studies, Brookings scholars are working to articulate principles of cooperative security in a post–Cold War world and to anticipate what fundamental policy changes will be required to reconcile global economic growth, population increase, income disparities, and environmental sustainability. This cooperative effort with the World Resources Institute and the Santa Fe Institute seeks to provide for basic human needs and increasing prosperity with improved standards of international equity while accommodating cultural differences and preserving fundamental environmental balances.

TACTICS

In its research, Brookings functions as an independent analyst and critic, committed to publishing its findings for the information of the public. In its conferences and other activities, Brookings serves as a bridge between scholarship and public policy, bringing new knowledge to the attention of decision makers and affording scholars a better insight into public policy issues.

Brookings works cooperatively with other research institutions, advocacy organizations, and professional associations. A current example is its work with researchers from Resources for the Future* on funding toxic waste cleanup in anticipation of Superfund reauthorization in 1994. It is also working with scholars from the American Enterprise Institute* in its study of congressional effectiveness.

The Center for Public Policy Education develops and sponsors programs for corporate executives, government officials, and others. Brookings conducts approximately fifty conferences and seminars for senior corporate executives each year; the programs share the goal of improving communication among leaders in business and government. Conferences on understanding federal government operations are held at least ten times a year to acquaint participants with federal government processes and business–government relations. International programs held around the globe are aimed at executives with international policy-making responsibilities. Special programs are arranged for individual corporations and universities. Programs for government officials reach more than 700 senior federal officials each year, bringing them together with scholars and corporate executives. Conference topics include business policy and operations, science and technology policy, American defense, and emerging issues in public management. Special programs are designed and conducted for individual federal agencies.

National issues forums designed for business leaders, government officials, private analysts and scholars, professionals, reporters, and the general public are one-day, on-the-record sessions on timely topics. In-depth, single-topic seminars bringing together senior business and government executives on issues such as the federal budget, energy policy, and industrial competitiveness are also part of the Institution's offerings. Since 1991 Brookings has joined with the Conference Board* in administering the Congressional Assistant Program, which provides one-year fellowships to high-potential corporate managers while they function as full-time staff in congressional offices. Brookings also reaches out to university faculty and graduate students, private-sector executives, and federal executives with guest appointments and fellowships.

FURTHER READING

Annual Report. Annual. Washington, DC: Brookings Institution.
Blair, Margaret M., ed. 1993. *The Deal Decade: What Takeovers and Leveraged Buyouts Mean for Corporate Governance.* Washington, DC: Brookings Institution.
Brookings Directory. Annual. Washington, DC: Brookings Institution.
Pastor, Robert A. 1993. *NAFTA as the Center of an Integration Process: The Nontrade Issues.* Washington, DC: Brookings Institution.

THE BUSINESS ROUNDTABLE

200 Park Avenue   1615 L Street N.W.
New York, NY 10166–0097   Washington, DC 20036–5610
(212) 682–6370   (202) 872–1260

ORGANIZATION AND RESOURCES

The Business Roundtable was founded in 1972 through a merger of the Construction Users Anti-Inflation Roundtable and the Labor Law Study Committee. These two groups were dedicated to countering the influence of organized labor, particularly in the construction business, and that continued as the original focus of the Business Roundtable. However, in mid-1973, while Washington was racked by the Watergate scandal and the business community faced serious political legitimacy challenges due to illegal campaign contributions, the Roundtable merged with an informal organization of chief executive officers of major companies known as the March Group. Bryce Harlow of Procter & Gamble, W. B. Murphy of Campbell Soup, Roger M. Blough of U.S. Steel, Fred J. Borch of General Electric, and John D. Harper of Alcoa were influential in shaping the merger and the new Business Roundtable. The new organization's focus widened to include the whole array of federal policy concerns of business; labor law affecting construction remained a concern but not the exclusive concern. Its membership shifted from a collection of large and medium-sized companies to the largest of the Fortune 500, earning the Roundtable the status as the elite big business lobby.

Present membership includes 211 companies and their chief executive officers. Membership is intended to be a diverse representation of categories of business and geographic location. The number of members has varied since 1972, dipping as low as 160 in the mid-1980s but generally around 200 companies. Amoco, Chase Manhattan, Dow Chemical, Ford, IBM, Metropolitan Life, Morgan Stanley, Pepsico, RJR Nabisco, Sears, and Xerox, to name just a few, give an impression of the membership roster.

Recent officers have included the chairmen of Union Pacific, AT&T, Aetna Life & Casualty, American Express, and Prudential. William L. Lurie is president; there are executive directors for public information, an education project, construction, and Washington operations. The staff totals eighteen persons; the organization declines to disclose its budget and only recently has disclosed its membership.

Chief executive officers of member firms work as part of task forces addressing specific issues. The task forces direct research conducted both by staffs of member companies and sometimes by prominent lawyers, academics, accounting firms, or lobbyists retained for specific projects. Research results in the preparation of position papers that recommend policy stands. In addition to the task forces of chief executive officers, there are a number of standing committees composed mostly of vice presidents of member companies. Activities and recommendations of both the task forces and standing committees are reviewed by the Roundtable Policy Committee, made up of eighty-three member chief executive officers. Position papers approved by the Policy Committee are circulated to members and to government decision makers, and are made available for use in the public discussion of issues.

POLICY CONCERNS

The Roundtable is motivated by the belief that business executives should take an increased role in debates about public policy. Its members examine public issues and develop positions that seek to reflect sound economic and social principles. The Roundtable believes that the basic interests of business closely parallel the interests of the American people, who are directly involved as consumers, employees, investors, and suppliers.

Current topics with which task forces are concerned include accounting principles; antitrust and government regulation; construction cost-effectiveness; corporate governance; education; the environment; the federal budget; health, welfare, and retirement income; human resources; international trade and investment; taxation; and tort policy. Construction, employee relations, public information, and Washington relations are the topics of present standing committees.

TACTICS

What sets the Business Roundtable apart from other groups is that its lobbyists are the chief executive officers of the nation's most powerful companies. It operates less visibly than most organizations; it does not seek to present testimony at congressional hearings, appear on the evening news, or mobilize grassroots campaigns. But its members' ability to gain direct access to members of Congress, the president, and members of the cabinet is unequaled. The president of General Motors will not be denied a request to meet face to face with any of these policymakers, nor will he have to work his way through layers of staff to get to them. Unique access, high status, and small numbers allow Roundtable members social lobbying opportunities with members of the Washington inner circle.

Among organizations that speak for producer interests, the Roundtable is regarded as more moderate and "establishment" than either the U.S. Chamber of Commerce* or the National Federation of Independent Businesses.* Its positions, in comparison to theirs, are more likely to represent the interest of business as a whole and to include positive proposals rather than only statements of opposition. Its opposition is less shrill, and most likely to be accompanied by a willingness to compromise quietly.

Although the Roundtable declines to claim credit for its lobbying prowess, it is regarded as one of the most influential organizations in Washington. It is credited with significant roles in preventing the establishment of a federal agency for consumer advocacy, weakening antitrust policy, defeating labor law reform, preventing criminal code revisions to include consumer fraud and other corporate crime provisions, and advocating reduction of regulation.

FURTHER READING

Behr, Peter. 1994. "Putting Principles Above Profits in China." *Washington Post*, national weekly edition, May 2–8, p. 22.
Business Roundtable. 1991. Washington, DC: Business Roundtable.
Edsall, Thomas Byrne. 1984. *The New Politics of Inequality*. New York: W. W. Norton.
Gottron, Martha V., ed. 1982. *Regulation: Process and Politics*. Washington, D.C.: Congressional Quarterly.
Green, Mark, and Andrew Buchsbaum. 1983. "The Corporate Lobbies: The Two Styles of the Business Roundtable and Chamber of Commerce." In Mark Green, ed., *The Big Business Reader: On Corporate America*. New York: Pilgrim Press.
Nader, Ralph, and William Taylor. 1986. *The Big Boys: Power and Position in American Business*. New York: Pantheon Press.
Schlozman, Kay Lehman, and John T. Tierney. 1986. *Organized Interests and American Democracy*. New York: Harper & Row.
Vogel, David. 1989. *Fluctuating Fortunes: The Political Power of Business in America*. New York: Basic Books.

BUYERS UP
c/o Public Citizen
2000 P Street
Washington, DC 20036
(202) 659–2500

ORGANIZATION AND RESOURCES

Buyers Up was founded in 1983 by Ralph Nader and Public Citizen.* It is a national nonprofit consumer advocacy organization whose members include some 9,000 households, commercial businesses, and organizations in the Washington, D.C., and Baltimore areas. The chief objective behind Buyers Up is to monitor energy issues affecting consumers and to administer a group purchasing program for home heating oil that negotiates discount prices for members. The organization publishes a quarterly newspaper called *Buyers Up*.

POLICY CONCERNS

The product of a time when consumers were concerned about energy costs and feared additional oil shocks, Buyers Up uses an established consumer response—collective buying power—to get lower prices on heating oil. Related energy issues affecting consumers include other problems consumers face with suppliers, regulatory issues facing the energy industry, and the role of government in forging and enforcing a national energy policy.

TACTICS

By negotiating with oil suppliers and service companies to allow members to purchase oil for a fixed markup over the wholesale price of oil, Buyers Up shows a set of tactics different from those of most consumer organizations. But although its roots are in an earlier decade, Buyers Up is in tune with the interest that consumer groups are currently showing American industries about individual buying power. It also is responsible for discussions and programs on energy; Sun Day, which it celebrated in 1992; and activities organized around a sustainable energy future, held on Earth Day.

FURTHER READING

Giese, William. 1989. "Radon-Testing Problems." *Changing Times,* April, pp. 28–29.
Southerland, Daniel. 1993. "Gasoline Prices Down Much Less Than Crude." *Washington Post,* December 31, p. C1.
Stewart, Thomas A. 1989. "The Resurrection of Ralph Nader." *Fortune,* May 22, pp. 106–108.

C /

CENTER FOR AUTO SAFETY (CAS)
2001 S Street N.W., Suite 410
Washington, DC 20009
(202) 328–7700

ORGANIZATION AND RESOURCES

The Center for Auto Safety was organized by Ralph Nader and Consumers Union* in 1970. The organization originally was under Nader's direction; in 1976 Clarence M. Ditlow III became executive director, and he has continued in that position. The Center became a membership organization in 1979 and now has over 12,000 members who pay dues of $15 annually. A five-person board of directors that includes Washington lawyers and traffic injury experts governs the organization. It operates on revenues of about $800,000 derived from grants (30 percent), membership contributions (25 percent), publications sales (17 percent), product liability research (9 percent), general contributions (9 percent), and other sources (10 percent). It employs a staff of fifteen and draws upon student interns and adult volunteers. The organization's goal is to advocate for the American consumer in order to achieve safer and more reliable automobiles.

POLICY CONCERNS

The Center's specific projects pursue vehicle safety, highway safety, and product liability issues. The vehicle safety project is intended to detect auto defects that pose safety or financial risks to consumers; letters from dissatisfied auto owners are a primary source of input for this project.

The highway safety project targets highway and bridge design, pavement composition, roadside barriers, signage, and truck and commercial vehicle standards. In the area of product liability, research aims at gathering and making available information usable both by the Center directly and by private product liability attorneys who in turn share data with the Center. The organization describes this interrelationship as helping to balance the tendency of the auto industry to deal unfairly with victims and to refuse to acknowledge defects by making it easier for victims and their lawyers to gain compensation.

The CAS is credited with involvement in a number of significant changes in consumer safety over its twenty-year history. Among them are mandates for passive restraints, extension of passenger car safety standards to light trucks and vans, bumper collision standards, mandatory child restraint systems, construction and safety standards for mobile homes, improved consumer warranty rights in the Magnuson-Moss Warranty Act, the Ford recall of the Pinto, the recall of Firestone 500 tires, "lemon laws" in forty-six states, and exposure of and suits against secret auto warranties.

TACTICS

The Center uses complaint information and research data as the basis for auto safety petitions to the Department of Transportation, the Federal Trade Commission, or the Environmental Protection Agency for recalls or tighter standards. It also provides help for individual consumers to proceed through negotiations and arbitration with manufacturers, and serves as a facilitator and clearinghouse for persons seeking to organize action groups. In some cases, it facilitates or files class action suits or petitions states' attorneys general to take action under state laws.

Providing congressional testimony, filing suits against the Department of Transportation, discussing highway hazards for media outlets, and coalescing with other groups such as Advocates for Highway and Auto Safety, Public Citizen,* Citizens for Reliable and Safe Highways, and the National Safety Council are among the tactics the Center uses to promote highway safety.

Data on defective or dangerous products are used by the Center to petition the National Highway Transportation Safety Administration for investigations. The Center shares data to support private product liability suits in order to help focus attention on manufacturer negligence and provide financial disincentives for dangerous or shoddy designs.

FURTHER READING

Brown, Warren. 1984. "Auto Safety: Chevy Service Manager's Son Is Leader of Recall Campaigns." *Washington Post,* January 29, p. H1.
———. 1991. "Letting Everyone in on the Secret." *Washington Post,* national weekly edition, September 30–October 6, p. 22.

Center for Auto Safety. 1990. *Center for Auto Safety: Twenty Years of Advocacy.* Washington, DC: Center for Auto Safety.

Kelley, Benjamin. 1992. "How the Auto Industry Sets Roadblocks to Safety." *Business and Society Review,* Fall, pp. 50–53.

Lemon Times. Quarterly. Washington, DC: Center for Auto Safety.

Nadel, Mark. 1971. *The Politics of Consumer Protection.* Indianapolis: Bobbs-Merrill.

Nader, Ralph, and Clarence Ditlow. 1990. *The Lemon Book: Auto Rights,* 3rd ed. Mount Kisco, NY: Moyer Bell.

Nader, Ralph, and William Taylor. 1986. *The Big Boys: Power and Position in American Business.* New York: Pantheon Books.

Victor, Kirk. 1994. "Clinton and Consumers." *National Journal,* January 15, p. 145.

CENTER FOR BUDGET AND POLICY PRIORITIES (CBPP)

777 N. Capitol Street N.E., Suite 705
Washington, DC 20002
Tel (202) 408–1080
Fax 202–408–1056

ORGANIZATION AND RESOURCES

Founded in 1981 by Bob Greenstein, who had headed the U.S. Department of Agriculture's Food and Nutrition Service during the Carter administration and was well known for his work at the Community Nutrition Institute, a Washington-based antipoverty and antihunger organization, the CBPP has 501 (c)(3) tax status. The organization's main objective is to analyze the effects of government programs and policies on low- and moderate-income Americans.

POLICY CONCERNS

CBPP gained attention in Washington policy networks for its authoritative information about the effects of the early Reagan administration's budget cuts on the buying power of poor families. As an effective advocate for liberal causes, it established a position in Washington by swimming against the tide of the conservative 1980s. For example, through studies and a regular *WIC Newsletter,* CPBB offers advice on complex issues like whether to increase funding of the USDA's Women's, Infants and Children's food program, which has survived the 1980s, by cultivating allies like cereal manufacturers. Through its efforts, now WIC coupons can be used at farmers' markets as well as supermarkets.

Other issues the Center has championed have included the need for subsidizing telephone costs for poor people, increasing the minimum wage, expanding the state and federal earned income tax credit, and strengthening state social service safety nets. The CBPP's reputation as an effective research and advocacy group for liberal causes will be tested in the 1990s by health care reform, especially the issue of how to improve the delivery system for poor people.

TACTICS

In pursuit of its objectives, the Center sponsors research and organizes conferences and seminars to analyze problems experienced by poor consumers and to discuss the fruits of the group's research projects. CBPP staffers testify at congressional hearings and monitor legislation and regulatory action, and the organization serves as a clearinghouse for others interested in issues associated with the reach and adequacy of government antipoverty programs.

FURTHER READING

Kellam, Susan. 1992. "Praise Is High, Funds Are Low for Welfare That Works." *Congressional Quarterly Weekly Report,* June 27, pp. 1876–1881.

CENTER FOR COMMUNITY CHANGE (CCC)
1000 Wisconsin Avenue N.W.
Washington, DC 20007
Tel (202) 342–0519
Fax 202–342–1137

ORGANIZATION AND RESOURCES

The Center for Community Change grew out of the movement to improve low-income and minority communities with the support of civil rights, antipoverty, and labor groups such as the United Auto Workers.* This movement pushed the Johnson administration for financial and legislative support for initiatives in this area in the 1960s. In 1968, the CCC absorbed the Citizen's Crusade Against Poverty, one of the major organizations that had served as a watchdog over the Office of Economic Opportunity and antihunger efforts under the jurisdiction of the U.S. Department of Agriculture. In the early 1990s CCC had thirty-four staff members, 501(c)(3) tax status, and an annual budget of more than $2 million. Headquartered in Washington, D.C., with a branch office in San Francisco, CCC publishes *Community Change* and the *CRA Reporter* on a quarterly basis.

POLICY CONCERNS

Since the 1960s the Center has carved out a niche for itself on low-income housing issues. Like organizations such as the Food Research and Action Center,* the National Coalition Against Misuse of Pesticides,* and the Citizens Clearinghouse on Hazardous Wastes, the Center for Community Change uses its Washington base and knowledge of Congress and the bureaucracy to provide information to a network of grass-roots groups on issues concerning the necessities of life. Specifically, CCC helps local groups help consumers use protections that Congress has established under the Community Reinvestment Act (CRA) and other low-income housing and citizen participation programs designed to prevent redlining.

TACTICS

CCC can be helpful in forming coalitions with and among local and national advocacy organizations supporting low- and moderate-income people in rural and urban areas. CCC advocates present testimony to committees of Congress, monitor and participate in regulatory decision making, and provide an information clearinghouse and related functions. The purpose is not just to get good laws on the books but to influence their implementation by governmental officials and to force banks to comply with requirements under such key consumer statutes as the CRA and the Housing Mortgage Disclosure Act.

FURTHER READING

U.S. Congress. House Committee on Banking, Finance, and Urban Affairs Subcommittee on Housing and Community Development. 1994. *Report on Chronology of Housing Legislation and Selected Executive Actions. 1982–1992.* Washington, D.C.: Government Printing Office.

Williams, Roger. 1987. "Centering on the Underdog." *Foundation News,* September–October, pp. 18–24.

CENTER FOR MARINE CONSERVATION (CMC)
1725 DeSales Street N.W.
Washington, DC 20036
Tel (202) 429–5609
Fax 202–872–0619

ORGANIZATION AND RESOURCES

Founded in 1972, the Center for Marine Conservation has successfully carved out a place for itself in a fairly narrow stream of public policy in Washington. It is included here as an organization that uses appeals to consumers in pursuit of environmental goals and reflects an increasing specialization in the American environmental community. The Center publishes the *Marine Conservation News* and conducts activities at sites in Austin, Texas; St. Petersburg, Florida; San Francisco; and Hampton, Virginia, focusing on dangers to whales, sea turtles, dolphins, manatees, and other marine animals and on protection of their natural habitats.

POLICY CONCERNS

Since its founding, the Center has moved away from its early focus on marine education to a broader activism. The organization's leaders pride themselves on being flexible and using an undogmatic approach. For example, Center staffers criticized shrimp industry practices but also worked with industry officials to get them to install devices to keep sea turtles from being caught in their nets.

This concern for protecting marine areas has meant attention to oil spill liability and cleanup issues. Fishery conservation issues have brought the organization into campaigns to protect tuna, swordfish, and whales in U.S., international, and other countries' territorial waters. Also, not surprisingly, the CMC weighs in during discussions about dangers to marine resources and the environment from oil and tanker industries, as shown in the *Exxon Valdez* spill.

Among the issues that may be new to wider publics are concern about problems caused by the rising tide of marine debris. Another issue that is gaining wider attention at the state level is the need for environmental cleanup of underwater lands and attempts to protect such lands from the dangers of overdevelopment. The CMC also seeks to strengthen state coastal management zones and improve compliance with water pollution legislation already on the books but, it believes, is not being well enforced.

TACTICS

The Center focuses on U.S. federal, state, and local governments, international bodies, and foreign governments. For example, the CMC has sent representatives to International Whaling Commission meetings since 1977 and currently enjoys the status of an official NGO (nongovernmental organization) in the Commission's deliberations. Other likely targets are trade associations representing fishermen and fish processors. Like many other environmental organizations, the CMC works for enactment of legislation in its bailiwick. Once a law is on the books, such as the Magnuson Fishery Conservation Management Act, Center staffers try to strengthen its provisions whenever it is due to be reauthorized.

Other important legislative authority with which the organization is concerned includes the Marine Mammal Protection Act and programs administered by the National Oceanic and Atmospheric Administration (NOAA). Center officials try to monitor the deliberations of industry trade groups when they work privately or when, as is the case with the South Atlantic Fishery Management Council, they report to the secretary of commerce (in this case, on efforts to work out a swordfish management plan).

The Center works to get bigger budgets for conservation agencies and programs like the National Marine Sanctuary Program, and monitors the actions of administrative agencies with regulatory authority over marine resources, such as the Coast Guard, the U.S. Fish and Wildlife Service (which is located in the Department of Interior), the National Marine Fisheries Service in the U.S. Department of Commerce, and state marine patrols. The CMC is also involved in creating coalitions with other organizations when that is useful to achieve its objectives. For example, CMC staffers helped organize the Coral Reef Coalition, which included local, state, and national environmental groups as well as diving and fishing industry representatives. A major goal is to get national marine sanctuary status for Florida coral reefs and to have NOAA develop a management plan for the area and its resources.

One of the CMC's main tactics has been to get school classes, civic associations, scout troups, and other children's groups to write to members of Congress in support of wildlife preserves, such as the Archie Carr National Wildlife Refuge in Florida, and to protect specific marine animal populations thought to be endangered by overfishing, urban and suburban development, and other perils. CMC has funded research and remains very involved in citizen education, especially through elementary and secondary schools.

FURTHER READING

"Dirty Dozen Beach Pollutants Listed." 1991. *Los Angeles Times,* May 24, p. A43.
Marine Conservation News. Quarterly. Washington, DC: Center for Marine Conservation.
Warren, Jennifer. 1994. "State Vulnerable to Oil Spills, Group Says." *Los Angeles Times,* March 25, p. A24.

CENTER FOR PUBLIC INTEGRITY (CPI)
1910 K Street N.W., Suite 802
Washington, DC 20006
(202) 223–0299

ORGANIZATION AND RESOURCES

The Center for Public Integrity was created in 1989 by Charles Lewis, a national network television investigative reporter. This nonprofit, tax-exempt educational organization has as its objective to bring a higher standard of integrity to the American political process and to government by combining the study of government with in-depth journalism.

POLICY CONCERNS

An issue that CPI tackled immediately upon its founding was the phenomenon of former White House trade officials registering as agents promoting foreign companies and governments. The organization also focused on other good-government or governmental process issues, such as elected officials taking leftover campaign funds for personal use, American research sold to foreign companies, and U.S. military restrictions on the media.

TACTICS

The Center conducts original research and investigations that result in the presentation of written material on important national issues. Government and industry are its chief targets, and among its allies are whistle-blowers working inside both kinds of organizations.

FURTHER READING

Novak, Viveca. 1993. "Passing the Hat." *National Journal,* October 23, pp. 2520–25.
Stone, Peter H. 1994. "Bonds of Gold." *National Journal,* January 29, pp. 238–41.

CENTER FOR SCIENCE IN THE PUBLIC INTEREST (CSPI)
1875 Connecticut Avenue N.W., Suite 300
Washington, DC 20009–5728
(202) 332–9110

ORGANIZATION AND RESOURCES

The Center for Science in the Public Interest was founded in 1971 by three scientists who sought to use their skills to build a better nation. Michael F. Jacobson, one of the three founders, still serves as executive director; another of the founders, now with the U.S. Agency for International Development, serves on the board of directors. The goal of the organization is to use science in the public interest, that is, for a better-informed citizenry, healthier people, a cleaner environment, improved corporate practices, and more enlightened governmental policies.

An eleven-person board of directors governs CSPI; nutrition professors, businesspersons, and consumer advocates are included. The staff numbers thirty-five and increases with summer interns. CSPI is a nonprofit organization with an annual budget of over $4 million and 250,000 members; both membership and revenues have grown dramatically since the mid-1980s. Three-fourths of its revenues come from memberships and member contributions, 10 percent comes from publication sales, 5 percent from foundation grants. It does not accept funding from government or business. Public education represents the largest share of its expenditures.

POLICY CONCERNS

Since 1971, CSPI has worked on issues ranging from toxic chemicals in the environment to national transportation policies, but in more recent years has focused on improving the safety and nutritional quality of the food supply and reducing the use of alcoholic beverages. Its current work is organized around the Nutrition Action Project, the Children's Nutrition Project, the Alcohol Policies Project, and Americans for Safe Food.* The goals of the Nutrition Action Project are to educate the public and health professionals, modernize government policies, and persuade companies to improve their products. Its future concerns include the effects of fat and sugar substitutes.

The focus of the Children's Nutrition Project is the impact on children's health of junk food and its marketing. It has prodded manufacturers to improve the wholesomeness of foods intended for children by reducing fat, sugar, and salt levels, and removing questionable additives. Through this project, CSPI has published guidelines for improving the nutritional quality of school lunches and has produced books and videos teaching young people about improved eating practices.

The Alcohol Policies Project aims to prevent alcohol problems by publicizing the industry's advertising strategies, working to restrict alcohol advertising, and advocating warning labels and heavy excise taxes. Dangerous contaminants in beer, wine, and liquor have been publicized by CSPI, and it has successfully persuaded several liquor companies to withdraw radio and television ads, and broadcasters to run more public service messages about the risks of alcohol.

Americans for Safe Food began in 1986 in an effort to increase the amount and availability of foods produced organically or with reduced amounts of pesticides, synthetic fertilizer, and veterinary drugs. It has sponsored conferences on organic and sustainable agriculture and has published manuals to assist in creating and expanding state sustainable agriculture programs.

CSPI publishes *Nutrition Action Healthletter* ten times a year; it provides information on personal nutrition and health, and launches petition and letter-writing campaigns. Posters, films, cookbooks for children, and computer software to analyze nutrition are among CSPI's numerous information and advocacy publications.

TACTICS

CSPI's core tactic is the research it conducts and disseminates to consumers, manufacturers, retailers, and government policymakers. A reputation for accuracy and careful cultivation of ties have yielded CSPI excellent relations with the mass media. Its staff members appear regularly on national talk shows, and its reports are widely covered by wire services, major newspapers, and the networks. CSPI makes nutrition science not only understandable but also newsworthy with a variety of tactics such as conferring its Bon Vivant Vichyssoise Memorial Award (named after a brand of canned soup that caused botulism deaths) to makers of junk foods, and displaying the amount of fat in a Burger King double Whopper with cheese in a graduated cylinder. This direct action strategy of focusing attention on the products and advertising of the fast food industry has prompted the industry to disclose ingredient and nutrition information and then to improve its products and offer healthier alternatives.

CSPI techniques include providing testimony at congressional committee hearings, formally petitioning executive regulatory agencies, and occasionally filing legal suits against government agencies. Among the outcomes attributed in part to its efforts is the *Dietary Guidelines for Americans,* published by the Departments of Agriculture and Health and Human Services. It has also contributed to a widespread campaign including state attorneys general to get the Food and Drug Administration and the Federal Trade Commission to move in the direction of more accurate labeling and advertising. The 1990 legislation requiring nutrition labeling of most packaged foods was a significant milestone in this effort. CSPI worked to restrict the use of sulfite preservatives, eventually persuading the FDA to ban most uses and to require other uses to be labeled. Its efforts also resulted in sodium labeling of processed foods, elimination of tropical oils from most processed foods, and listing of sugar content on breakfast cereals. It has petitioned the FTC to ban junk food advertising on children's television and continues to work on this issue.

Coalescing with other organizations is further illustrated in CSPI's efforts on alcohol. Here it has been joined by a wide range of organizations, including parent groups and physicians, and has won legislation requiring warning labels on every alcoholic beverage container. Grass-roots tactics are also part of CSPI's repertoire. The Americans for Safe Food campaign was launched with efforts to request pesticide-free foods in grocery stores and petitions to Congress for national organic farming standards.

The organization's expertise is brought to bear in ongoing oversight of executive implementation of programs. The Center's Safe Food Project takes credit for helping win 1990 legislation that set a national definition of organic food, and continues to oversee its implementation by the states and the U.S. Department of Agriculture, which opposed the legislation.

FURTHER READING

Berry, Jeffrey M. 1977. *Lobbying for the People: The Political Behavior of Public Interest Groups.* Princeton: Princeton University Press.
Center for Science in the Public Interest 1971–1991. 1991. Washington, DC: Center for Science in the Public Interest.
Ippolito, Pauline M. and Alan D. Mathios. 1993. "New Food Labeling Regulations and the Flow of Nutrition Information to Consumers." *Journal of Public Policy and Marketing,* Fall, pp. 188–205.
Nutrition Action Healthletter. Monthly. Washington, DC: Center for Science in the Public Interest.
Pertschuk, Michael. 1982. *Revolt Against Regulation: The Rise and Pause of the Consumer Movement.* Berkeley: University of California Press.

CENTER FOR STUDY OF RESPONSIVE LAW
P.O. Box 19367
Washington, DC 20036
(202) 387–8030

ORGANIZATION AND RESOURCES

The Center for Study of Responsive Law was founded by Ralph Nader in 1968 as the institutional home for the teams of zealous young lawyers known as Nader's Raiders. It was originally funded by foundation grants and later by the out-of-court settlement paid by General Motors to Nader in his suit against them for their investigation into his private life. General Motors' fruitless effort to "dig up dirt" discrediting Nader was launched in response to his critique of the corporation's commitment to consumer safety, published in *Unsafe at Any Speed: The Designed-in Dangers of the American Automobile.* Although Nader has subsequently founded many other consumer organizations, the Center still serves as his own institutional base. Its staff size fluctuates between ten and twenty individuals, and it is funded by foundation grants and publication sales. Its mission is to raise public awareness of consumer issues and to encourage public and private institutions to be more responsive to the needs of citizens and consumers.

POLICY CONCERNS

The Center's concerns have mirrored the wide range of issues that have risen to the top of the consumer protection agenda since the late 1960s. Among these concerns are food safety, workplace safety, the relationship of administrative agencies to private-sector interests they govern, administrative effectiveness, freedom of information, nuclear power safety and cost, business response to consumer complaints, whistle-blowing, corporate accountability, and purchasing cooperatives. Specific current issues pursued by the Center include nursing home conditions, postal services, banking deregulation, insurance, meat inspections, toxic waste, management of taxpayer assets, and discrimination against women.

TACTICS

The Center sponsors a freedom-of-information clearinghouse, but its principal mode of operation is to conduct research and disseminate the results as widely as possible through publications, conferences, seminars, and the mass media. It issues a newsletter, *Buyer's Market,* ten times a year, and publishes reports with provocative titles such as *Returning to the Jungle: How the Reagan Administration Is Imperiling the Nation's Meat and Poultry Inspection Program* (1983). It also assists with grass-roots organizing and initiative and referendum campaigns. One of the characteristic strategies it promotes is consumer checkoff funding of committees to serve as watchdogs of utilities or financial service organizations such as banks. The Center also monitors legislative and regulatory processes and joins coalitions with like-minded organizations.

FURTHER READING

Bollier, David. 1989. *Citizen Action and Other Big Ideas: A History of Ralph Nader and the Modern Consumer Movement.* Washington, DC: Center for Study of Responsive Law.

Nader, Ralph. 1965. *Unsafe at Any Speed: The Designed-in Dangers of the American Automobile.* New York: Grossman.

Kaufman, Leslie. 1991. "America's New Mr. International." *International Economy,* July/August, pp. 35–37.

Torry, Saundra. 1994. "Harvard Law Group Tackles Social Injustice." *Washington Post,* February 18, p. A3.

CHILDREN'S DEFENSE FUND (CDF)
122 C Street N.W.
Washington, DC 20001
Tel (202) 628–8787
Fax 202–783–7324

ORGANIZATION AND RESOURCES

The Children's Defense Fund has a well-earned reputation in Washington for its effective advocacy in behalf of the most disadvantaged members of the U.S. consumer society, poor and disadvantaged children. Founded in 1973 by antipoverty and civil rights activist Marion Wright Edelman, as a follow-on organization to her Washington Research Project, CDF has a staff of over 100 (1993) and a budget of almost $9 million annually. Besides its headquarters in Washington, it has branch offices in three states. The organization publishes *CDF Reports* monthly, *The State of America's Children* annually, and numerous reports on problems that children and their families face.

POLICY CONCERNS

Current and long-standing concerns focus on child health and welfare, prevention of adolescent pregnancy, child care and development, and related issues. Like other governmental watchdog groups established in the wake of increased social activism in the 1960s and 1970s (e.g., FRAC* and the Center for Community Change*), the Children's Defense Fund seeks enactment of new programs and policies and full implementation of those already on the books.

TACTICS

State and national government agencies serving children and their families or whose programs affect them are CDF's chief targets. Examples are the Department of Health and Human Services and its Children's Office, Aid to Families with Dependent Children, Medicaid, food assistance, and Social Security officials. As a player in Washington politics, CDF has a reputation for leveraging its resources by putting together and participating in coalitions with consumer and social welfare activists, as well as with such unlikely partners as business, professional organizations, and women's groups like the Junior League. A recent example was CDF's participation in a coalition in support of malpractice reform, the National Medical Liability Reform Coalition. It included about forty organizations, such as the National Association of Manufacturers,* the American Medical Association,* and the American Hospital Association.*

FURTHER READING

Bernard, April. "First Mother." *Lear's,* 6:88–91 (March).
Bouton, Katherine. 1987. "Marian Wright Edelman." *Ms.,* July/August, pp. 98–100.
Hood, John. 1992. "Children's Crusade." *Reason,* June, pp. 32–35.
Kaus, Mickey. 1992. "The Godmother." *New Republic,* February 15, pp. 21–25.
Kosterlitz, Julie. 1991. "Malpractice Morass." *National Journal,* July 6, pp. 1682–1686.
Seligman, Daniel. 1993. "And Now, Speaking for the Grownups." *Fortune,* April 19, pp. 159–160.
Shapiro, Joseph P. 1990. "The Unraveling Kids' Crusade." *U.S. News and World Report,* March 26, pp. 22–24.

CITIZEN ACTION FUND (CAF)

1406 West 6th Street	1300 Connecticut Ave. N.W.
Suite 200	Suite 401
Cleveland, OH 44113	Washington, DC 20036
Tel (216) 861–5200	Tel (202) 857–5153
Fax 216–698–6904	Fax 202–857–4937

ORGANIZATION AND RESOURCES

Renamed in 1989, this organization was originally founded in 1979 as Citizen Action. Nearly three-quarters of the organization's budget comes from its 4.5 million members, who are organized into eight branches and connected with over thirty affiliated grass-roots organizations. The Fund, which has 501(c)(4) tax status, claims a staff of thirty-five.

POLICY CONCERNS

The organization's chief objective—to work to enhance citizen participation in economic, environmental, and political decisions—remains the same. Officials concentrate on achieving greater input by local communities in issues affecting their neighborhoods and pocketbooks, such as state and national debates over energy conservation and new energy technologies, insurance reform, toxic and solid waste, and similar issues.

TACTICS

CAF officials lobby, testify before congressional committees, and help organize coalitions with other organizations advocating for the interests of low- and moderate-income consumers. CAF is also active in campaigns to reform state insurance systems along the lines of the legislation enacted after voter approval of a ballot proposition in California, promoted through door-to-door and telephone canvassing. This reform package includes creation of state consumer insurance advocates, rollbacks of rate increases, and changes intended to prevent the roadblocks that the California insurance industry put up against implementation in that state.

FURTHER READING

Barnes, James A. 1991. "Liberal Democrats Feeling Their Oats." *National Journal,* January 5, p. 25.

CITIZENS FOR TAX JUSTICE (CTJ)
1311 L Street N.W.
Washington, DC 20005
(202) 626–3780

ORGANIZATION AND RESOURCES

Citizens for Tax Justice is a nonprofit, nonpartisan coalition of labor, public interest, and grass-roots citizens groups working for fairer taxes at the federal, state, and local levels of government. It was formed in 1979 with support from organized labor and Ralph Nader for the purpose of giving ordinary people a greater voice in tax policy so that they could compete with the lobbyists for special interests and the wealthy. CTJ fights for more equitable treatment for middle- and low-income families based on the belief that people should pay taxes according to their ability to pay.

A thirty-two-person board of directors governs the organization; members represent prominent labor, consumer, and community organizations. Among these are Lane Kirkland of the AFL-CIO,* Albert Shanker of the American Federation of Teachers, Steven Brobeck of the Consumer Federation of America,* Joan Claybrook of Public Citizen,* Maude Hurd of ACORN,* three state Citizen Action* representatives, Benjamin Hooks of the National Association for the Advancement of Colored People,* and Susan Lederman of the League of Women Voters.* The six staff members are directed by Robert S. McIntyre.

CTJ publishes studies on taxation that are available to members and others. Among these are *Corporate Taxpayers & Corporate Freeloaders, A Far Cry from Fair: CTJ's Guide to State Tax Reform,* and *Inequality and the Federal Budget Deficit.* Fact sheets on more limited topics are also published and available; some of these titles are "Indexing Capital Gains Is a Very Bad Idea," "The Facts About Jerry Brown's Proposed Flat-Rate Income Tax & National Sales Tax," and "Bill Clinton's Tax Record as Governor." It has also begun publication of a newsletter, *CTJ Update,* which is available nine times a year for $10; it also comes with membership ($25 per year).

CTJ's studies on corporate tax avoidance have been widely cited for their key role in the enactment of the Tax Reform Act of 1986, which curbed tax shelters for corporations and the wealthy and cut taxes for poor and middle-income families. Its research on state taxes has helped make tax fairness an issue in state reform debates as well. Thus, its reputation for presenting relevant, persuasive data that make a difference on the side of progressive taxation is its most important resource.

POLICY CONCERNS

The overriding concern of CTJ is to achieve a more progressive system of taxation in the United States at all levels of government. "Progressive" is defined as meaning that the share of income paid out in taxes should rise as income rises. CTJ argues that tax progressivity was official national policy until the 1980s, when it began to be eroded at both federal and state levels. It does not advocate reduced taxation overall; in fact, it argues that taxes are necessary to pay for public services. However, it points out that not all taxes are equal in their impact, and that the public ought to understand the ramifications of the choices made in this complex policy arena. Its initial focus was on the federal tax system, particularly the corporate income tax and how many leading, profitable companies managed to pay little or nothing in federal taxes. CTJ advocated closing the loopholes that allowed corporations to evade taxation, instituting a minimum corporate tax, and reducing the income tax on middle- and lower-income individuals.

Since the enactment of the federal tax reform legislation of 1986, CTJ has focused on state taxation and on the federal budget. Its study of state taxes, *A Far Cry from Fair,* decries the overreliance on regressive sales and excise taxes and individual and corporate income taxes that are insufficiently progressive. Its prescription for reform advocates greater reliance on more progressive income taxes, strengthening corporate income taxes, and targeting property tax relief to low- and middle-income families.

Inequality and the Federal Budget Deficit documents the tax and budget impact of supply-side economics through the 1980s. It portrays the growing federal deficit alongside the growing inequality in incomes and wealth to argue that the deficit is due to the reduced tax burdens on the rich. To counter the conservative argument that the deficit is due to increased spending, especially on entitlements, the study points out that most federal spending, excluding Social Security, has actually fallen as a share of GNP. While programs for education and training, roads and transportation, the environment, and welfare were reduced, spending on defense, interest on the debt, and the savings and loan bailout increased. Thus persons of low and middle income are paying an increased share but receiving less in government services than before the supply-side experiment.

The supply-side notion of trickle-down is attacked as well; savings, investment, and trade have not improved in spite of increased resources in the hands of the wealthy. CTJ calls on the federal government to raise additional revenue for needed public investment by taking back the tax giveaways to the richest 1 percent of the population and plugging remaining corporate tax loopholes, such as accelerated depreciation write-offs, capital gains tax breaks, and tax subsidies for leveraged buy-outs and for multinational companies that send manufacturing jobs outside U.S. borders. CTJ opposes a value-added tax on the grounds that it is regressive, cannot easily be made progressive, would not have positive effects on the trade imbalance, would be no easier to administer than the income tax, and would encourage more special interest lobbying on the federal tax code. It favors the luxury tax on jewelry, automobiles, yachts, private airplanes, and expensive furs.

TACTICS

CTJ's primary tactic is to research tax incidence and report it persuasively to policymakers and the interested public. Research for its initial studies on the federal corporate income tax was conducted by painstaking analysis of individual corporate annual reports by Robert McIntyre. What gave the CTJ studies such an impact was that they listed names of prominent corporations and the amounts they had paid in federal taxes. A long list of large corporations that had paid no federal income taxes in at least one year studied particularly caught the public's eye. Facilitating the impact of *Corporate Taxpayers and Corporate Freeloaders* (1985) was the fact that the chief executives of some of the corporate "freeloaders" were prominent critics of wasteful government spending.

CTJ's study of state taxation included analysis of the tax systems of the fifty states and the District of Columbia, with detailed tables for each state showing the impact of each type of tax on each income group. States with the highest taxes on poor and middle-income families are dubbed "The Terrible Ten." CTJ also provides research support for state advocacy groups by analyzing proposals that come before state legislatures or other policymakers.

Besides undertaking massive long-term research like the three-and-a-half-year study of state taxation, CTJ is able to produce rapid responses to alternatives raised as debates evolve in the states and in the Washington policy community. For example, as the reexamination of federal taxes and the deficit evolved in 1991, the option of a European-style value-added tax became the favorite of some policymakers. CTJ quickly responded with research, a fact sheet, testimony, and news releases on the probable incidence of a national value-added tax. It also analyzes and comments on specific tax legislation as it is proposed.

The stature enjoyed by CTJ is evident in its direct relationship with prominent members of Congress. Its 1991 study on the federal budget deficit was released in a joint press conference with House Majority Leader Richard Gephardt. It is frequently invited to present testimony before congressional committees.

CTJ enjoys excellent media relations—its studies get prominent news coverage when they are released, and it provides ongoing news releases targeted to specific states and issues. Articles written by CTJ staff members frequently appear in the *New York Times*, the *Washington Post*, the *Los Angeles Times*, *The New Republic*, and other prominent publications as well as many smaller publications around the country. Its articles have appeared in *Roll Call*, a magazine widely read on Capitol Hill. Robert McIntyre is frequently a featured guest on television and radio news and call-in shows. CTJ's expertise is sought by news organizations that request analyses of specific tax proposals.

Allying with like-minded organizations extends CTJ's reach. Its study on state taxation was simultaneously released by tax activists in many of the states, including citizen action, labor, and tax reform associations. Staff members, including McIntyre, travel around the country speaking to organizations that might be receptive to their progressive message.

FURTHER READING

Annual Report. Annual. Washington, DC: Citizens for Tax Justice.

Berry, Jeffrey M. 1989. *The Interest Group Society*. 2nd ed. Glenview, IL: Scott, Foresman.

Birnbaum, Jeffrey, and Alan S. Murray. 1987. *Showdown at Gucci Gulch: Lawmakers, Lobbyists, and the Unlikely Triumph of Tax Reform*. New York: Random House.

CTJ Update. Monthly. Washington, DC: Citizens for Tax Justice.

McIntyre, Robert S. 1991. *Inequality and the Federal Deficit*. Washington, DC: Citizens for Tax Justice.

McIntyre, Robert, S., et al. 1991. *A Far Cry from Fair: CTJ's Guide to State Tax Reform*. Washington, DC: Citizens for Tax Justice.

"Soaking the Poor: Study Finds State and Local Taxes Very Regressive." 1991. *Dollars and Sense*, July/August, pp. 9–11.

COMMON CAUSE
2030 M Street N.W.
Washington, DC 20036
(202) 833–1200

ORGANIZATION AND RESOURCES

Common Cause is a nonprofit, nonpartisan citizens' group that works to improve the way federal and state governments operate. It was founded in 1970 by John Gardner, former head of the Carnegie Foundation; secretary of health, education and welfare under President Johnson; and chairman of the Urban Coalition. Gardner successfully tapped widespread anxiety about how the nation was being run, asserting that "everybody's organized but the people." More than 100,000 people responded within a six-month period to mass mail and newspaper advertisement invitations to join in a citizen's lobby to advance the well-being of the nation. Membership peaked at about 340,000 in August 1974, the month Richard Nixon resigned the presidency. Gardner served as chairman until 1977, when he was succeeded by Nan Waterman, a Common Cause activist. In 1980, Archibald Cox, the Watergate special prosecutor fired by President Nixon, became chairman; Fred Wertheimer became president in 1981.

The group is supported by dues and small contributions from 275,000 members. Regular membership is $20, student membership $10, family membership $30 annually. The organization's annual budget is over $11.7 million. Approximately 40 percent of its revenue comes from dues, and an additional 55 percent from member contributions and bequests in addition to dues. It accepts no corporate or union contributions of more than $100. A sixty-member national governing board is elected by members to set issue priorities and policy. An annual issues poll of the entire membership, in-depth surveys of samples of members, and staff recommendations guide the board in policy setting.

Common Cause has 49 state units, 300 active congressional district branches, and 115 full-time employees in its national and state offices. It has devoted substantial effort to teaching its activists to lobby by coaching them in letter writing, appropriate behavior in direct meetings with candidates, and other topics. In addition to staff, the organization makes use of a large number of volunteers, sometimes as many as 200 at a time. Volunteers work as reporting observers of congressional meetings and hearings, as telephone liaison with congressional district volunteers, and as collectors and tabulators of campaign finance data. Volunteers support regular staff in publication of *Common Cause Magazine,* a monthly release until late 1991 that reemerged in 1992 as a leaner quarterly publication. The magazine reports organizational news, hard-hitting exposés of current issues, congressional voting records, and action alerts to members. Occasional special studies are published separately; recent examples include *Missing Money: A Common Cause Study of Federal Tax Expenditures* and *Public Advisers/Private Interests.*

POLICY CONCERNS

Common Cause is guided by five key principles: (1) self-government cannot work unless citizens make it work; (2) governance issues require long-term commitment and constant vigilance; (3) efforts to hold public officials accountable and persuade them to enact reforms involve tension and conflict; (4) the way we govern ourselves is central to the daily lives of citizens and the nation's well-being; and (5) honest and accountable government is essential to democracy. While its specific concerns range across many issues, they all relate to these guiding principles.

In its first decade Common Cause successfully pressed Congress to end or weaken its seniority system, open committee hearings, and reform campaign finance. It was among the groups that focused public opposition to the Vietnam War on the strategy of ending the appropriations that supported the conflict. Its careful monitoring of campaign behavior and finance involved Common Cause in the Watergate scandal; it sued Nixon's Committee to Re-Elect the President, forcing it to disclose the list of donors solicited for $20 million before the disclosure deadline.

Common Cause issues were part of the reform wave of the mid-1970s. It was involved with the passage of open meeting laws in forty-eight states, financial disclosure laws in more than thirty states, and public financing measures in some states. The Ethics in Government Act, requiring financial disclosure by officials in all three branches of the federal government, signed by President Carter in 1978, was one to which Common Cause had devoted tremendous effort.

The 1980s is described by Common Cause as an era of "Ask not what you can do for your country, ask what you can do for yourself." It was a decade in which, like many citizens' groups, Common Cause struggled to protect gains made in the previous decade. It led the coalition against the MX missile and was part of the effort to block the Strategic Defense Initiative. It supported the Equal Rights Amendment, voting rights and statehood for the District of Columbia, the 1982 extension of the Voting Rights Act, the 1988 Civil Rights Restoration Act, and the Americans with Disabilities Act, and helped defeat the nomination of Robert Bork as Supreme Court justice. Common Cause became part of the Reagan administration "sleaze watch," opposing the confirmation of Edmund Meese as attorney general, criticizing the Federal Election Commission's failure to regulate "soft money" (that raised by parties outside the federal campaign reporting system) and enforce election laws, and chronicling the savings and loan scandal. Common Cause prodded the Senate Ethics Committee to initiate an investigation of the "Keating Five," and used the climate of ethics concern to press again for campaign finance reform.

Looking into the 1990s, Common Cause will continue to lobby for reform of campaign financing. It sees four elements as essential to real reform: spending limits, publicly funded alternative resources, aggregate limits on receipts from political action committees, and an end to "soft money" abuses. President Bush vowed to veto any bill providing public funding or imposing spending limits; President Clinton supports reform, but getting legislation out of Congress will still be a significant challenge. Easing voter registration as a means to raise voter turnout is an issue Common Cause has been involved with for a long time. Neither President Carter's effort nor the 1990 House bill was successful, but Congress passed, and President Clinton signed, a "motor voter" bill early in 1993.

TACTICS

The foundation of Common Cause's wide repertoire of tactics is the classic grass-roots letter-writing or telephone campaign. This tactic is comprised of an active, educated membership, groomed with careful topical research, and activated by direct mail or telephone alerts from the national office down a telephone tree to thousands of members. For example, in the five weeks before the House of Representatives voted on a campaign finance reform bill in November 1991, Common Cause members made more than 6,000 phone calls to House offices. Members also meet on a regular basis in their home districts with their elected representatives, attend public forums to raise Common Cause issues, and sometimes ask their representatives to take a written pledge of their position on an issue of importance to Common Cause. Letters to the editors of local newspapers are also coordinated from the national office. Charts showing how members of Congress voted on the group's issues are published in *Common Cause Magazine,* but members are not rated or endorsed.

Although on the one hand Common Cause is highly regarded for its professionalism, it is also noted for occasionally turning on its usual allies. Its motto is "No permanent friends, no permanent enemies." Even usual allies may find themselves embarrassed by full-page ads in the *Washington Post* or their district newspaper, urging them to stop blocking campaign finance reform or whatever issue they are not moving along quickly enough.

Common Cause enjoys very high regard for its research, particularly that relating to campaign finance data. It is able to release meaningful reports based on data filed with the Federal Election Commission before anyone else, including the Federal Election Commission. Its reports are widely published in the mass media, although Common Cause as an organization may not get much attention as the source of the report. Background papers supplied by the organization sometimes become the basis of news articles or editorials. Investigatory reports published in *Common Cause Magazine* also appear in other publications, such as the *Washington Post,* the *San Francisco Chronicle,* and *Reader's Digest.*

Lobbyists for Common Cause work directly with staff and members of Congress, planning strategy, providing research, and presenting testimony. Common Cause has sometimes requested special investigations of issues or behavior, as it did with the savings and loan "Keating Five." Board of governors members from all over the country spend time in Capitol Hill offices, working to persuade their senators and representatives. Common Cause carefully oversees the work of the Federal Election Commission and other executive agencies administering issues of concern to it. In addition to publicizing agency behavior, it may file complaints and, as a last resort, may sue. Most of the resources used for litigation have been directed at the area of campaign finance regulation.

FURTHER READING

Alston, Chuck. 1989. "Common Cause: A Watchdog That Barks at Its Friends." *Congressional Quarterly Weekly Report,* August 26, pp. 2204–2207.

Common Cause. 1990. *20 Years of Citizen Action: Common Cause 1970–1990.* Washington, DC: Common Cause.

————. 1992. Financial Statements. December 31, 1990 and 1991. Washington, DC: Common Cause.

Common Cause Magazine. March/April 1988 through January/March 1992.

Cooper, Kenneth J. 1993. "Campaign Finance Reform? Maybe Next Year." *Washington Post,* national weekly edition, November 8–14, p. 11.

Gardner, John. 1972. *In Common Cause: Citizen Action and How It Works.* New York: W. W. Norton.

McFarland, Andrew S. 1984. *Common Cause: Lobbying in the Public Interest.* Chatham, N.J.: Chatham House.

Sammon, Richard. 1993. " 'Motor Voter' Rides a Fast Track Through the House." *Congressional Quarterly Weekly Report,* February 6, p. 264.

THE CONFERENCE BOARD

845 Third Avenue	1775 Massachusetts Ave. N.W.
New York, NY 10022–6601	Washington, DC 20036
(212) 759–0900	(202) 483–0580

ORGANIZATION AND RESOURCES

The Conference Board was founded in 1916 during an era of tension and violence between American management and labor. Originally called the National Industrial Conference Board, it was intended to improve the public image of business by looking objectively at solutions to industrial conflict that would serve the public interest. Its current mission is to improve the business enterprise system and to enhance the contribution of business to society. It strives to be the leading global business membership organization that enables senior executives from all industries to explore and exchange ideas impacting business policy and practice. To support this activity, the Board provides a variety of forums and a professionally managed research program that identifies and reports objectively on key areas of changing management concern, opportunity, and action. The accuracy and independence of its research and publications have earned it respect, but the organization has also remained in touch with top business executives.

The activities of the Conference Board are overseen by a thirty-member board of trustees whose numbers include chief executive officers of such corporations as 3M, Unilever, Philip Morris, and IBM. Preston Townley is its president and chief executive officer, directing a staff of 250 with an annual budget of more than $22 million. Until the late 1980s, almost two-thirds of Conference Board operating revenue came from general subscription support, but that share has declined to approximately one-half, with meeting revenue increasingly making up most of the difference. In addition to its New York office, the Conference Board has offices in Chicago, San Francisco, and Washington, D. C. The Conference Board of Canada has offices in Ottawa. The Conference Board Europe has offices in Brussels and staff representatives in the United Kingdom, France, Scandinavia, Germany, and Spain.

Participating in Conference Board councils is one of the most significant benefits of membership. Councils on 39 specific topics bring together more than 1,300 senior executive members with interests in those subjects in informal, off-the-record settings that facilitate the development of personal networks. Newly created council topics include a European council on managing the environment, services marketing, and corporate communications. The Board's growing number of councils reflects a strategy of focusing on high-priority business issues and forging a more global perspective.

Conference Board conferences are held around the world; the 72 conferences, seminars, and workshops in 1991 attracted more than 8,500 executives, an increase over previous years, despite the recession. Research produced by the Board's staff included thirty-three research reports, two white papers, and regular issues of twenty-nine periodicals. Among their research reports are *Corporate Directors' Compensation, Encouraging Employee Self-Management in Financial and Career Planning, Employee Buy-in to Total Quality,* and *Corporate Support of National Education Goals.* Periodicals include *Global Business Briefing* and *Human Resources Briefing;* the economics periodicals are their best-known, including the *Consumer Confidence Survey.* Time-sensitive research results are available through the Board's fax service and a personal computer information service. Members also have access to the Conference Board Information Service, which links them with a business library of 15,000 reference works, 1,000 periodicals, and on-line data bases. The Information Service answers more than 20,000 business questions each year.

POLICY CONCERNS

The Conference Board has long been attentive to corporate practice in internal governance, compensation, contributions, and public affairs. Its program priorities for the 1990s and beyond focus on six key issues—quality and productivity, the work force, global management, economics, corporate practices, and business and education. The globalization of the marketplace and rising consumer expectations place pressure on companies to gain organizationwide commitment to excellence and to improving products and services. Board research on quality management asks such questions as whether quality is compatible with corporate restructuring, how companies motivate employees, and what distinguishes quality companies. In the face of a changing work force, the Conference Board examines how employers are responding to the challenge of diversity as compared with the traditional white male work force. Concerns of this research include how to design policies that are flexible but equitable and whether child care, family leave, and other work–family programs are cost-effective.

In the contemporary drive toward globalization, Board research analyzes events that have current and future impacts on business management. Particular attention is focused on trade negotiations, German reunification, Japan, and the former Soviet Union. While the Board has long been regarded as a significant source of data on trends in the American economy, it is also striving to integrate an increasingly broader view of international financial trends into its information so that it is able to provide current intelligence on global, national, and regional markets.

How corporations function and how they relate to society have always been areas of interest to the Conference Board. Trends in compensation, contributions, response to environmental regulations, and corporate governance, particularly the shift in ownership from individual to institutional shareholders, are issues of concern for Board research and publications. Finally, the Board attends to the involvement of business leaders in efforts to reform and improve education. It voices concerns about the national crisis in education, particularly that large numbers of young people leave high school early or unprepared to meet job requirements. Business faces a shrinking pool of adequately trained workers and a future in which it must provide remedial training for employees. The Board's position is that business is in a unique position to provide the strong leadership to overcome educational inertia.

TACTICS

In a wide variety of venues, Conference Board meetings bring together business and political leaders from throughout the world to examine critical business issues. Its reputation for sound economic reporting means that its research is used by business, the media, and government policymakers. Its research councils offer networking at its highest level; council members have access to practical, competitive information and the opportunity to test new ideas in an off-the-record environment with people whose opinions count. The Conference Board's media relations are excellent, and it may well be the world's most widely quoted business organization. It is cited in more than 15,000 news stories a year on worldwide television and radio, and in magazines, newspapers, and wire services.

The Board has long been a major force in shaping economic ideas and providing forward-looking analysis of business trends. What is now known as the U.S. Consumer Price Index was pioneered by the Conference Board; in 1969 it began publishing its own Index of Consumer Confidence, which is included in the federal government's leading economic indicators. The significance of Conference Board data has increased as the quality of government data has deteriorated and business has faced intensifying competition. Conference Board forecasts have been more accurate than most others in projecting short- and long-term interest rates and changes in the value of the dollar. Its Index of Consumer Confidence, the Business Executives' Expectations Index, the International Economic Scoreboard, and the Help-Wanted Index are proprietary products and valuable planning tools. The credibility of Conference Board data stems in part from the Board's unique access to senior management around the world, which provides it a superior data base comprised of high response rates to surveys and early warning cues about events on the horizon.

Finally, the organization supports a hands-on program for business executive involvement in the nation's capital. Direct experience for executives on Capitol Hill is provided through the Board's Congressional Assistant Program, in which individuals are placed in one-year assignments on committees' or members' staffs.

FURTHER READING

The Conference Board. n.d. New York: Conference Board.
The Conference Board at 75: Annual Report 1991. 1991. New York: Conference Board.
Research Program: Strategies and Tactics for Business in the Nineties and Beyond. n.d. New York: Conference Board.
Whiting, Meredith, ed. 1993. Washington Dialogue: The New National Agenda. Washington, DC: Conference Board.
Who We Are, What We Do, How You Benefit, What We Provide. n.d. New York: Conference Board.

CONSUMER ALERT
1024 J Street, Room 425
Modesto, CA 95354
(209) 524–1738

1555 Wilson Blvd., Suite 300
Arlington, VA 22209
(703) 875–8644

ORGANIZATION AND RESOURCES

Consumer Alert was incorporated in 1977 by Barbara Keating-Edh, who continues to be its president and executive director. It is a nationwide, nonprofit membership organization for persons concerned about the growing regulatory climate in our national and state capitals. The organization was founded to advance the cause of competition as the best regulator of business, individual choice as the best expression of consumer interest, and economic accountability as the best policy of government intervention.

Ms. Keating-Edh was the 1974 Conservative candidate for the U.S. Senate from New York. She subsequently worked as a special assistant to Senator James Buckley, and in 1980 headed the Reagan administration's transition team for the Consumer Product Safety Commission. The organization operates with a staff of four and draws on volunteers and interns. Consumer Alert itself is a 501(c)(3) organization but has a lobbying arm, Consumer Alert Advocate Fund. Its annual budget of about $360,000 is obtained from membership dues (33 percent); gifts, grants, and contributions (33 percent); and subscriptions and sales of publications (33 percent). Membership is confined to individuals who pay annual dues of $20; the group has over 6,000 members from every state in the nation. Publications, including a newsletter, press releases, testimony, surveys, and reprints of excerpts from prominent conservative publications such as Milton and Rose D. Friedman's *Free to Choose,* are available to corporate subscribers. Consumer Alert makes a point of accepting no government funding except reimbursement for members invited to testify before congressional committees.

POLICY CONCERNS

Consumer Alert regards the regulation advanced as consumer protection to be threatening to individual freedom to choose and to the economic well-being of the nation. Climbing consumer prices caused by compliance costs, science that unjustifiably appears to discredit technology and hinder advancement, and regulation for the sake of regulation are the targets of the organization. It defends the wisdom of private ownership, allocations made by the competitive marketplace, and the ability of consumers to protect themselves. These principles are said to be the basis of the American way of life, and the core interest of consumers is to see that they are preserved. Their motto is that free enterprise does benefit most of the people most of the time.

Current concerns include expansion of free trade, Environmental Protection Agency reviews of health risks associated with chemicals such as dioxin, blocking increases in Corporate Average Fuel Economy standards, and promoting oil exploration in the Arctic National Wildlife Refuge.

TACTICS

Consumer Alert's overall strategy is to voice the conservative position in the war of ideas. It conducts opinion research on attitudes and abuses, provides information to the media, sponsors conferences, comments on proposed federal regulations, and presents testimony at congressional hearings. It also acts as a conduit to public interest law firms such as the Pacific Legal Foundation and the Atlantic Legal Foundation. For the 1989 National Consumers Week, Consumer Alert organized a National Consumer Coalition that brought together thirty like-minded policy groups including Accuracy in Media,* Americans for Tax Reform, Citizens for a Sound Economy, the Heritage Foundation,* and the National Center for Privatization. Consumer Alert received funding for the forum from corporate sources including Pfizer, Philip Morris, and Adolph Coors. Highlighting the Coalition program was the warm acceptance by outgoing Consumer Alert board chairman John Sununu of a compilation of policy recommendations for the incoming Bush administration.

Consumer Alert frequently is aligned against Ralph Nader-inspired organizations and positions; "Nader-needling" is a noticeable theme in its newsletter features. The organization was instrumental in bringing about litigation to end the mandatory fee system that supported university Public Interest Research

Groups.* A Consumer Alert survey of students about the fee practice brought forth a student plaintiff for whom a suit was pursued by the MidAtlantic Foundation against Rutgers University. Consumer Alert subsequently persuaded the University of California Board of Regents to end the negative check-off fee collecting arrangement that had been substituted after the court ban on mandatory fees.

FURTHER READING

Annual Report. Annual. Modesto, CA: Consumer Alert.
Consumer Alert. n.d. Modesto, CA: Consumer Alert.
Consumer Comments. Newsletter of Consumer Alert.
Vogel, David. 1989. *Fluctuating Fortunes: The Political Power of Business in America.* New York: Basic Books.

CONSUMER BANKERS ASSOCIATION (CBA)
1000 Wilson Boulevard, 30th floor
Arlington, VA 22209–3908
(703) 276–1750

ORGANIZATION AND RESOURCES

The Consumer Bankers Association provides a Washington voice for retail banks and thrift institutions. It was founded in 1919 as the Morris Plan Bankers Association and changed its name in 1946. Its members total 722, including single banks, holding companies, holding company banks, savings and loans, and nonbanks. Substantial effort has been devoted to retaining and recruiting members since 1988 through special visits to member institutions, enhanced direct communications with individual leaders in member institutions, and other methods of highlighting the value of membership in CBA.

An eighteen-member board of directors governs the organization; the staff of seventeen is directed by Joe Belew, the president. Revenue for CBA totals approximately $3 million annually; member dues account for 44 percent of revenue, 22 percent comes from conferences, and another 22 percent from the Graduate School of Bank Management. The latter offers course work in economics, finance, marketing, and human resource management; it includes a two-week resident session each summer at the University of Virginia.

The goal of CBA is to facilitate an exhange of information and ideas among its members, to provide education, and to act for retail banking interests in government relations at the national level. Member committees are concerned with government relations, communications, education, home equity lending, automobile finance, education funding, electronic funds transfer, small business banking, and consumer affairs. Members receive *CBA Reports,* a monthly newsletter that keeps them posted on Association activities, and may attend regular conferences on such topics as automobile finance and small business banking.

POLICY CONCERNS

Salient national attention to numerous banking issues has kept the CBA active in national policy. CBA participated with other banking associations in considering ways to recapitalize the Federal Deposit Insurance Corporation's Bank Insurance Fund and endorsed the industry position of avoiding direct use of taxpayers' dollars to resupply the fund. CBA supported the Bush administration's proposal for comprehensive banking reform, especially interstate branching and cross-sell authority for all financial products. It strongly opposed consumer amendments, particularly those for mandatory cashing of government checks and basic banking. CBA takes the position that these requirements are unnecessary and unduly interfere with a bank's conduct of business. Provisions allowing banking institutions to price these basic services to cover their costs plus a 10 percent profit also were opposed by CBA; it supported an amendment to allow banks to self-certify these pricing policies rather than requiring the Federal Reserve to police them. As an alternative to mandatory cashing of government checks, the Association supports the elimination of paper-based distribution of benefits payments. CBA also is working to ensure that banks will not incur costs or liabilities in electronic transfer of benefits.

The Truth in Savings Act, which was part of the congressional effort at banking reform in 1991, was opposed by CBA each time it was proposed since 1972. The 1991 version included more uniform balance and interest calculation and disclosure methods, to which the CBA was strongly opposed, arguing that the variations among banks would be very difficult and costly to report uniformly.

CBA is active in protecting the role of its members in providing guaranteed student loans under the Higher Education Act of 1965, which is reauthorized on a five-year cycle. Recent attention to the allowance to lenders, and proposals to replace the bank role in lending with direct loans by schools, brought the Association strongly in opposition to direct government provision of education loans.

Looking toward the future, among the issues on which the group expects to face challenges are privacy considerations for customers who use telephone banking systems to access account information and transfer funds. Resolution of disputed credit report data is also getting attention from CBA and other banking and credit associations.

TACTICS

While it has been a top priority of CBA to oppose congressional mandates for services to low-income populations that the group regards as burdensome, it has worked to promote voluntary provision of services. Community Reinvestment Act workshops on profitable community development lending programs have been offered; CBA also has become part of a group of financial industry leaders who seek more public recognition for their efforts in community development. This sort of coalition work was exemplified by CBA's organizing a banking industry response to proposals by the Treasury Department for electronic benefits transfer.

The Association conducts studies and does research both for the use of its members and for presentation to public policymakers. These are often the foundation for CBA's work with members of Congress and their staffs and for its testimony before congressional committees and subcommittees. CBA also reviews and comments upon proposed regulations from executive branch agencies that impact members' business.

CBA resources support member media relations and relate to the media directly on behalf of the industry. Grass-roots tactics include bringing members to meet directly with their representatives in the House and Senate and to educate them on more effective contacts with policymakers.

FURTHER READING

Annual Report. Annual. Arlington, VA: Consumer Bankers Association.
CBA Reports. Monthly. Arlington, VA: Consumer Bankers Association.
Meier, Kenneth J. 1985. Regulation: Politics, Bureaucracy, and Economics. New York: St. Martin's Press.
U.S. Congress. House Committee on Banking, Finance, and Urban Affairs Subcommittee on General Oversight, Investigations, and the Resolution of Failed Financial Institutions. 1994. Hearing on Community Development Proposals and CRA Reforms. Washington, DC: Government Printing Office.

CONSUMER FEDERATION OF AMERICA (CFA)
1424 16th Street N.W., Suite 604
Washington, DC 20036
(202) 387–6121

ORGANIZATION AND RESOURCES

The Consumer Federation of America is the nation's largest consumer advocacy organization, including more than 240 organizations from throughout the nation with a combined membership exceeding 50 million. Member organizations include grass-roots consumer groups, senior citizen organizations, labor unions, cooperatives, and other national, state, and local organizations. CFA is dedicated to ensuring that all consumers have a reasoned, articulate voice in the policy decisions that affect their health, safety, financial welfare, and quality of life. The federation was founded in 1967 to inform its constituent organizations about pending legislative and administrative actions; it originated out of a coalition of groups called the Consumer Clearing House, which began holding a national consumer assembly. Activists from labor unions, the President's Consumer Advisory Council, and Consumers Union* were instrumental in formalizing the federated coalition. Since then its functions have expanded, its staff has grown to 14 persons, and its budget is more than $900,000.

The Federation is governed by a board of directors elected by CFA members.

Policy committees oversee specific issues including energy, food, health, product safety, communications, antitrust, the disabled, finances, low income consumers, insurance, transportation, and the environment. Policy resolutions are debated and adopted at an annual meeting held in conjunction with the consumer assembly. The group's advocacy program, based on those resolutions, is implemented by its staff under the directorship of Stephen J. Brobeck.

CFA publishes three newsletters. *CFAnews,* issued eight times a year, reports on organization advocacy efforts, conferences, and publications. *CPSNewsletter* covers regulatory activities, congressional activities, and new information on product safety; it is distributed quarterly to members of the Consumer Product Safety Network. *Indoor Air News* is issued four times a year and covers legislative and administrative action relating to clean indoor air. CFA testimony, special legislative alerts, news releases, *Congressional Voting Record,* and pamphlets on consumer topics are available to Information Service subscribers. Informational pamphlets cover such topics as consumer savings options, store brands, dangers of formaldehyde, and indoor air quality. Consumer guidebooks based on staff research are also available; recent titles include *How to Fly, The Bank Book, The Childwise Catalog,* and *The Product Safety Book.*

POLICY CONCERNS

CFA has been involved in every major consumer issue since its founding. Since the early 1980s, it has sounded the alarm at what it describes as the federal government turning its back on marketplace abuses that harm consumers. CFA is prominent among those who criticize an economic policy that has eroded the means of the poor and near poor while bestowing benefits on the wealthy. It has advocated strong and equitable measures to stabilize the economy and to protect consumers by assuring that the marketplace promotes competition, safe products and services, and protection against fraud and abuse. It has supported effective deregulation only in those economic sectors where meaningful competition exists. CFA is particularly sensitive to the needs of low-income consumers whose resource limitations make them vulnerable to economic hardships.

The staff of CFA has provided advocacy leadership in recent years on product safety, including hazardous chemicals in household products, toy safety, and reform of the Consumer Product Safety Commission. Financial services reform has witnessed CFA urging caution about expanded bank powers and sounding warnings about the risks of home equity loans, aggressive credit card marketing, and excessive interest rates on credit cards. They advocate truth in savings, lifeline services (free or low-cost basic services), usury ceilings, insurance disclosures, and community reinvestment standards and reporting. As telephone services have undergone regulatory changes, CFA has lobbied against unnecessary price increases and for affordability, especially for low-income households. While some business and manufacturing sectors have worked to change product liability law, CFA has worked to protect the rights of victims to seek redress in the courts for dangerous or defective products. The affordability of basic necessities such as electricity is an ongoing issue for CFA; in recent years its attention has been drawn to railroad rates for coal shipments because those rates affect electric utility pricing. Other core issues for the Federation include health care access, quality, and cost, and indoor air pollution, including airliner cabin air quality.

CFA has also been involved with a number of salient issues on which allies have taken the leading roles. These include food safety, drug safety, pesticide legislation and regulation, low-income energy assistance, long-term health care financing, corporate mergers, and campaign finance reform.

TACTICS

Research and dissemination of information are the bases of CFA's efforts. Staff members conduct original research that is published, usually in report form, and made available to members and the public. Often the information collected will become the basis for new consumer legislation. Consumer information also takes the form of pamphlets and book-length guides. Spokespersons for CFA frequently are invited to testify before congressional committees and provide input to regulatory agencies and executive departments. Special legislative alerts to members and news releases through the media are an integral part of CFA's tactics. Detailed analyses of votes on key consumer issues are published as *Congressional Voting Record,* rating members as consumer heroes or villains.

CFA coordinates ongoing communication and advocacy among hundreds of consumer and community organizations around the country, including, but not limited to, its state and local grass-roots members. The Consumer Product Safety Network, operated by CFA, keeps more than 900 activists, educators, and professionals up to date on events and urges them to contact members of Congress and submit comments on proposed regulations. It also forms smaller coalitions of both member and nonmember organizations on issues before Congress and the regulatory agencies.

Consumer Assembly, an annual conference of leading advocates including labor, senior citizen, and rural leaders is sponsored by CFA. The Assembly provides consumer advocates a unique forum for the exchange of views and information on consumer priorities with government, academic, and industry leaders. CFA also sponsors a full schedule of single-issue conferences each year; these allow consumer advocates and representatives of government and industry to discuss emerging issues. Distinguished service awards for public service, media achievement, and consumer service are presented at its annual awards banquet. CFA pays travel expenses to enable eligible grass-roots members to attend the Consumer Assembly, single-issue conferences, and board meetings.

FURTHER READING

Berry, John M., and Albert B. Crenshaw. 1991. "Paying for the Privilege." *Washington Post,* national weekly edition, April 15–21, pp. 19–20.
CFAnews. n.d. Washington, DC: Consumer Federation of America.

Courtless, Joan C. 1993. "Trends in Consumer Credit." *Family Economics Review,* 6: 3, pp. 8–17.

Jacquez, Albert S., and Amy S. Friend. 1993. "The Fair Credit Reporting Act: Is It Fair for Consumers?" *Loyola Consumer Law Reporter,* Spring, pp. 81–90.

Nadel, Mark V. 1971. *The Politics of Consumer Protection.* Indianapolis: Bobbs-Merrill.

Tolchin, Susan J., and Martin Tolchin. 1983. *Dismantling America: The Rush to Deregulate.* Boston: Houghton Mifflin.

Veron, Ilyse J. 1992. "In a Year of Election Uncertainty, Score Cards May Sway Voters." *Congressional Quarterly Weekly Report,* May 2, pp. 1135–1137.

Why You Need CFA. n.d. Washington, DC: Consumer Federation of America.

CONSUMERS FOR WORLD TRADE (CWT)

1726 M Street N.W., Suite 1101
Washington, DC 20036
(202) 785–4835

ORGANIZATION AND RESOURCES

Consumers for World Trade, an organization founded in 1978, works for greater liberalization of world trade, a goal it believes benefits both producers and consumers. Great attention by the organization goes to showing the costs to the average consumer of the effects of what CWT believes to be artificial trade barriers developed to benefit special interests. It is organized as a nonprofit foundation under Section 501(c)(4) of the Internal Revenue Code and draws its membership from U.S. international trade experts. Thus, its members often come from the law, think tank, business, educational, and public policy communities. During the Reagan and Bush administrations, its officials often sat on committees advising the president on trade matters. The organization publishes *Window on Washington* (monthly) and *Consumers for World Trade Newsletter.*

The organization provides a voice for industries that themselves are consumers involved in world trade. It is governed by a board of directors elected every two years by individuals who contribute to CWT. Financial support comes from grants and contributions by U.S. individuals, corporations, or foundations.

POLICY CONCERNS

CWT's chief concerns in the early 1990s are a successful—in the organization's terms—completion of the General Agreement on Tariffs and Trade's (GATT) Uruguay Round and the North American Free Trade Agreement (NAFTA) negotiated by the Bush administration and subsequently ratified by the Clinton administration and the U.S. Congress.

CWT officials and members are also concerned about implementation of trade legislation, especially what the group considers a rash of protectionist legislative initiatives taken (or urged) against other countries' products that result in higher prices to consumers of products such as Japanese cars. CWT also opposes antidumping laws as protecting U.S. firms from competition without considering the price to consumers, and voluntary restraint arrangements where they feel the big losers are industrial consumers, who purchase materials to produce manufactured goods, and ultimately the American consumer.

TACTICS

Besides providing public information contained in newsletters, press releases, special studies, and other publications, members testify before Congress and seek to influence executive branch decision making on issues like the ones discussed above, as well as "managed trade" and industrial policies, which are seen as forms of protectionism. In these and other legislative activities, the organization uses alerts to mobilize grass-roots mail, participates in coalitions with like-minded organizations, and seeks consumer representation on governmental advisory bodies involved in trade policy and in international conferences, in order to influence other governments' policies.

During the Reagan-Bush years, CWT often found itself on the same side as the administration and increasingly critical of what it believed to be a growing protectionist sentiment in the Congress. In the early 1990s, it opposed environmental and consumer organizations and their trade union allies on issues like NAFTA.

FURTHER READING

Bovard, James. 1991. *The Fair Trade Fraud.* New York: St. Martin's Press.
Consumers for World Trade Newsletter. Monthly. Washington, DC: Consumers for World Trade.

CONSUMERS UNION (CU)

101 Truman Avenue
Yonkers, NY 10703–1057
(914) 667–9400

2001 S Street N.W.
Washington, DC 20009
(202) 462–6262

ORGANIZATION AND RESOURCES

Consumers Union is a nonprofit organization established in 1936 to provide consumers with information and advice on goods, services, health, and personal finance, and to initiate and cooperate with individual and group efforts to maintain and enhance the quality of life for consumers. CU buys all the products it tests on the open market and accepts no advertising for any of its publications; it does not allow its reports or ratings to be used in advertising or for any other commercial purposes. Thus, it asserts, it is not beholden to any commercial interest.

An eighteen-member board of directors governs the organization; notable consumer activists such as Joan Claybrook are members. Rhoda H. Karpatkin is executive director of the staff, which includes 383 full-time employees. Most of the staff is located in Yonkers, New York, but small advocacy offices are located in Austin, Texas, San Francisco, and Washington, D.C. Mark Silbergeld directs the Washington office with a staff of nine. Annual revenues for CU total approximately $100 million, 95 percent of which comes from subscriptions, newsstand sales, and contributions.

CU bases its product reports on laboratory tests, controlled-use tests, and expert judgments. *Consumer Reports,* published monthly, is the primary vehicle for communicating with consumers seeking information; its circulation is over 4.8 million. Among the prominent features of *Consumer Reports* is the report on automobiles, but it also includes comparative test reports on other products, medical subjects, and financial products and services. The Technical Department, responsible for testing, is the organization's largest, with 127 members.

In addition to *Consumer Reports,* CU publishes numerous books on topics ranging from how to buy a car or house to male sexual health. Special newsletters on health and travel are available; *Zillions* is aimed at making children better-informed consumers. CU also produces a newspaper column, radio and television programs, and specials. A new program offers free sets of *Zillions* to schools in economically disadvantaged areas; a publishing program with a textbook company is designed to use CU product-testing projects to teach consumer science to junior high students.

POLICY CONCERNS

CU's program for economic justice focuses on issues that affect low- and moderate-income consumers. It has researched and reported on health care costs and access problems, and has provided testimony before congressional committees on these issues. It also advocates for the interests of low-income consumers on housing and banking legislation, for example, supporting proposals to require banks to offer low-cost checking accounts and check-cashing services to consumers with incomes below $20,000.

The Consumer Policy Institute works on specific projects in environmental quality, public health, and social equity relating to production and use of consumer products. It is seeking to develop models for community right-to-know legislation as a means of preventing toxic emissions and chemical accidents. Reducing pesticide use and encouraging sustainable agriculture globally are also among the objectives of the Institute.

CU is concerned with vigorous enforcement of existing legislation, such as the Consumer Product Safety Act and antitrust laws. It has opposed changes in product liability laws that it views as anti-consumer in intent.

TACTICS

CU works primarily as a source to be consulted for its product and service expertise. That expertise is the basis for its frequent testimony before committees of Congress and regulatory agencies. The widespread dissemination of its product and service test results through its own publications and the mass media are its other primary tactic. Not only does it reach numerous consumers directly, but its expertise is the basis for excellent relationships with the mass media, which report its results.

CU's work in national policy-making often finds it allied with other consumer organizations, most frequently Consumer Federation of America,* Public Citizen,* and the American Association of Retired Persons.*

Consumers Union was instrumental in founding the International Organization of Consumers Unions in 1960; it now has more than 180 member organizations in 64 countries. It works to advance the global consumer interest by sharing information, fostering new organizations, and lobbying before global bodies whose work affects the consumer interest. With the globalization of world markets, this is an effort of enormous potential significance.

FURTHER READING

Berry, Jeffrey M. 1977. *Lobbying for the People.* Princeton: Princeton University Press.
Board of Director's Financial Report to the Members of Consumers Union of United States, Inc. Annual. Yonkers, NY: Consumers Union.
Consumer Reports. Monthly. Yonkers, NY: Consumers Union.
Executive Director's Report to the Annual Meeting of Consumers Union. Annual. Yonkers, NY: Consumers Union.
Nadel, Mark V. 1971. *The Politics of Consumer Protection.* Indianapolis: Bobbs-Merrill.
Pertschuk, Michael. 1982. *Revolt Against Regulation: The Rise and Pause of the Consumer Movement.* Berkeley: University of California Press.
Starobin, Paul. 1993. "Make 'Em Pay." *National Journal,* July 24, pp. 1856–61.

CONTINENTAL ASSOCIATION OF FUNERAL AND MEMORIAL SOCIETIES (CAFMS)
6900 Lost Lake Road
Egg Harbor, WI 54209–9231
(414) 868–3136

ORGANIZATION AND RESOURCES

The Continental Association of Funeral and Memorial Societies was founded in 1963 as a network of nonprofit, volunteer-run local memorial societies. These local societies help people plan in advance for simple and dignified funerals, often at substantial savings as compared to what people usually experience in making funeral arrangements. More than 150 local societies with over 500,000 members are part of the CAFMS; it extends to 39 states, the District of Columbia, and 8 Canadian provinces. Member societies are screened to make sure they are democratic, nonsectarian, nondiscriminatory, and committed to freedom of choice in funeral arrangements. These nonprofit societies were organized by church and consumer groups and are not in the undertaking business; they work with local funeral directors and encourage members to plan before a death occurs. Individuals may become members for a small fee, and their membership may be transferred if they move or if their death occurs away from home.

John Blake is the executive director of the CAFMS. The elected leadership includes executive officers and thirteen committees, each reporting to an executive officer. The societies belonging to the CAFMS are endorsed by major religious, consumer, senior citizen, and labor organizations. Official recognition has been given by the Administration on Aging, the U.S. Office of Consumer Affairs, and the Cooperative Extension Service of the U.S. Department of Agriculture. Recognition has been accorded the Canadian societies by similar organizations and agencies in that country.

CAFMS publishes books on dealing with death and caring for the dead without use of an undertaker. Its pamphlets describe how to talk about death and related decisions, dealing with grief, funeral planning, funeral prepayment, cremation, body donation, earth burial, and how to beat the high costs of dying. Forms available from CAFMS include a durable power of attorney for health and "Putting My House in Order," which lists information needed at the time of death.

POLICY CONCERNS

CAFMS attends to issues identified with consumer abuses by the funeral industry. Its position is that the best way to assure dignity, simplicity, and economy in funeral arrangements is to be a member of a memorial society and to preplan death-related decisions. It focuses on efforts by the Federal Trade Commission to regulate the funeral industry, state regulatory efforts, consumer complaints, and legislation at both federal and state levels. Among the issues that have surfaced repeatedly are the availability of itemized price information from undertakers, access to cremation without requiring purchase of a coffin, written explanation of charges for services, and advertising of prices. After more than seven years of study, the Federal Trade Commission put the Funeral Rule into place in 1984. It requires that funeral directors initiate price disclosure to clients, that price information be given over the telephone, and that written explanations of charges for items not selected be given.

TACTICS

CAFMS operates at several tactical levels. It serves as a critic of the funeral industry and its regulation. For example, a recent newsletter for board members describes the weak and slow enforcement of the Funeral Rule by the FTC. It acts as a consumer voice and a clearinghouse for complaints about the conventional funeral industry. It also offers a real alternative for persons seeking to avoid or to deal more carefully with funeral homes. Although it does relatively little direct recruiting, its work with the media and other organizations does bring inquiries from interested potential members. For example, mentions in newspaper advice columns, on television talk shows, and articles in consumer magazines generate a flow of mail to CAFMS or member societies.

FURTHER READING

Directory of Memorial Societies. Annual. Egg Harbor, WI: Continental Association of Funeral and Memorial Societies.

Pertschuk, Michael. 1982. *Revolt Against Regulation: The Rise and Pause of the Consumer Movement,* Berkeley: University of California Press.

Publications. Annual. Egg Harbor, WI: Continental Association of Funeral and Memorial Societies.

Tolchin, Susan J., and Martin Tolchin. 1983. *Dismantling America: The Rush to Deregulate.* Boston: Houghton Mifflin.

CO-OP AMERICA

2100 M Street N.W., Suite 403
Washington, DC 20063
Tel (202) 872–5307
Toll-free (800) 424–2665

ORGANIZATION AND RESOURCES

Founded in 1982, Co-op America is a nonprofit membership organization that provides information on socially responsible products and services in tune with a cooperative economy. Its publications include *The Co-op American Catalog, Co-op America's Socially Responsible Investment Opportunities,* and *Boycott Action News.* Co-op America has a staff of 22 and claims over 60,000 members. Its budget in the early 1990s was approximately $2 million, about 80 percent of which came from members, which can be individuals or groups.

POLICY CONCERNS

The organization's aim is to provide information so that people can join and form cooperative organizations that will help bring about progressive social change. After the oil spill in Prince William Sound, Alaska, Co-Op America's executive director authored a set of guidelines, known as the "Valdez Principles," that companies are urged to embrace to show their commitment to the environment. The organization also combines its interest in the environment with the effects of industrial development on Third World countries.

TACTICS

By obtaining information, people can act on their own or in concert with others sharing their views as informed consumers buying environmentally safe products and services, and investing in companies that act responsibly toward the environment and their employees. Many of the organizations featured in this volume that urge consumers to show their concern for how products are made and/or how companies are run are operating firmly in the tradition of an earlier generation of consumer activists who showed their support for the fledgling labor movement by boycotting companies whose goods did not display a union label. In the 1960s the United Farm Workers Union, under the leadership of César Chávez, sought to get consumers to boycott lettuce and grapes harvested by nonunion laborers.

FURTHER READING

Franklin, Erica. 1990. "Kinder, Gentler Toys: New Board Games Teach Cooperation and Social Values." *American Health,* July/August, p. 89.
Ludwig, Dean C., and Judith A. Ludwig. 1992. "The Regulation of Green Marketing: Learning Lessons from the Regulation of Health and Nutrition Claims." *Business and Professional Ethics Journal,* Fall/Winter, pp. 73–91.

COUNCIL ON ECONOMIC PRIORITIES (CEP)

30 Irving Place   1601 Connecticut Avenue N.W.
New York, NY 10003   Washington, DC 20009
Tel (212) 420–1133   Tel (202) 745–2450
Fax 212–420–0988   Fax 202–387–6298

ORGANIZATION AND RESOURCES

The New York-based Council on Economic Priorities has served as an information clearinghouse on corporate social responsibility for individual and institutional consumers since it was formed in 1969. With a budget of $1.3 million in 1990, CEP has been run by Alice Tepper Marlin since its inception. Activities by the staff of twenty include publication of the monthly *CEP Newsletter* and the annual shopping guide, *Shopping for a Better World.* Publication sales are a major fund-raising source for this organization. CEP also gave rise to a spin-off organization, INFORM, devoted to exposing companies' responsibility for severe environmental problems like toxic waste, in 1977.

POLICY CONCERNS

CEP added national security issues to its list of concerns after it absorbed the Committee for National Security. This has involved CEP in issues like defense conversion in the United States and countries of the former Soviet Union, but the organization's main focus is still corporate social responsibility, allowing consumers to vote their ideologies when they make purchases of stocks and bonds or groceries.

TACTICS

This focus on providing consumers with information makes CEP's publications second only to Consumers Union's *Consumer Reports* in significance. Its quarterly reports, updating social responsibility ratings for some 300 companies are provided to clients who invest money for institutions. Besides these projects and in-depth studies of individual companies or industries that have led to changes in corporate behavior, CEP testifies before Congress, and is involved in coalition formation, training, and technical assistance.

FURTHER READING

Mano, D. Keith. 1987. "Corporate America Sucks Up." *National Review,* May 8, pp. 55–57.
Meeks, Fleming. 1991. "The Greening of Graham and Dodd." *Forbes,* April 15, p. 90.
Shopping for a Better World: A Quick and Easy Guide to Socially Responsible Super-market Shopping. Annual. New York: Council on Economic Priorities.

CRITICAL MASS ENERGY PROJECT
215 Pennsylvania Avenue S.E.
Washington, DC 20003
(202) 546–4996

ORGANIZATION AND RESOURCES

Critical Mass is one of the subsections of Public Citizen,* the public interest organization founded by Ralph Nader in 1971. Critical Mass focuses on the safety, economic, and waste problems posed by nuclear power compared with alternative energy technologies. The group's goal is the rapid phaseout of nuclear power in the United States in favor of clean and safe energy options. Critical Mass has a staff of four persons plus a director, Bill McGavern; its 1991 expenses were about $144,000. In both staff size and budget it is the smallest of the five subsections of Public Citizen; the others are the Litigation Group,* the Health Research Group,* Congress Watch,* and Buyers Up.*

POLICY CONCERNS

Critical Mass is an active nuclear safety watchdog. Recurring report topics under the heading of nuclear power plant safety include the number and frequency of accidents, near accidents, emergency shutdowns at plants, exposure of workers to health-threatening conditions, and the safety records of various plants over time. Critical Mass has challenged Nuclear Regulatory Commission efforts to accelerate the licensing of plants by reducing opportunities for public access and participation and its efforts to restrict the release of nuclear safety information to the public. It has also used a variety of tactics to get the NRC to develop guidelines for the training of nuclear power plant workers rather than let the industry regulate itself in this matter. It works not only to convince the general public that nuclear power must be phased out but also to make plants less dangerous while they still operate. After Hurricane Andrew hit the Turkey Point nuclear plant in southern Florida, Critical Mass petitioned the Nuclear Regulatory Commission to keep the plant closed until there were reasonable emergency evacuation plans to protect the public in the event of an accident at the plant.

Nuclear economics themes in Critical Mass reports include the poor reliability of U.S. nuclear reactors, the costs of operating, maintaining, and decommissioning plants, and efforts by utility companies to circumvent statutory or regulatory obligations by means such as bankruptcy. The Price–Anderson Act, which limits the nuclear industry's liability in case of accidents, has been a constant target for reform or repeal. Critical Mass also keeps nuclear waste issues on the agenda by reporting on the types, amounts, and radioactivity levels of waste generated by nuclear facilities. It details the health risks posed by radioactive waste, the safety hazards in shipping it, and the failure of government officials to develop technically sound, long-term storage facilities for it. It was involved in the effort to include in the 1992 Energy Policy Act provisions striking down the Nuclear Regulatory Commission decision to allow low-level radioactive waste to be disposed of in sewers, landfills, and incinerators or recycled into consumer products. Local groups opposed to low-level waste dumps in their communities have been supported by Critical Mass, as have opponents of the Yucca Mountain repository in Nevada.

While keeping up a running opposition to nuclear energy development, Critical Mass promotes renewable energy technologies and conservation. Its reports point out the growing contribution of geothermal, wind, biomass, hydroelectric, photovoltaic, solar thermal, and solar building technologies to meeting energy needs. The group also advocates a national energy policy that would further stimulate development of renewable technologies and reward conservation. Despite the unresponsiveness of national energy policy to the public's willingness to conserve and to shift from nuclear and fossil fuels, Critical Mass continues to be committed to a strategy of grass-roots campaigns.

TACTICS

Critical Mass conducts research that it shares with a wide network of grass-roots citizen and environmental organizations; studies are often released by Critical Mass and these groups simultaneously. Fifteen hundred groups nationwide are part of the grass-roots network with which it is in regular contact. It also works through the mass media to draw public attention to its research results, brings together coalitions, presents information to Congress, advocates in the regulatory process, and uses litigation techniques. It has helped coordinate referenda and other types of local campaigns to close down or halt construction of specific nuclear facilities.

Studies and ratings of presidential and congressional candidates on energy matters have been compiled and released by Critical Mass at election times. The organization took advantage of the shift in partisan control of the White House after the 1992 elections by presenting detailed energy recommendations to the Clinton-Gore transition team.

FURTHER READING

Annual Report. Annual. Washington, DC: Public Citizen.

Magavern, Bill, 1993. ''Prospects Dim for Nuclear Power Plants.'' *Public Citizen,* September/October, pp. 22–24.

''Sun Power.'' 1991. *Public Citizen,* November/December, pp. 18–23.

Tolchin, Susan J., and Martin Tolchin, 1983. *Dismantling America: The Rush to Deregulate.* Boston: Houghton Mifflin.

D
———————————— / ————————————

DIRECT MARKETING ASSOCIATION (DMA)

11 West 42nd Street   1101 17th Street N.W.
New York, NY 10036–8096   Washington, DC 20036–4704
(212) 768–7277   (202) 347–1222

ORGANIZATION AND RESOURCES

The Direct Marketing Association represents member companies who market goods and services to consumers through direct mail, catalogs, telemarketing, magazine and newspaper ads, and broadcast advertising. It was established in 1917 by merger of the Direct Mail Marketing Association and the Direct Mail Advertising Association. The Association is governed by a 37-member board of directors; a staff of 136 is directed by Jonah Gitlitz, president and chief executive officer. The Washington office includes ten professional staff; Richard A. Barton is senior vice president for government affairs. An annual budget of $17.4 million is derived from meeting revenues (50 percent), membership dues (40 percent), staff-generated revenue such as lectures and publications, and other sources.

DMA's 3,400 member corporations may participate in the organization in a variety of ways. Fifteen member councils address such specialized interests as alternate response media, insurance, microcomputer marketing, and telephone marketing. Member councils provide specialized programs, hold conferences, conduct research, and communicate through their own newsletters. Five groups for agency leaders, business-to-business leaders, catalog leaders, computer service bureau leaders, and list leaders hold specialized forums, conduct research, and meet with legislators in Washington. The Association as a whole holds an annual conference as well as multiple specialized conferences, totaling eighteen in 1991. Speakers at its Government Affairs Conference have included the chairman of the Federal Trade Commission, the director of the U.S. Office of Consumer Affairs, the postmaster general, and a member of the House Subcommittee on Postal Operations and Services.

DMA provides professional development and training for member staffs through structured courses on both basic topics such as telemarketing and statistics, and more specialized courses such as direct marketing of insurance. Courses are offered both at its seminar center in New York and at locations around the country. Member companies may sponsor in-house seminars for their own employees in order to assure customization, consistency, and confidentiality.

The world's largest collection of direct marketing reference files, books, periodicals, videocassettes, and catalog samples is maintained by DMA. An in-house computerized information system supports staff responses to member inquiries. Research and publication programs provide practical support for members on topics such as rental list practices, seasonal catalog performance, and telemarketing technology. DMA's publications include *Postal Rate Strategies Resource Guide, Environmental Resource Collection,* and *Statistical Fact Book on Direct Marketing.* The affiliated Direct Marketing Educational Foundation works to establish and support direct marketing education and academic research. It holds educators' conferences and seminars, grants cash awards to authors, funds internships, and has established an on-campus career program.

Members are kept informed through a wide variety of communications. A monthly newsletter, *Direct Line,* presents an overview of DMA governmental initiatives, public affairs and media campaigns, and conference and seminar opportunities. *Directions,* a quarterly journal, features analyses of direct marketing and management issues by industry leaders. *Dateline: DMA,* also quarterly, is tailored for international members. *Washington Weekly* provides immediate updates on federal and state legislative and regulatory issues; *Washington Report* provides more detailed analysis on a monthly basis. *Washington Alerts* informs members of government issues requiring urgent action. DMA testimony, lobbying, and government representation data are compiled in *Compendium of Government Issues Affecting Direct Marketers;* legislation from each state is included in *The Telemarketer's Guide to State Laws.*

POLICY CONCERNS

DMA's policy concerns center on postal rates, consumer issues, use taxes, privacy, and the environment. The organization's general position is that third-class mail is of economic and social value to the American public and should be treated favorably. It seeks to develop and protect work sharing and automation discounts with the U.S. Postal Service (USPS), and supports changes in the Postal Reorganization Act provisions on rate-setting procedures. Mailers are urged to participate in alternate delivery systems so that the USPS has competition; this is particularly important for catalog companies like J.C. Penney and Land's End. DMA works cooperatively with the USPS on issues such as implementing drop-ship regulations, address quality, standardizing business-to-business addresses, eligibility of nonprofit mailers, and environmental concerns.

Ethics and consumer affairs programs maintained by DMA demonstrate the industry's commitment to self-regulation. Its Committee on Ethical Business Practice hears cases on violations of standards and works with the companies to correct improper practices. The Ethics Policy Committee analyzes consumer concerns and formulates principles for industry behavior; for example, it recently approved a position supporting clear prior disclosure of the costs of 900-number calls. DMA's core consumer services are mail and telephone preference services that allow consumers to have their names removed from mail or telephone solicitation lists used by member companies. Mail Order Action Line is a consumer complaint resolution service that claims to successfully resolve over 90 percent of consumer mail order complaints; the balance are referred to regulatory agencies. In time for National Consumers Week in 1991, DMA installed a device that allows hearing-impaired customers to reach its consumer services by telephone. It also published a brochure, *Tips for Telephone Shopping,* for Asian and Hispanic markets.

Proposals to regulate or restrict telemarketing practices have come forth in many states in recent years. Some states propose requiring a signed contract for any telephone sale, but that approach is countered by DMA lobbying for exempting sales when the customer has return or refund privileges. DMA is also active in the Alliance Against Telemarketing Fraud and maintains communication with the National Association of Consumer Agency Administrators, the National Association of Attorneys General,* and the Postal Inspection Service.

State efforts to impose use tax collection responsibilities on out-of-state direct marketers have been a serious concern for DMA in recent years. The organization's position is that these are unconstitutional, and it has provided both direct and indirect support for opposing them. State and federal court decisions have helped direct marketers avoid these taxes; decisions that have gone against them are being appealed.

Privacy issues have been a major concern for direct marketers at state and federal levels of government and internationally. State legislatures have attempted to require marketers to gain approval from consumers before information can be transferred for marketing purposes. DMA opposes all bans on the release of customer or subscriber files, and thus far has succeeded in protecting that position. Proposals to regulate electronic monitoring in the workplace, for caller identification, for creation of a national data protection board, and to have the Federal Communications Commission create a national "do not call" list have all been successfully opposed by DMA. However, privacy proposals in general, and particularly those to restrict the use of public records and protect consumer credit information, are considered an ongoing threat by direct marketing interests. The organization is working with the European Community on proposed directives that it regards as interfering with the direct marketing process.

Attention to direct mail's contribution to solid waste has brought DMA to promote environmental awareness and responsibility in direct marketing. Its task force on environmental issues has produced a guide for members on environmental management, printing and production, paper and packaging, marketing, mailing lists, and community education. DMA is working with the USPS, New York City, and the Northeast Recycling Council to promote voluntary action to minimize waste and avoid legislative solutions.

TACTICS

DMA is able to draw upon its own staff talent, the expertise and contacts of its members, and outside consultants on major concerns like postal rates and taxation. The organization has excellent access to relevant policymakers and substantial persuasive resources; USPS management, the USPS Board of Governors, and the Postal Rate Commission viewed DMA's video presentation on the value of third-class mail to the American public. DMA is a regular intervenor in Postal Rate Commission proceedings. It appeals to the Board of Governors on those occasions when it opposes what the Commission recommends, and also appeals beyond the Board to the federal courts.

Staff members monitor state and federal legislative and regulatory proposals. State legislative initiatives have been particularly prolific in recent years; DMA staff analyzes their potential impact as well as their likelihood of passage. DMA provides testimony in all these venues regularly, and its approach is often to describe its efforts at self-regulation as sufficient to address the issues. It maintains close contacts with government agencies and consumer officials. For example, with the United States Office of Consumer Affairs and the Council of Better Business Bureaus it cosponsors a twice-yearly dialogue program to build positive relationships between direct marketers and state regulatory and consumer officials.

DMA engages its members in lobbying, for instance, to persuade state governors to stop enforcing state tax levies on out-of-state marketers. In its "Write the Wrong" campaign, DMA mailed over 5,000 action kits to direct marketers to assist them in writing to their governors; lobbying teams were also organized in thirty-two states to follow up the letters with face-to-face meetings.

Improving direct marketing's public image is a top priority of DMA. It cultivates producers and editors, supplying story ideas about direct marketing and arranging live appearances by DMA staff and industry advocates. Positive stories are placed in high-circulation magazines, major national newspapers, wire services, consumer magazines, and syndicated columns. Media tours around the country generate interviews; attention is further stimulated by sending member catalogs and other DMA materials to lifestyle reporters. DMA staff monitors and analyzes more than 12,000 news clips per year from the consumer and business press, and transcripts from radio and television programs. It responds to misleading stories by sending editors and producers correct information and positive story ideas. The association is helping member companies build their own media response programs with a public affairs publication, *Managing Today's Issues: A Communications Handbook.* DMA also answers reporters' inquiries and reaches out to the media with press releases, media advisories, weekly news briefs, and issue-specific press kits.

FURTHER READING

Challenges/Solutions: 1991 Annual Report. 1992. New York: Direct Marketing Association.
1993 Directory of Major Mailers and What They Mail. 1993. Philadelphia: North American Publishing Co.
Statistical Fact Book 1992–93: Current Information About Direct Marketing. 1992. New York: Direct Marketing Association.

E
/

EARTH ISLAND INSTITUTE (EII)
300 Broadway, Suite 28
San Francisco, CA 94133
Tel (415) 788–3666
Fax 415–788–7324

ORGANIZATION AND RESOURCES

Earth Island Institute was formed in 1982 by David Brower, who had left the Sierra Club* in a policy dispute and later headed a new organization, Friends of the Earth (FOE).* Later, as a result of policy differences, Brower and some associates left FOE to form EII, which now, along with Greenpeace,* has established itself as one of the more activist and antiestablishment of U.S. environmental organizations. With 18 staffers and 33,000 members, the group publishes *Earth Island Quarterly.* It is registered as a 501(c)(3) organization and has established Earth Island Action Group as a separate lobbying arm.

POLICY CONCERNS

Earth Island Institute is included here to recognize the kinds of appeals that environmental organizations are making to consumers in the 1990s to take into account ethical and social responsibility issues when they make choices in the supermarket. Calls for consumer boycotts led the three major tuna canners and processors—Star-Kist (Heinz), Chicken of the Sea (Van Camp), and Bumble Bee—to agree in 1990 not to buy tuna caught by fleets whose fishing practices included methods that also killed dolphins. Other concerns are climate protection and international issues, including degradation of Lake Baikal in Russia.

TACTICS

In keeping with its willingness to use boycotts and other direct action tactics to achieve its objectives, EII is seen as one of the most aggressive environmental organizations operating on the national scene.

FURTHER READING

Green, Lee. 1991. "Man of the Earth." *Modern Maturity,* April/May, p. 22.
Kriz, Margaret E. 1990. "Shades of Green." *National Journal,* July 28, pp. 1826–1831.
Lindsey, Marina. 1993. "David Brower Speaks Out." *Buzzworm,* July/August, pp. 31–32.
Rauber, Paul. 1992. "Trading Away the Environment." *Sierra,* January/February, pp. 24–26.

EDISON ELECTRIC INSTITUTE (EEI)
701 Pennsylvania Avenue N.W.
Washington, DC 20004–2696
(202) 508–5300

ORGANIZATION AND RESOURCES

The Edison Electric Institute was formed in 1933 and has since absorbed two other trade associations, the Electric Energy Association in 1975 and the National Association of Electrical Companies in 1978. Today, as the trade association for almost 200 electric utilities nationwide, its staff of 300 manages a range of services for its member companies, providing them with information and helping them to shape public policies and public opinion on issues of interest and concern to investor-owned electric utilities. EEI's balance sheet for 1991 showed operating expense totals of $61.7 million, about 12.5 percent of which was expended for governmental affairs. EEI publishes *Electrical Perspectives* monthly, and member companies contribute to POWERPAC, a political action committee.

POLICY CONCERNS

In past years EEI has been involved in the debate over nuclear power, a subject that continues to take various forms. Since 1985, the industry has spent money to clean up Three Mile Island through voluntary contributions to the utility principally involved. EEI also has been involved in national energy legislation enacted in response to the oil price shocks of the 1970s and the controversy over decontrol that preoccupied Congress, industry, and state regulators in the early 1980s.

Issues on which EEI members currently seek to lead public policy include those noted above (e.g., nuclear cleanup responsibilities) and environmental and consumer issues that have come onto the policy agenda more recently, such as global climate change. Will a switch to electrical power reduce the emissions of carbon dioxide, the principal global warming gas, into the environment? Electrical utilities would like to be able to convince government and other attentive publics that new technologies which use electricity rather than fossil fuels deserve support.

Other new technology issues promise to be important in the 1990s. These include the possibility of using electrical energy to power automobiles, and research and development of technologies to power trains using electricity and magnetic fields. Several major high-speed rail projects using TGV (trains a grande vitesse) and maglev (magnetic levitation) technology are being actively pursued in different parts of the country, but these proposals are raising concerns about whether exposure to electromagnetic fields may cause leukemia, lymphomas, brain cancer, and other dire medical conditions. So far, research data are scant and inconclusive. In the meantime, light rail, freight rail electrification, and research and development on new products such as advanced batteries are going ahead more quickly.

EEI members and their Washington representatives are involved in policy debates over renewal of the Clean Water and Clean Air acts. Reconciling the different legislative vehicles involved in clean air and acid rain policy during passage of major legislation in 1990 consumed large amounts of attention and public resources. Also of perennial interest to the industry are tax issues and electric and natural gas legislative and regulatory issues. Finally, electric utilities must pay attention to the requirements of environmental legislation such as the Resource Conservation and Recovery Act.

Another important set of issues pits EEI companies against other suppliers of electric service to consumers, mostly local, state, and national public power producers and rural electric cooperatives. EEI claims that investor-owned utilities serve approximately three-fourths of all electric customers in the United States. EEI and its members enter into negotiated agreements to provide transmission services to third parties but oppose mandatory transmission access (called ''wheeling'') agreements.

TACTICS

Governmental targets include the Department of Energy, the Federal Energy Regulatory Commission, the Nuclear Regulatory Commission, the Environmental Protection Agency, and the Treasury Department. Also important, sometimes as an ally and sometimes as an adversary, is the professional association of state government regulators, the National Association of Regulatory Utility Commissioners (NARUC).* For example, EEI and NARUC worked together on guidelines for judging Clean Air compliance plans.

Since tax, rate, and regulatory issues are the big concerns in Washington, EEI is interested in both legislative and executive branch decision making. The industry lost an important battle in which consumer and environmental advocates claimed victory in 1978 when amendments to the Public Utility Regulatory Policies Act (PURPA) forced utilities to buy power from cogenerators. But this situation, which pitted small operators and consumers against EEI, is unusual. To further member interests on these and other issues, EEI, like other Washington-based trade associations, likes to practice coalition politics. Examples of coalitions in which EEI joins with industry include the Global Climate Coalition, which is made up of companies and associations representing important sectors of the U.S. economy, and the Clean Coal Technology Coalition, whose aim is promoting advanced coal-burning technologies.

Other coalitions to which EEI belongs are more eclectic in membership, drawing in organizations representing consumers and others. Examples include the Electric Transportation Coalition and Transit Now, which supported national programs to promote the development and marketing of electric vehicles and electric transportation. EEI also led a coalition seeking to make tax-exempt to residential utility consumers payments made by a public utility for energy conservation measures or services.

In these and other cases, EEI supplements its lobbying activities with public information campaigns, media "hits" on news programs, and arguments to place industry activities in a favorable light. To this end, EEI can call on the research performed by the Electric Power Research Institute.

FURTHER READING

Annual Report. Annual. Washington, DC: Edison Electric Institute.

Idelson, Holly. 1992. "Conferees at Last Find Harmony on National Energy Strategy." *Congressional Quarterly Weekly Report,* October 3, pp. 3030–3033.

Matlack, Carol. 1991. "It's Round Two in Clean Air Fight." *National Journal,* January 26, pp. 226–227.

Morgan, Granger. 1991. "Flying Blind: The Making of EMF Policy." *Science,* October 5, pp. 23–25.

Pool, Robert. 1990a. "Electromagnetic Fields: The Biological Evidence." *Science,* September 21, pp. 1378–1381.

————. 1990b. "Is There an EMF-Cancer Connection?" *Science,* September 7, pp. 1096–1097.

ENVIRONMENTAL DEFENSE FUND (EDF)

257 Park Avenue South   1875 Connecticut Ave. N.W.
New York, NY 10010   Washington, DC 20009
Tel (212) 505–2100   Tel (202) 387–3500
Fax 212–505–2375   Fax 202–234–6049

ORGANIZATION AND RESOURCES

The Environmental Defense Fund was founded in 1967 in suburban Long Island, New York, by Victor Yannacone and several other volunteer conservationists and scientists. Now headquartered in New York City, EDF also has offices in Washington, D.C.; Oakland, California; Boulder, Colorado; Raleigh, North Carolina; and Austin, Texas. EDF has a membership of about 200,000 and a budget that topped $18.5 million in 1991. Activities in which the organization and its 120-person staff are involved can be seen in the *Letter* that is sent to those who pay the $10 yearly membership fee. EDF's staff includes over fifty full-time personnel, supplemented by volunteers whose expertise in such fields as science, economics, and law is crucial to the organization.

POLICY CONCERNS

One of EDF's first battles was over the pesticide DDT's health effects on consumers and on populations near sprayed areas on suburban Long Island. The organization is profiled here because, like other established environmental organizations active in Washington, EDF analyzes the economic as well as the scientific claims that industries make to Congress and other governmental decision makers (e.g., the courts and major regulatory agencies) on important environmental policy issues.

Economic and scientific evidence is important to consumer and other audiences on such current issues as energy regulation and development, and the effects of toxic chemicals on people, wildlife, and the environment. EDF has recently expanded its attention into the arena of international politics, focusing on issues such as global warming and ozone depletion, acid rain, tropical rain forest depletion, toxic waste cleanup, protecting Antarctica, and related issues.

TACTICS

Since the late 1960s, EDF has been involved in a wide range of environmental issues but now uses a broader variety of tactics than litigation (as in the DDT case). Getting good scientific evidence into the debate was crucial in many of these cases. It helped in 1979 when the issue was getting a national recall of hair dryers containing asbestos. EDF also can take credit for helping policymakers understand the link that scientists are beginning to make between sulfur emissions and acid rain.

EDF has always targeted industry behavior and government laws and regulations, but in the 1990s the organization is recognized by industry as an organization with which it can resolve some disputes without getting government involved. An example of EDF's negotiation with industry (for which the organization takes criticism from more radical environmental groups) is its agreement with McDonald's in 1990 to phase out foam packaging. That decision came as a result of a task force of EDF and McDonald's experts.

After adding economists to its experts in the 1980s, EDF is now known for creating alliances with business and industry on important issues. EDF explains these changes by referring to a "third stage" of environmental activism in which it is necessary to work with former foes to get solutions. A good example of this combination of science and environmental goals is the "emissions-trading" section of the revised Clean Air Act. Other evidence can be seen when public officials invoke economic arguments such as those EDF made as to why New York should not contract for power with Hydro-Quebec. In his decision to cancel the state's $17 billion contract from the Great Whale project, Governor Mario Cuomo of New York expressed ideas similar to those EDF and New York's Pace University Center for Environmental Legal Studies had put forward earlier: that it would be cheaper for the state to rely on conservation.

But EDF still occasionally does "sue the bastards," the informal slogan for which the organization was known in its early years. An example is a case brought to seek implementation of California's consumer referendum, Proposition 65. Under terms of the resulting settlement, several large hardware stores agreed to stop selling products containing the carcinogen methylene chloride.

The hard issues facing environmental groups like EDF during the period of recession in the early 1990s shows in debates like that over reauthorization of the Endangered Species Act, one of the cornerstones of U.S. environmental policy. Business groups like those in the National Endangered Species Act Reform Coalition charge that environmentalists use that legislation as a no-growth act in addition to its original purpose of protecting certain endangered species. Thus, organizations like EDF feel they need their economists to argue the usefulness of new and existing legislation.

FURTHER READING

Browning, Graeme. 1992. "Biotech Politics." *National Journal,* February 29, pp. 511–514.

Davis, Phillip A. 1992a. "Economy, Politics, Threaten Species Act Renewal." *Congressional Quarterly Weekly Report,* January 4, pp. 16–18.

————. 1992b. "Environment: Protection's Costs Must Be Reconciled." *Congressional Quarterly Weekly Report,* September 26, pp. 2908–2910.

EDF Annual Report. Various years. New York, NY: Environmental Defense Fund.

Kriz, Margaret E. 1990. "Shades of Green." *National Journal,* July 28, pp. 1826–1831.

Matlack, Carol. 1991. "It's Round Two in Clean Air Fight." *National Journal,* January 26, pp. 226–227.

The Supermarket Diet: Watching Our Waste. n.d. New York, NY: Environmental Defense Fund.

U.S. Congress. Senate Committee on Agriculture, Nutrition, and Forestry. 1993. *Hearing on National Academy of Sciences Report on Pesticides and Children.* Washington, DC: Government Printing Office.

F
/

FOOD MARKETING INSTITUTE (FMI)
1750 K Street N.W., Suite 700
Washington, DC 20006
Tel (202) 452–8444
Fax 202–429–4519, 4529, 4549

ORGANIZATION AND RESOURCES

The Food Marketing Institute represents the interests of 1,600 member grocery retailers and wholesalers, or about 17,000 stores, which claim to account for about half of all U.S. grocery sales. FMI officials also claim to be working on behalf of food consumers. The organization was founded in 1977 through a merger of the National Association of Food Chains, founded in 1934, and the Supermarket Institute, whose activities date from 1937. This trade association publishes both a monthly *Issues Bulletin* and a weekly *Washington Report* for its members.

POLICY CONCERNS

In the 1980s, FMI was actively involved in trucking deregulation issues and worked to develop a coalition to work on the Anti-Tampering Act of 1983. Washington policy issues in which its members have taken interest in recent years have included taxation and labor-management concerns, health care reform, farm and food policies, and food safety.

TACTICS

FMI lobbies on behalf of its members, monitors regulatory decision making, and engages in a wide range of trade industry activities. Food industry companies also contribute to a political action fund called FMIPAC.

FURTHER READING

Byal, Nancy. 1989. "Good Food, Good Health: Project LEAN." *Better Homes and Gardens,* September, pp. 46ff.
Pinstrup-Andersen, Per, ed. 1993. *The Political Economy of Food and Nutrition Policies.* Baltimore: Johns Hopkins University Press.

FOOD RESEARCH AND ACTION CENTER (FRAC)
1875 Connecticut Ave. N.W., Suite 540
Washington, DC 20009
Tel (202) 986–2200
Fax 202–986–2525

ORGANIZATION AND RESOURCES

Founded in 1970, the Food Research and Action Center, a 501(c)(3) organization, focuses on hunger issues and the problems of people receiving governmental food assistance in meeting their families' needs with their food budgets. This concern with the (in)ability of low-income people to purchase one of life's necessities makes FRAC an interesting example of how social welfare advocacy organizations approach consumer policy and politics.

FRAC started as a public law firm advising lawyers working for the Community Services Administration (CSA) of the Office of Economic Opportunity, the Johnson administration's controversial antipoverty program. In the 1990s, FRAC is still a nonmembership organization but offers subscriptions to its bimonthly *Foodlines* for $25 yearly. It operates with a $1.2 million budget funded by grants and donations, and a staff of about twenty. FRAC still advises Legal Services Corporation lawyers but has expanded its activities by providing a range of information about government programs to national and community groups working with grass-roots low-income organizations.

POLICY CONCERNS

FRAC is recognized as the principal organization in Washington focusing on the federal food aid programs, such as food stamps, school lunch, school breakfast, WIC (women, infants, and children), and surplus foods donated by the U.S. Department of Agriculture. Each program operates separately, and in order to focus them on particularly vulnerable populations such as children, FRAC has worked with other organizations in the Campaign to End Childhood Hunger to make better use of the programs.

A major accomplishment was the passage in August 1993 of the Mickey

Leland Childhood Hunger Relief Act as part of the Omnibus Budget and Reconciliation Act. It was the most important achievement in over a decade and a half in helping remove the barriers that food stamp recipients face. Other goals include expanding food stamp coverage for the elderly. Another special problem is the homeless; FRAC believes that programs must be changed to reflect their unique needs.

TACTICS

FRAC's activities require a variety of techniques. It (1) researches and documents the extent of hunger, malnutrition, and nutritional risk; (2) monitors legislative, judicial, and regulatory decisions affecting food aid policy; (3) provides support for a variety of organizations and officials at the local level (e.g., food pantries and other emergency food providers, food program directors, etc.); (4) provides legal advice and technical assistance for the Legal Services Corporation, the successor of the CSA; and (5) shapes media and public opinion on food policy issues.

At the beginning the main technique used was lawsuits, such as the one that contributed to the requirement of universal coverage for a family food program. That is, every state must operate either a food stamp or a commodity distribution program to feed the poor in all counties. This issue of universal coverage—and ensuring that enough money was appropriated by Congress to make that a reality—has remained. In 1973, in *USDA* v. *Moreno,* the U.S. Supreme Court agreed with FRAC that an expanded definition of "household" was necessary. In 1976 FRAC successfully headed off a Department of Agriculture plan to reduce food stamp benefits.

FRAC knows the importance of getting useful information into the media and before sympathetic members of Congress, as could be seen in 1981, when the organization publicized a USDA regulatory proposal that would have changed the nutritional requirements Congress had placed on the school lunch program. Cartoonists soon had a field day with the idea that catsup could be considered a vegetable under the new rules, and the proposal was quickly withdrawn.

The main focus of FRAC's activities is Congress and the U.S. Department of Agriculture, but the group also must follow the interests that White House officials have in food aid policy, a task that has always been complicated by real or imagined budgetary contraints. That was clear when FRAC and other antihunger groups had to react to the Reagan administration in 1981.

Other organizations involved with aspects of food aid include the Community Nutrition Institute, Public Voice for Food and Health Policy,* and the Children's Defense Fund.* Other organizations at work on appropriations bills include Bread for the World, the National Association of WIC Directors, and the Center for Budget and Policy Priorities.* Recent antihunger initiatives such as the Leland bill could not have succeeded if not for the important support received from the Congressional Black Caucus.

FURTHER READING

Berry, Jeffrey. 1984. *Feeding Hungry People.* New Brunswick, N.J.: Rutgers University Press.
Demkovich, Linda. 1984. "FRAC: A Lean, Mean Hunger Machine Fueled by Research, Action, Controversy." *National Journal,* January 28, pp. 169–173.
Maney, Ardith. 1989. *Still Hungry After All These Years: Food Assistance Policy from Kennedy to Reagan.* Westport, Conn.: Greenwood Press.
Pinstrup-Andersen, Per, ed. 1993. *The Political Economy of Food and Nutrition Policies.* Baltimore: Johns Hopkins University Press.

FOUNDATION ON ECONOMIC TRENDS (FET)
1130 17th Street N.W., Suite 630
Washington, DC 20036
Tel (202) 466–2823
Fax 202–429–9602

ORGANIZATION AND RESOURCES

Founded in 1977 to counter arguments by industry spokespersons about the rosy future of biotechnology, the organization has been led throughout its existence by Jeremy Rifkin, an enterprising and controversial consumer activist. FET sees its mission as a monitor of the environmental, economic, and ethical impact of this kind of scientific progress. The organization also serves as an information clearinghouse for groups and individuals concerned about these and related issues and as a support arm for Rifkin. But this is a small organization, with only two other principal staffers, a lobbyist and a litigator, the latter formerly with the Environmental Defense Fund.*

POLICY CONCERNS

FET is best known in the 1990s for Rifkin's Beyond Beef campaign, which has drawn fire from agribusiness and agricultural producer groups, such as the National Cattlemen's Association,* and Rifkin's calls for boycotts of major retail restaurant outlets such as McDonald's.

Other Rifkin concerns have shown a knack for drawing the attention of other organizations. For example, women's organizations worked with Rifkin on his campaign against surrogate motherhood. His concerns about the use of biotechnological techniques to develop "superpigs" and other farm animals have enjoyed support from some farm groups. When FET mounted a campaign against using human genetic material in other species for research purposes, Rifkin was joined by leaders from some religious groups. FET has been concerned about the possible use of biotechnology to develop new germ weapons.

TACTICS

FET emphasizes its role of providing information to the public on biotechnology issues. Rifkin keeps a busy schedule of speeches and lectures, especially on college campuses, and the organization operates as almost a "one-man band." Rifkin's activities are not always followed by the national media, but his speeches before university audiences get local attention and draw people who have strong opinions about him—pro and con. He has proved to have a knack for discovering new issues and putting together inventive and unlikely coalitions. Examples include a coalition to monitor industry and government actions to introduce bovine growth hormone (BGH) onto the market that is made up of family farmers, the Moral Majority, and animal rights activists. Besides this International Coalition Against BGH, other such coalitions include the Global Greenhouse Network, the International Coalition Against Biological Warfare, and the National Coalition Against Surrogacy.

Rifkin's efforts face determined opposition from supporters of agribusiness on the congressional agriculture committees and at the U.S. Department of Agriculture, although FET does have congressional support for some of its initiatives. Other targets include government agencies that have regulatory power over biotechnology products, such as the Food and Drug Administration and the National Institutes of Health. Corporate targets include the Animal Health Institute, the Association of Biotechnology Companies,* conservative science watchdog groups, and individual manufacturers of biotechnology products such as Monsanto, Lilly, Upjohn, and American Cyanamid.

FURTHER READING

Matlack, Carol. 1991. "Barnyard Brawl over Cow Hormone." *National Journal,* April 6, pp. 807–808.
Rifkin, Jeremy. 1980. *Entropy.* New York: Viking Press.
Tivnam, Edward. 1988. "Jeremy Rifkin Just Says No." *New York Times Magazine,* October 16, pp. 38–46.

FRIENDS OF THE EARTH (FOE)
218 D Street S.E.
Washington, DC 20003
Tel (202) 544–2600
Fax 202–543–4710

ORGANIZATION AND RESOURCES

Friends of the Earth was created in 1990 as a merger of three existing organizations, Friends of the Earth (1969), the Environmental Policy Institute (1972), and the Oceanic Society (1972). Headquartered in Washington, D.C., with a staff of thirty, it also has offices in Seattle and Manila, Philippines. This 501(c)(3) organization claims 50,000 members and supporters. It operated on an annual budget for fiscal year 1992 of $2.8 million. Financial support is from membership fees, donations, and foundation grants.

FOE participates in federal, state, and local workplace charitable campaigns along with other groups that are part of Earth Share. Members and supporters can also contribute financially to a political action committee, FOEPAC. FOE publishes *Friends of the Earth* on a monthly basis. Besides this general newsletter, the organization's staff puts together *Atmosphere,* a quarterly newsletter on global climate issues, and *Community Plume,* a newsletter on chemical safety issues that appears periodically.

Unlike environmental groups that focus on a particular set of issues such as the wilderness or animal protection, Friends of the Earth consciously chose the planet as its chief focus. It also represents both change and continuity because it reflects a coming together again for people in FOE and the Environmental Policy Institute after an earlier split and an attempt to shift focus to membership support from dependence on foundation money. The new organization will be well positioned on international issues because it will benefit from affiliation with the thirty-three-member Friends of the Earth International, which is active on issues like protecting the ozone layer, saving tropical forests, preserving oceans and marine life, and assisting environmental groups in developing nations and the former Soviet Union.

FOE was reconstituted after a faction of the existing organization, led by David Brower, left to form Earth Island Institute.* In 1969 Brower had led a similar dissident faction out of the Sierra Club* that became the core of Friends of the Earth when it was originally established in 1969. The "new" FOE emphasizes that it is committed to advocacy globally—that is, activity locally, nationally, and internationally. FOE also works with an affiliated organization, Oceanic Society Expeditions, which organizes vacation travel for FOE's members and supporters.

POLICY CONCERNS

The variety of policy concerns that environmental organizations have in the 1990s is well illustrated in the case of FOE. That wide agenda has taken many of the organizations into the realm of consumer policy. It also has contributed to a shakeout among the ranks of environmental activists as some move on to new groups, and existing organizations search for and try out new issues and missions. In this profile the emphasis is on the many initiatives that FOE has been involved with since its reorganization in 1990. Some of the major emphases reflect continuing environmental concerns including groundwater, mining, nuclear weapons, and oceans.

FOE and other organizations worked hard to thwart legislation pushed by energy companies and their congressional supporters to open up Alaska's Arctic National Wildlife Refuge to oil and gas drilling. FOE also works on mining issues under the auspices of its Citizens Mining Project, designed to monitor implementation of the Surface Mining Control and Reclamation Act (first enacted in 1977). FOE also has been involved with the Antarctic and Southern Coalition to ban mineral and oil development in the Antarctic region for fifty years. This coalition's work helped lead to an international treaty signed in 1991.

Other issues represent newer concerns. FOE's international agenda includes the devastation done to Kuwait by the oil fires set by Iraq during the Persian Gulf War in 1991. FOE worked with National Wildlife Federation, the Natural Resources Defense Council,* the Environmental Defense Fund,* the National Audubon Society,* and other environmental groups in the Coalition for Action to Protect the Environment in preparation for the United Nations Conference on the Environment and Development held in June 1992.

A final set of emphases represents concerns that FOE shares with consumer, citizens, and grass-roots activists. For example, FOE's Environmental and Social Justice Project represents the organization's involvement in the National People of Color Environmental Leadership Summit organized by the United Church of Christ's Commission on Racial Justice (then led by Ben Chavis). FOE is also pursuing a Toxics Project, a Nuclear Weapons Production Project, a Corporate Accountability Project, and a Tax Reform Project.

TACTICS

Some of FOE's current work echoes its early legislative successes in Washington, such as halting government participation in the development of the supersonic transport aircraft. Campaigns for ecotaxes (i.e., the tax reform initiatives that would institutionalize environmental concerns into the tax code) and "green appropriations" (i.e., ensuring funding for environmental and human services programs as part of Congress's response to defense downsizing), however, take the organization before a different set of congressional decision makers than those on the committees that authorize traditional environmental and natural resources legislation (e.g., Surface Mining Control and Reclamation Act, Clean Water Act, Resource Conservation and Recovery Act, Safe Drinking Water Act). FOE also uses court cases where necessary to advance its agenda, as a recent case supporting shareholder activism has shown.

Many of FOE's new projects illustrate how the organization extends its resources by working in coalitions. Sometimes, as on the issue of how to spend the peace dividend, FOE is the only environmental organization to join. This was the case with the Coalition of Human Needs, most of whose members specialized in the problems of low-income people. FOE also belongs to Invest in America, a coalition of 120 organizations that seeks to increase overall funding for domestic programs. In other cases organization officials participate with citizen and environmental groups like the National Toxic Campaign's* Military Toxics Network and the 20/20 Vision National Project formed to earmark more money to clean up contaminated military bases.

Finally, FOE, like other public interest organizations operating in Washington, uses its publications to provide information to members and other interested persons about how to live a "green" lifestyle and shop as consumers concerned about the environment. These publications also refer readers to other organizations that specialize in important issues beyond FOE's resources. An example might be how to care for your lawn without using chemical pesticides or tips for "greening your office."

FURTHER READING

Brower, David. 1990. *For Earth's Sake: The Life and Times of David Brower.* New
    York: Peregrine Smith.
Green, Lee. 1991. "Man of the Earth." *Modern Maturity,* April/May, p. 22.
"Group Says 11 Billion Gallons of Oil Wasted." 1993. *Los Angeles Times,* May 18, p.
    D2.
Kriz, Margaret E. 1990. "Shades of Green." *National Journal,* July 28, pp. 1826–1831.
Ludwig, Dean C., and Judith A. Ludwig. 1992. "The Regulation of Green Marketing:
    Learning Lessons from the Regulation of Health and Nutrition Claims." *Business
    and Professional Ethics Journal,* Fall/Winter, pp. 73–91.
Lippman, Thomas W. 1993. " 'Earth Budget': Waste Not, Want Not: Group Urges Re-
    directing $14 Billion in Spending." *Washington Post,* February 4, p. A19.

FUND FOR A FEMINIST MAJORITY (FFM)

1600 Wilson Blvd., Suite 801
Arlington, VA 22209
Tel (703) 522–2214
Fax 703–522–2219

ORGANIZATION AND RESOURCES

The Fund for a Feminist Majority was formed by Eleanor Smeal and a group
of people long identified with the National Organization for Women (NOW).
The organization pursues a wide range of concerns surrounding the full empowerment of women—economically, politically, and socially—in American society. The Fund has 501(c)(4) status and gets the preponderance of its financial
assistance from over 40,000 members and supporters. FFM publishes *Feminist
Majority Report,* a quarterly newsletter, and works out of a branch office in Los
Angeles as well as its Washington base.

POLICY CONCERNS

Although the Fund for a Feminist Majority has interests in getting women
into important levels of government and society, enacting gender-balance laws
and rules, and protecting abortion rights and related women's rights policies,
the organization is included here because of its work on consumer issues. FFM,
along with Planned Parenthood of America and other organizations, has been
interested in getting the French birth control medication RU-486 introduced into
the American pharmaceutical market.

TACTICS

On this issue FFM is working with the French company, Roussel Uclaf, and
is opposed by right-to-life groups and other abortion and reproductive rights
opponents. FFM, NOW, and other women's rights groups have undertaken economic boycotts with mixed success in order to advance their agenda.

FURTHER READING

Allen, Charlotte Low. 1989. "The Mysteries of RU-486." *The American Spectator,* October, pp. 17–20.
Leary, Warren E. 1993. "Maker of Abortion Pill Reaches Licensing Pact with U.S. Group." *New York Times,* April 20, p. A18.

G
/

GREENPEACE, USA
1436 U Street N.W.
Washington, DC 20009
(202) 462–1177

ORGANIZATION AND RESOURCES

Greenpeace, founded in 1971 in Canada to protest underground nuclear testing in nearby Alaska, now has a membership of around 900,000 in the United States and over 2.7 million around the world. Dues for American members, some of which is donated yearly to support Greenpeace, International, is $25. There is also a 501(c)(4) organization, Greenpeace Action. Greenpeace USA has 300 staff members and publishes *Greenpeace* on a quarterly basis.

POLICY CONCERNS

Greenpeace is of interest because of its innovative strategies to draw public attention to the need to halt nuclear testing and for its work protecting the marine habitat. For example, Greenpeace is very concerned about implementation of the Marine Mammal Protection Act. Also at the center of the organization's field of focus are problems of acid rain, protection of Antarctica, and disposal of toxic waste at sea.

Recently, one of the issues on which Greenpeace has been active shows a different side to the organization. Greenpeace has been trying to work with government, industry, and other interested parties on behalf of environmental organizations and other paper consumers who want to recycle but lack information. This attempt to help paper consumers "green" the paper industry has led the organization to engage in activities with the American Soybean Association (which would like to see more of its product used in soy ink) and the Recycling Advisory Council, a body formed by the Environmental Protection Agency. The target is the American Paper Institute, which represents the paper industry.

TACTICS

For many years Greenpeace had a daredevil image, drawing much interest away from more conventional environmental groups. To some extent that is still true, although new organizations like Earth First! and Sea Shepherds, which eschew Greenpeace's commitment to nonviolence, have positioned themselves as more extreme. Greenpeace is best known for its direct actions protecting seals, whales, and other endangered species from the whaling and hunting industries. Another private-sector target is toxic waste dumping as well as companies seeking to dump garbage and other wastes into the seas.

Government is another frequent target, as may be seen when the group tries to stop nuclear tests by sailing their ships into nearby waters. Actions like that taken against the French government led to a much-publicized attempt on July 10, 1985, by one of the French security services to destroy the organization's ship, the *Rainbow Warrior*. Greenpeace, which is very active outside of the United States, does seek to influence policy-making by Congress and other national government decision makers in more conventional ways.

FURTHER READING

Broad, William J. 1993. "Disaster with Nuclear Subs in Moscow's Fleet Reported." *New York Times*. February 26, p. A2.

Browning, Graeme. 1991. "Taking Some Risks." *National Journal*, June 1, pp. 1279–1281.

Darnton, John. 1993. "Norwegians Claim Their Whaling Rights." *New York Times*, August 7, p. A1.

The Greenpeace Guide to Paper. n.d. Washington, DC: Greenpeace.

Harwood, Michael. 1988. "Dividends for the Environment." *New York Times Magazine*, October 2, pp. 72–75.

Kamen, Al. 1993. "Greener Than Thou." *Washington Post*, September 24, p. A21.

Kriz, Margaret E. 1990. "Shades of Green." *National Journal*, July 28, pp. 1826–1831.

Pollack, Ellen Joan. 1993. "Incinerator Suit Dismissed." *Wall Street Journal*, November 22, pp. B2, B8.

Russell, Dick. 1987. "The Monkeywrenchers." *Amicus Journal*, 9:4, 28–42 (Fall).

GROCERY MANUFACTURERS OF AMERICA (GMA)
1010 Wisconsin Avenue N.W.
Washington, DC 20007
Tel (202) 337–9400
Fax 202–337–4508

ORGANIZATION AND RESOURCES

Originally founded in 1908, the Grocery Manufacturers of America is a trade association made up of the manufacturers and processors of food and nonfood products sold in retail grocery stores throughout the United States. The organization's members annually sell several hundred million dollars of products to American consumers. Like other trade associations, GMA offers a variety of services to its members, including promotion of the importance of the grocery manufacturing industry to Washington policymakers and the general public. The organization is governed by a board of directors and assisted by numerous committees and task forces, including the Industry Productivity Council and the Government Affairs Council. Among the organization's publications are the weekly *Washington Report* and the weekly *State Legislative Report.*

POLICY CONCERNS

GMA members are concerned about the costs and administrative burdens that government regulations place on them. These companies are affected by federal legislation mandating new product labels, increased concern about food safety, and consumer fears about the security of food and medical products. GMA members take a keen interest in federal programs providing food assistance to low-income consumers since the largest of these, the food stamp program, operates by subsidizing food purchases by consumers who would not otherwise be able to afford the food products that manufacturers and processors offer for retail sale.

In recent years, organization spokespersons have testified on issues associated with disposal of solid waste—especially on plans for recycling grocery containers—as well as Food and Drug Administration enforcement of advertising and labeling legislation. Member companies have been very concerned about the requirements that they would face under the tougher nutritional labeling legislation passed by Congress in 1990.

TACTICS

Besides pursuing policy issues in Washington, GMA increased the attention it pays to the actions of state government decision-making bodies in the 1980s. GMA also works with other trade organizations such as the Food Marketing Institute,* the American Frozen Food Institute, and organizations representing snack foods on issues such as product safety and tampering prevention to reassure consumers.

FURTHER READING

Gottlieb, Daniel W. 1982. "Business Mobilizes as States Begin to Move into the Regulatory Vacuum." *National Journal,* July 31, pp. 1340–1343.

Ippolito, Pauline M., and Alan D. Mathios. 1993. "New Food Labeling Regulations and the Flow of Nutrition Information to Consumers." *Journal of Public Policy and Marketing,* Fall, pp. 188–205.

H
/

HALT—AMERICANS FOR LEGAL REFORM (HALT)
1319 F Street N.W., Suite 300
Washington, DC 20004
(202) 347–9600

ORGANIZATION AND RESOURCES

HALT—Americans for Legal Reform is concerned about the high cost of legal services and sees itself as a watchdog over lawyers and the legal profession. Founded in 1977, HALT claims to have over 100,000 members, a budget of $2.5 million, and a Washington staff of 10. One source of income is sale of books providing simple legal advice and forms that consumers can use to draw their own divorces, wills, and other legal papers.

POLICY CONCERNS AND TACTICS

Although HALT is not a small organization by the standards of some better-known groups in the consumer community, it keeps a low public profile. By trying to make consumers better shoppers for legal services and taking an interest in issues like no-fault insurance, HALT has succeeded in specializing as a watchdog for an industry that can take large chunks out of a consumer's pocketbook in times of crisis.

FURTHER READING

Smith, Wesley J. 1993. "Obedience School for Lawyers." *Home Office Computing,* February, pp. 54–56.

HANDGUN CONTROL, INC. (HCI)
1225 Eye Street N.W., Suite 1100
Washington, DC 20005
Tel (202) 898–0792
Fax 202–371–9615

ORGANIZATION AND RESOURCES

Handgun Control, Inc., was founded by Pete Shields in 1974, after his son had been killed by a handgun. HCI has 501(c)(4) status from the U.S. Internal Revenue Service and works with the Center to Prevent Handgun Violence, a 501(c)(3) group. HCI claimed over 250,000 members at the beginning of the 1990s and had a budget of $6.5 million. The organization publishes *Handgun Control—Washington Report.*

POLICY CONCERNS

HCI's chief policy aim for over a decade has been to get Congress to enact the Brady Bill, which would require a nationwide seven-day waiting period before a consumer could purchase a firearm. In 1993 a version of the bill was passed by Congress and signed into law by President Clinton, with James and Sarah Brady and other gun control advocates in attendance. The couple became the chief public spokespersons for the organization after Jim Brady was severely wounded in the assassination attempt on President Ronald Reagan in 1981.

TACTICS

HCI's chief opponent has been the National Rifle Association, whose lobbyists acknowledge HCI's growing political savvy. HCI's work also has been opposed by the Citizens' Committee for the Right to Keep and Bear Arms. The group has had important help from the nation's police chiefs, and its successes have been prefigured by passage of assault weapons bans and state laws calling for waiting periods. HCI has endorsed and campaigned for congressional and state candidates through its political action committee, the Handgun Control Voter Education Fund.

FURTHER READING

King, Wayne. 1990. "Target: The Gun Lobby." *New York Times Magazine,* December 9, pp. 42–45.
Rosenbaum, Ron. 1991. "The Brady Offensive." *Vanity Fair,* January, pp. 66–72.

HEALTH INSURANCE ASSOCIATION OF AMERICA (HIAA)
1025 Connecticut Avenue N.W.
Washington, DC 20036–3998
(202) 223–7780

ORGANIZATION AND RESOURCES

The Health Insurance Association of America is the dominant trade association for companies in the accident and health insurance business in the United States. It was formed in 1956 by the merger of the Bureau of Accident and Health Underwriters and the Health and Accident Underwriters Conference. Its 285 member companies include the giants of the industry, such as Prudential, Metropolitan Life, and Aetna, as well as small and medium-sized companies; a twenty-person board of directors reflects the mix of membership. Bill Gradison became president of the Association early in 1993, resigning from the House of Representatives after being elected to his tenth term to take the HIAA position. Gradison heads an HIAA Washington staff of 150 with an annual budget of $20 million. The organization also draws on the resources of member companies with task forces of corporate experts created to study and recommend positions on developing issues and by bringing company personnel into Association staff as temporary "fellows" to enhance efforts on emerging issues.

The HIAA collects data and conducts research on health insurance topics at both state and federal levels. Research compilations are used to support specific policy positions and are published as periodic reference sources, such as *The Source Book of Health Insurance Data* and topical *Research Bulletins.* Public opinion monitoring for insurers is conducted on a regular basis and published as *Monitoring Attitudes of the Public.* State and federal legislative and regulatory developments are monitored and made available to members through an interactive real-time computerized information system, called HI-WIRE, that includes access to testimony transcripts, research output, and calendars. Claims information from more than 150 major contributors including insurers, third-party administrators, Blue Cross and Blue Shield plans, and self-insured groups is available to subscribers as the Prevailing Healthcare Charges System. Med Track provides members with telephone access to insurance-related medical information on emerging technologies, therapies, and other topics.

The HIAA develops public relations strategies for the industry that it takes to the media and directly to consumers. For example, it conducted a satellite tour of television stations in thirteen markets to address questions about long-term-care insurance and marketing. It disseminates newspaper editorials and magazine and journal articles, and responds to requests for representatives to appear on radio and television. Consumer booklets such as *The Consumer's Guide to Disability Insurance* are made available through member companies, agents, and the media. Together with the American Council of Life Insurance (ACLI), the HIAA supports the Center for Corporate Public Involvement, which aids members in promoting and claiming credit for their community service activities.

Health insurance education is also a priority for the HIAA. It conducts its own programs, enrolling 32,000 students a year in courses on topics such as medical coverage, flexible benefits, underwriting, and managed care. Study courses on new topics such as long-term care are sometimes developed with advisory groups made up of consumer and provider representatives. Topical conferences are jointly developed with other organizations such as the American Association of Homes for the Aging and the International Association for Financial Planning. HIAA also participates with the ACLI in supporting basic medical research and scholarships for advanced degree candidates.

POLICY CONCERNS

Prominent among the issues bringing the HIAA into the national policy arena since the 1980s are "medigap" insurance, long-term care, and access to health care. "Medigap" refers to policies designed to supplement Medicare by paying its deductibles and coinsurance, and charges it does not cover. The value of such plans and the ways they are marketed and sold have come onto the congressional agenda periodically since 1978, when Representative Claude Pepper launched an undercover investigation that disclosed cases of misrepresentation, scare tactics, and sales of duplicate policies. Consumers Union* has also been an active investigator and critic of industry practices. HIAA has responded with its own surveys, worked cooperatively with the National Association of Insurance Commissioners* (NAIC) to develop model state regulations and educate companies and agents for compliance. Evidence of continuing abuses has spurred Congress to set more stringent federal standards in spite of HIAA's urging national policymakers to wait and measure the effect of state regulations.

While the Congress debated and then passed the short-lived catastrophic care program, the HIAA was trying to persuade national policymakers to deal instead with needs of the elderly in long-term care, which it characterized as more pressing. It lobbied against the catastrophic care proposal at the outset, on the grounds that most Medicare beneficiaries already had supplemental private insurance or were eligible for Medicaid. However, once catastrophic care was passed, the HIAA assisted the industry in making the rapid, extensive adjustments to comply. When Congress then considered repeal, the HIAA position was to urge caution because of the resulting confusion and costs to the industry and consumers of rapid redesign.

Since 1989, the HIAA has been a player in the national debate on access to health care for the 37–41 million Americans without health insurance. Its research has provided industry rebuttals to the claims of proposals such as those for community rating or a single-payer system modeled on Canada's, some versions of which would eliminate the private health insurance business. HIAA's own plan proposes an expansion of Medicaid giving priority to primary and preventive care for children, insurers being allowed to offer more affordable coverage by elimination of state-mandated benefits, coverage of uninsurable individuals and groups through state pools, and 100 percent tax deduction for the self-employed individuals. It has also devoted substantial effort to the industry response as the states move ahead with their own access reforms. Prominent among the HIAA's state proposals is its call for small-employer market reform, including continuity of coverage, guaranteed coverage for individual high-risk employees, and premium pricing limits.

AIDS, AIDS testing, and risk classification continue to be matters of concern for the industry. Implications of genetic testing are an emerging issue of focus for the HIAA, as is the impact of emerging medical technologies and precedures, and their effect on reimbursement decisions.

TACTICS

HIAA tactics range from meeting with cabinet officers to confronting demonstrators outside its Washington headquarters. Gradison and member company executives have been invited by the secretary of health and human services to participate in working groups on health care financing reform and administrative costs. Staff and member company executives testify frequently before congressional committees, work with staff on drafting legislation, and plan strategy. Issue advertising targeted at the districts of significant members of Congress conveys the health insurance industry position on legislative proposals.

Task forces of member company experts and HIAA staff develop proposed model bills for consideration by the NAIC. Recent model bills designed to stabilize the small-employer insurance market and to increase access for small business were adopted by the NAIC. HIAA staff members also work directly to persuade state policymakers to adopt such proposals. State legislators participate with health association executives and industry experts in symposia and seminars sponsored by HIAA.

HIAA not only forges unified policy positions among health insurance companies but also forms coalitions that extend outside the industry. For example, it coalesced with the National Association of Manufacturers,* the U.S. Chamber of Commerce,* the National Federation of Independent Business,* and others to oppose employer-mandated health benefits. It sometimes uses the courts, as it did in *HIAA* v. *Corcoran,* to defend the use of HIV testing for underwriting purposes.

FURTHER READING

Annual Report. Annual. Washington, DC: Health Insurance Association of America.
Brostoff, Steven. 1989. "Senate Pares Catastrophic Care After House's Repeal." *National Underwriter,* October 16, p. 1.
Fisher, Mary Jane. 1989a. "Kinder, Gentler HIAA Plan Expands Medicaid Eligibility." *National Underwriter,* April 3, p. 3.
———. 1989b. "New Coalition Fights Mandated Health Benefits." *National Underwriter,* July 3, p. 21.
———. 1990. "NAIC, Health Associations Oppose Stark's Medigap Reform Bill." *National Underwriter,* March 26, p. 1.
Gart, Alan. 1994. *Regulation, Deregulation, Reregulation: The Future of the Banking, Insurance, and Securities Industries.* Somerset, NJ: Wiley.
Rice, Thomas, Katharine Desmond, and Jon Gabel. 1989. *Older Americans and Their Health Coverage.* Washington, DC: Health Insurance Association of America.

Rovner, Julie. 1990. "Climbing Medigap Premiums Draw Attention on Hill." *Congressional Quarterly Weekly Report,* February 17, pp. 527–531.

Rubin, Alissa J. 1993. "Special Interests Stampede to Be Heard on Overhaul." *Congressional Quarterly Weekly Report,* May 1, pp. 1081–1084.

THE HERITAGE FOUNDATION
214 Massachusetts Avenue N.E.
Washington, DC 20002–4999
(202) 546–4400

ORGANIZATION AND RESOURCES

The Heritage Foundation was created in 1973 to articulate conservative ideas and devise and propose conservative policies. Joseph Coors of the Adolph Coors Brewing Company helped found the organization, which is committed to individual freedom, private initiative, and limited government. The Heritage Foundation describes itself as conducting warfare in the battle of ideas, and is frequently credited with being the source of recommendations that have found their way into executive and legislative proposals, particularly since 1980.

A fourteen-member board of trustees is responsible for Heritage Foundation leadership; Edwin J. Feulner, Jr., is president and directs more than 150 researchers, scholars, fellows, managers, and supporting staff. Among Heritage fellows are William Bennett, former secretary of education and chairman of the National Endowment for the Humanities, and Edwin Meese III, former attorney general, who holds the $2.5 million endowed Ronald Reagan fellowship in public policy. The organization's 1991 income was over $19 million, half of which came from individuals, one-quarter from foundation grants, and 13 percent from corporations. More than 170,000 businesses, foundations, and individuals contribute to the Heritage Foundation; it accepts no government contracts or grants, and performs no sponsored research.

The Heritage Foundation research program is organized into the department of domestic policy studies, the Roe Institute for Economic Policy Studies, the Center for International Economic Growth, the department of foreign policy and defense studies, the Institute for Hemispheric Development, and the Asian Studies Center. The Foundation publishes *Policy Review,* a quarterly journal with a paid circulation of 14,000, and offers lecture and seminar programs. It publishes more than 250 major monographs and policy studies a year, ranging from brief commentaries to full-length books. It also publishes specialized newsletters, including the monthly *Business/Education Insider* and *SDI Report.* Its studies are available in print and electronically on NEXIS.

POLICY CONCERNS

Issues on which the Heritage Foundation is currently active range from the Strategic Defense Initiative to health care. In the domestic and economic policy arena, attention is devoted to taxes, the federal budget, health care, housing, education, welfare, trade, regulatory affairs, and the environment. On the budget and taxation, the Heritage Foundation advocates tax- and budget-cutting strategies for reinvigorating the economy. It is critical of the budget process, which it decribes as a fraudulent disguise of record-setting growth in government spending. For the health care crisis, the Foundation prescribes a consumer-driven national health system, scrapping the existing financing system of government- and employer-provided insurance, and making individuals responsible for paying for their own health care, using tax credits and vouchers to help finance the costs. Consumers, it contends, would thus shop for more economical coverage and providers would compete for their business. In education policy, the Foundation advocates reforms allowing parents to choose the schools their children attend. It pursues the theme of individual consumer empowerment in other domestic issues, such as housing and welfare policy, with arguments that government regulations raise prices and contribute to the problem rather than the solution. Rather than have government attempt to redistribute income, it would have government get out of the way of expanding opportunities for the poor.

In foreign policy and defense, the Heritage Foundation argues that the emergence of reform in eastern Europe and the Commonwealth of Independent States offers an unprecedented opportunity for free-market, privatization, and democratic strategies. In spite of warmer relations with the former Soviet Union, it continues to devote serious attention to national security issues, taking credit for having launched the public debate over strategic defenses in the 1980s and promoting the Strategic Defense Initiative with more than sixty monographs, studies, and lectures. The Foundation advocates free trade and hopes to help spread it throughout the western hemisphere, and eventually the globe. It supported "fast track" negotiating conditions for the trade agreement with Mexico, arguing that real reform is more likely to occur without congressional involvement. The Heritage Foundation's U.S. Congress Assessment Project is examining institutional problems of the Congress and has supported the national term limitation movement by bringing together leaders of state-based term limit organizations and drawing national media attention to the issue.

TACTICS

The Heritage Foundation is distinct from more academic research organizations in that it devotes more attention to what it calls real-world research and to activity on events as they occur. It describes this as an entrepreneurial approach to public policy. This was particularly visible during the Persian Gulf War, when a series of Foundation papers, describing how the war should be fought, laid groundwork for Bush administration thinking on how to conduct the war. The Foundation also targets its research, combining scholarship with salesmanship in order to make an impact on policy; the organization includes four departments responsible for marketing—to Congress and the executive branch, national and international news media, the academic and policy advocacy communities, and the corporate community. Congress and the executive branch are the intended primary audience of the Foundation's work; it maintains close contact with members, staff, cabinet, and subcabinet officials, providing topical research and in-depth briefings. In addition, it recommends qualified conservatives for administration positions.

The Foundation reaches out to academics by providing resident positions for scholars to work on projects, by providing a network among academic research centers and policy organizations, and by helping nonprofit conservative policy institutes to raise funds. It is also working to develop a more conservative curriculum in higher education through a series of graduate-level seminars on the foundations of U.S. conservatism.

Heritage Foundation research teams bring together experts from other Washington think tanks, other conservative groups, Capitol Hill, the executive branch, universities, embassies, and the business community for off-the-record working group discussions on major issues. Its lectures and seminars serve as a forum for discussion in Washington and beyond by means of extensive media coverage, including being broadcast over C-SPAN. Its prominence allows the Heritage Foundation to bring together notable conservatives such as Phyllis Schlafly, speaking on women in combat, and Arthur Laffer, on tax cuts, as well as persons from across the ideological spectrum.

Articles by Heritage Foundation researchers appear in leading publications, for example, articles on the Foundation's health care proposal appeared in the *Journal of the American Medical Association.* Conservative spokespersons from the Foundation provide the media with its position on any issue and frequently appear on major television programs and in the print media. The Heritage Speakers Bureau provides a conservative perspective for business and civic groups, including the American Farm Bureau Federation, and universities, including Harvard and St. John's College.

The Foundation sponsors issue-focused conferences around the country, as it did to rally the attention of business leaders to become more involved in supporting school choice initiatives in Pennsylvania, New York, and Michigan. Reform plans for the leaders of newly emerging democracies in eastern Europe and the Commonwealth of Independent States have been crafted by Foundation authors, translated into multiple languages, and shared by means of seminars and study sabbaticals for leaders of those countries.

The Foundation's Third Generation Project cultivates young people who became politically aware during the Reagan years; they meet fortnightly for lectures and debates, and hold an annual retreat to discuss future issue priorities. The New Majority Project seeks to communicate conservative ideas to African-Americans, Hispanics, and other minorities through fellowships, lecture series, and a Traditional Values Coalition made up of black ministers.

FURTHER READING

Felten, Rice. 1993. *The Ruling Class: Inside the Imperial Congress.* Washington, D.C.: Regnery Gateway.

The Heritage Foundation: Annual Report. Annual. Washington, DC: Heritage Foundation.

Soley, Lawrence. 1991. Right Thinking Conservative Think Tanks. *Dissent,* Summer, pp. 418–20.

HUMANE SOCIETY OF THE UNITED STATES (HSUS)
2100 L Street N.W.
Washington, D.C. 20037
Tel (202) 452–1100
Fax 202–778–6132

ORGANIZATION AND RESOURCES

Besides headquarters in Washington, D.C., the Humane Society of the United States has ten regional offices and an educational division called the National Association for Humane and Environmental Education (NAHEE). Since its founding in 1954, HSUS has been one of the most important and visible animal protection groups. Recently, with the appearance of more extreme animal rights organizations, HSUS has broadened its activities, which are supported by memberships, contributions, bequests, and grants.

Regional HSUS offices serve as contact points to hear about animal protection issues and alert national headquarters. The organization's grass-roots role can be seen in its mission, to "assist animals, the groups that seek to help and protect them, and you." That means concern for the welfare of companion animals (or pets), wildlife living in zoos and the wild, laboratory animals, animals used in circuses and other entertainments, and farm animals.

POLICY CONCERNS

HSUS is involved in a wide range of animal protection measures, including the traditional work for which the organization is known: its campaigns against what HSUS believes to be cruel treatment of animals, some commercial uses of fur and animal parts (e.g., whaling), gaming such as cockfights, and concern for animal habitats. A large amount of organizational resources go to prevent the overpopulation of companion animals through spaying/neutering.

HSUS provides advice and support to state humane societies, veterinarians, and animal shelters. In addition, Humane Society International is involved in endangered species activities worldwide and HSIEurope has an agenda of animal protection issues that come before the European Union and its member countries that parallels the organization's objectives in the United States.

HSUS publications cite the organization's work on a wide range of legislative achievements since the 1970s, including the Endangered Species Act in 1973. The organization's director of federal legislative affairs prepares status reports on pending legislation, which may include appropriations bills for federal agencies (e.g., the Food and Drug Administration and the departments of Agriculture, Interior, Labor, Education, and Health and Human Services). Current concerns include issues concerning companion animals (e.g., helping consumers recover the costs of vet bills for pet shop puppies) and captive wildlife.

Issues recently coming onto the organization's agenda reflect a broader focus on environmental issues generally and include biodiversity, support for a Department of the Environment, and the environmental effects of international trade. HSUS officials got involved in the legislative battles over the General Agreement on Tariffs and Trade and the North American Free Trade Agreement, especially issues that concerned animal and environmental protection.

HSUS is increasingly active on agriculture issues that concern animals, farm production, and the environment. That means becoming knowledgeable about technical legislative language contained in the Packers and Stockyards Act, which is supposed to protect nonambulatory animals (otherwise known as "downers"), extralabel animal drug use, pesticide usage, and concern for humane slaughter practices. Concern for animal health and well-being has led the organization to come out against the use of BGH, the bovine growth hormone.

Another set of issues comes under the authority of the U.S. Department of Interior. It includes hunting (e.g., concern about inhumane traps), the state of the country's refuge system, whether hunting should be permitted on federal lands, and whether airborne hunting should be permitted. This long list of issues touches the jurisdiction of many congressional committees. Targets of particular interest include Senate and House committees such as Merchant Marine and Fisheries, Agriculture, Foreign Affairs, and Interior.

HSUS publishes *Animal Activist Alert,* which appears quarterly. This magazine profiles issues and urges members to contact their representatives in Washington in support of bills the organization favors. Allies include local humane societies, animal shelters, and animal control agencies. The organization also has participated with a wider network of environmental organizations through the work of the Endangered Species Coalition.

TACTICS

In Congress there is evidence that HSUS officials sometimes have to walk a fine line when the actions of more extreme animal rights groups are criticized. HSUS tries to take a middle-ground position, deploring cruelty while recognizing that animal research is necessary. HSUS deplores acts of lawbreaking by the more extreme groups. The organization supports legislation addressing the problem of pet overpopulation and responsible pet ownership (e.g., pet licensing, spay/neuter programs, and breeding moratoriums). HSUS has been involved in court cases. For example, it filed a friend of the court brief supporting the city of Hialeah, Florida, in a widely reported case involving the killing of animals in a religious ritual.

HSUS uses investigations and other forms of direct action to generate publicity about the plight of animals and help bring redress. The organization hosts a trade show, Animal Care Expo, that attracts people from animal care professions and industries (e.g., the pet food industry, animal breeders, the licensing-

and-control industry, animal drug and other research organizations, companies manufacturing and selling animal care products). Public education is also an important HSUS tactic. In 1993 the organization launched a new campaign against any breeding of cats and dogs until all in shelters are adopted: "Until There Are None—Adopt One!"

Like other public interest organizations, HSUS has supported consumer boycotts, a case in point being that called on Norwegian products to protest that country's resumption of commercial whaling. HSUS is very keen to reach the next generation of consumers in another way. NAHEE develops curriculum materials for humane education for children in schools, and publishes *KIND News Primary, KIND NEWS Jr.,* and a Spanish-language version, *KIND News Internacional.*

FURTHER READING

"Humane Society Urges End to Slaughtering of Horses." 1994. *New York Times,* May 6, p. A13.

Lockwood, Randall. 1993. "A Day in the Lives." *HSUS News,* Summer, p. 32.

Matlack, Carol. 1991. "Animal-Rights Furor." *National Journal,* September 7, pp. 2143–2146.

Palmer, Elizabeth A. 1992. "Animal Lab Protection Bill Advances to Judiciary." *Congressional Quarterly Weekly Report,* April 4, p. 873.

"Rights for Farm Animals." 1992. *Science,* March 2, pp. 914–922.

Tomsho, Robert. 1993. "Ranchers Howl Over Halt in Killing Coyotes." *Washington Post,* April 21, p. D1.

I

/

**INDEPENDENT BANKERS ASSOCIATION OF AMERICA
(IBAA)**
One Thomas Circle N.W., Suite 950
Washington, DC 20005–5802
(202) 659–8111

ORGANIZATION AND RESOURCES

IBAA provides a Washington voice for small and medium-sized community banks. Its goal is to advance and protect the interests of that segment of the financial services industry. Community banks are represented as essential building blocks of the towns and countries they serve, crucial to economic development, and critical for lending to the small businesses that create more than 80 percent of new jobs each year. IBAA was founded in 1930 and now has approximately 6,300 members, a staff of 45, and an annual budget of about $10 million. A ninety-member board of directors, led by a six-person executive committee, governs the organization; Kenneth A. Guenther is the executive vice president.

The Washington office has the largest staff and is responsible for legislative and regulatory access as well as information services. A "Main Street" office in Sauk Centre, Minnesota, is responsible for educational programs, meetings, membership recruitment, and accounting services. There is a Western regional office in Newport Beach, California, and a Rocky Mountain regional office in Denver. Arlington, Virginia, offices are responsible for the Community Banking Network, a wholly owned subsidiary of the IBAA that provides bankcard, securities, and mortgage services to community banks. *Independent Banker* is the

IBAA's monthly magazine; it also publishes a weekly newsletter, *Washington Weekly Report,* and special supplements on rapidly developing issues. The *IBAA Compliance Deskbook* and *Compliance Bulletin* updates provide in-depth information on the major regulations with which banks must comply; disclosure forms and suggested compliance action plans are included.

IBAA offers educational programs for community bank executives and their staffs on such topics as residential mortgage lending, consumer lending, fair lending compliance, funds marketing, and bank holding company issues. Annual offerings consist of thirty to forty seminars and workshops. A certification program in internal auditing is under development, and plans are under way to expand to additional subject areas. Videotapes and publications for continuing education purposes are developed and sold by IBAA.

POLICY CONCERNS

Recent policy concerns of IBAA have centered on federal regulation and competition from other providers of financial services. Community banks were opposed to the deregulatory movement of the national government during the late 1970s and early 1980s. Their assessment of the direction set by the Bush administration was that it wanted to consolidate the nation's financial services, to buttress Wall Street at the expense of Main Street. IBAA argues that those interests are separate, that community banks require the protection of deposit insurance for multiple individual accounts, barriers between banking and commerce, and continued restrictions on branch banking.

It has worked to cooperate with other banking interests on recapitalizing the bank insurance fund, maintaining deposit insurance at its existing level, and defeating consumer initiatives that banks regard as onerous and costly. Among the consumer proposals that IBAA has cooperated to defeat are those calling for government check cashing or ''lifeline'' banking (basic services at low or no charges) and truth-in-savings proposals. IBAA guards the market of its members by documenting credit union efforts to expand beyond their allowable members to compete with local banks while enjoying tax and deposit insurance advantages not shared by those banks.

The role of community banks in agriculture is defended by IBAA involvement in legislation providing for crop insurance, and creation and regulation of a secondary market for guaranteed agricultural real estate and rural housing mortgage loans. The impact of the Community Reinvestment Act requirement for public ratings of banks continues to be a concern of IBAA. It has worked to educate its members about compliance requirements and is working with regulatory agencies to assure that customers understand the difference between reinvestment ratings and bank safety and soundness. An additional regulatory concern of community banks is the Americans with Disabilities Act and its impact on employment, public accommodations, and services.

TACTICS

IBAA uses a wide range of tactics to influence the policy process. The executive committee of its board of directors meets periodically with the full Board of Governors of the Federal Reserve System. It assembles expert analyses of proposals that are submitted to and used by the Treasury Department for reference in its development of reports and further proposals. It has similar ongoing relationships with the Internal Revenue Service, Small Business Administration, Financial Accounting Standards Board, American Institute of Certified Public Accountants, and many others. Its executive director is a well-known figure on Capitol Hill, and community bankers present testimony before congressional committees and meet with individual members. Surveys of the potential impact on members of proposed legislation is one way of conveying to policymakers the concerns of their districts' community banks. IBAA staff and members travel to statehouses around the country to acquaint governors with their positions; they also work with the National Governors Association on financial issues.

Community banks are assisted in engaging in grass-roots lobbying by IBAA provision of statement stuffers to inform customers about issues such as deposit insurance, and postcards for customers to send to the president or their members of Congress. IBAA gets the message of community banking to the mass media through issues advertising, news releases, press conferences, and one-on-one conversations with journalists around the country.

Prominent members of Congress, such as Banking Committee chairmen, are invited to speak to IBAA annual meetings and committee meetings. IBPAC, the IBAA political action committee, contributes to sympathetic members of both parties, incumbents in vital positions, and challengers who express support for community banking. Funds raised by IBPAC grew more than 70 percent between 1986 and 1990; it boasts a "batting average" of 89 percent, meaning that 89 percent of candidates it supported won their elections.

Coalition building is among IBAA's tactics. Perhaps its best-publicized alliance was with the American Association of Retired Persons* (AARP) on the 1991 Treasury proposal to overhaul the financial services industry. This alliance was the core of the Main Street Coalition created to oppose interstate branching and consolidation of service providers. IBAA joined with the 33 million-member AARP, not a usual ally, because it needed support in what it described as "the fight of its life." AARP agreed to support existing levels of deposit insurance, and in exchange, IBAA agreed not to oppose "lifeline" banking and government check cashing for a bank's own customers. The success of this unusual and highly visible alliance was evident in the Senate Banking Committee outcome.

FURTHER READING

Alston, Chuck. 1991. "Lobbyists Storm Capitol Hill, Clash over Banking Bill." *Congressional Quarterly Weekly Report,* August 24, pp. 2313–2318.

Annual Report. Annual. Washington, DC: Independent Bankers Association of America.

Campagna, Anthony S. 1994. *The Economy in the Reagan Years.* Westport, CT: Greenwood Press.

Gart, Alan. 1994. *Regulation, Deregulation. Reregulation: The Future of the Banking, Insurance, and Securities Industries.* Somerset, NJ: Wiley.

Independent Banker. Monthly. Washington, D.C: Independent Bankers Association of America.

Meier, Kenneth J. 1985. *Regulation: Politics, Bureaucracy, and Economics,* New York: St. Martin's Press.

Washington Weekly Report. Weekly. Washington, DC: Independent Bankers Association of America.

INFACT
256 Hanover Street
Boston, MA 02113
Tel (617) 742–4583
Fax 617–227–7704

ORGANIZATION AND RESOURCES

INFACT has been monitoring corporate behavior and attempting to influence policies that affect people's health first as a coalition and then as a separate organization since it was founded in 1977. It operates as a 501(c)(3) organization and has a staff of about forty. INFACT claims to have 30,000 members, and its Boston-based staff coordinates activities for four other offices. INFACT publishes *Nuclear Weapons Campaign Update,* a quarterly newsletter.

POLICY CONCERNS

INFACT's first major campaign was directed against the marketing practices of the Swiss food products manufacturer Nestlé, which has subsidiaries in the United States. INFACT led a coalition of organizations that opposed the company's marketing of its baby food products in Third World countries. Since alerting world opinion and international organizations to these practices and having some measure of success in changing Nestlé's policies, INFACT has become fully occupied with a campaign against General Electric to force it to clean up the sites where it manufactures nuclear weapons under government contract and to get out of the nuclear weapons business altogether. This second campaign has not been as successful as the first, but the organization may be able to take advantage of the end of the Cold War and the movement toward defense conversion to achieve victory in the future.

TACTICS

INFACT's chief tactic has been the consumer boycott, supported by grassroots organizing, coalition building, and creative use of national and international media. INFACT's General Electric campaign draws on allies and sympathizers in the religious community.

FURTHER READING

"Activist Group Is Planning Boycotts of Tobacco Firms." 1994. *Wall Street Journal*, April 13, p. B9.

Driscoll, Lisa. 1991. "The Gnat Trying to Sting an Elephant Called GE." *Business Week*, June 24, pp. 44–45.

Ryan, James. 1992. "Deadly Reception." *Buzzworm*, July/August, p. 13.

Sethi, S. Prakash. 1994. *Multinational Corporations and the Impact of Public Advocacy on Corporate Strategy: Nestle and the Infant Formula Controversy*. Norwell, MA: Kluwer Academic Publishing Group.

Wald, Matthew. 1991. "G.E. Boycott Is Working, Group Says: But Company, Target of Nuclear Protest. Says Its Sales Are Up." *Wall Street Journal*, June 13, p. C3.

Wang, Penelope. 1986. "Taking a Shot at Goliath." *Newsweek*, July 7, p. 43.

Zheutlin, Peter. 1990 "Doctors Join GE Boycott." *The Bulletin of the Atomic Scientists*, (November), p. 8.

INSURANCE INSTITUTE FOR HIGHWAY SAFETY (IIHS)
1005 North Glebe Road
Arlington, VA 22201
(703) 247–1500

ORGANIZATION AND RESOURCES

The Insurance Institute for Highway Safety is an independent, nonprofit research and communications organization dedicated to improving highway safety by improving drivers, motor vehicles of all types and sizes, and roadways both urban and rural. It is wholly supported by the American Insurance Highway Safety Association, the American Insurers Highway Safety Alliance, the National Association of Independent Insurers Safety Association, and individual insurance companies including Aetna, Allstate, GEICO, Nationwide, Prudential, State Farm, Transamerica, and Travelers. A twenty-person board of directors governs the organization; Brian O'Neill directs a staff of fifty-five members. The Institute took its present identity in 1969, when it was restructured to focus on research and communications.

IIHS conducts both short-term and long-term research. Among its long-term projects is an in-depth investigation of crashes in a seven-county area around Charlottesville, Virginia. Begun in 1987, the work involves vehicle investigation, information from people injured, hospital reports, and other sources providing more detailed data than is otherwise available. Since 1969 IIHS has conducted and filmed low-speed crash tests that are a primary source of data on the performance of auto bumpers; some manufacturers use the Institute's tests for product development and improvement.

Status Report, the Institute's biweekly communication on ongoing research, sometimes includes dramatic accounts of accidents related to issues on which the research is focused. Special issues of the newsletter report research outcomes. Full research reports are published separately as independent volumes, such as *The Injury Fact Book,* which analyzes injuries of all types by cause, age, sex, race, socioeconomic status, geographical area, and time of day. IIHS research is also reported in trade journals such as the *Journal of Safety Research.*

Affiliated with the IIHS is the Highway Loss Data Institute, which collects and analyzes insurance claims and coverage information to report on the injury, collision, and theft losses of cars by make and model. It publishes *Injury and Collision Loss Experience* and other statistical reports about vehicle damage, injury claim frequencies, and theft losses of recent model cars. Its annual reports on theft frequencies by model and city receive widespread media coverage, as do its reports on injury claims by auto and driver type. Its consumer brochures on the effect of damage susceptibility on insurance costs for various vehicles may soon be available in new car showrooms.

POLICY CONCERNS

Since 1969, IIHS has systematically considered a complete range of highway loss reduction options relating to human, equipment, and environmental factors. Its low-speed crash test series has documented the advantages of damage-resistant auto bumpers; the organization supported the 1979 federal requirement that prohibited all but minor cosmetic damage in 5 mph front and rear collisions, and has documented the effects of the 1982 regulatory decision to change the federal standard to 2.5 mph. Its work also has led to the inclusion of light trucks, vans, and multipurpose vehicles under the same safety standards as cars.

IIHS was an early sponsor of research on the diagnosis and treatment of trauma patients and the recognition and certification of emergency care physicians. The group has been active in many aspects of alcohol-impaired driving, including the development, testing, and use of more effective screening instruments for roadside alcohol breath tests. Its research on legal sanctions against drunken driving concludes that probable apprehension, swift punishment, and tough penalties are important for a powerful sanction. The effectiveness of police sobriety checkpoints and of swift driver's license revocation are supported by their research. The Institute also has documented the effects of changes in the age requirements for purchasing alcohol; its research was influential in federal and state decisions to restore the legal drinking age to twenty-one.

IIHS has studied the use of safety belts since its founding and was one of the first groups to endorse mandatory seat belt laws. It continues to investigate the reasons for variance in use of seat belts. The Institute has promoted the use of air bags and considers it a great victory that auto manufacturers now not only must supply them but also have discovered that buyers want them. Its research on motor vehicle death rates of children has been influential in getting all fifty states to enact child restraint laws; it continues to conduct research on the effectiveness of these laws.

Institute studies on fuel tank ruptures, leaks, and fires led to federal requirements that autos meet test requirements with little or no fuel leakage. The hazards presented by large trucks on the highways have been researched by IIHS;

it supports guard structures on the backs of tractor-trailers to prevent autos from sliding under the trailers, and antilock brakes, and is opposed to double trailers. It has been concerned with truck drivers—how much time they actually spend behind the wheel compared with how much time is recorded in their logs, and their use of drugs and alcohol. IIHS has taken the lead in researching travel speeds and fatality increases under the recently enacted 65 mph speed limits on rural interstate highways. Its focus on enforcement of speed limits has led it to oppose the use of radar detectors and to demonstrate the usefulness of electronic radar detector-detectors by police.

One of the more controversial positions taken by the Institute is in support of the safety of larger, as opposed to smaller, cars. Thus, in the debate over tougher fuel economy standards, IIHS advocates not downsizing vehicles.

TACTICS

The central approach used by IIHS is to conduct sustained research and keep the results before policymakers, with the understanding that response may take a number of years. The group devises research methods that get beyond apparent outcomes to measure real outcomes; for example, its research on the impact of high school driver education courses found that they did not reduce crash likelihood but did encourage teenagers to get their licenses sooner than they would have otherwise. An Institute survey found three out of four truck drivers violating work hour regulations, and one in five reporting falling asleep at the wheel one or more times per month. While most of the Institute's research is devised on its own initiative, it occasionally engages in counterresearch to refute misinformation presented by others, as it did when the Federal Highway Administration claimed that raising speed limits does not affect travel speeds. It has been actively responding to misinformation on air bags as their use becomes more widespread.

IIHS support for air bags illustrates a wide range of tactics, including direct consumer education through brochures, graphic film footage of crash tests shown on television news programs, testimony before Congress, federal regulators, and state legislators and regulators, and a conference for purchasers of corporate fleet cars that resulted in thousands of orders being placed for cars equipped with air bags. Slow-motion film footage of crash tests on unrestrained children has been widely distributed and shown by the media. IIHS has excellent media relationships; it is a respected source, its staff members appear on television as experts, and reporters call when they need data on the extent of a problem that has come to their attention. IIHS monitors advertising related to highway safety; its critical response to ads that glorified speeding persuaded a television network to require the auto manufacturer to change the ad.

IIHS research on the benefits of antilock brakes led the Department of Transportation to initiate a fleet study of such brakes and legislation requiring the department to report to Congress on whether they should be mandated for commercial vehicles. Its research sometimes is used in a direct petition to a federal agency, as was the case with its study on how much time truck drivers actually spend behind the wheel.

Direct involvement with local and state law enforcement agencies is illustrated by the group's work on radar detectors. As part of a 1990 research project, the Institute equipped Virginia police with radar detector-detectors and helped them use the equipment to spot motorists using illegal detectors.

The Institute sometimes pursues its goals in alliance with other organizations. Its work on alcohol-impaired drivers has found it allied with Mothers Against Drunk Driving* in support of increasing the likelihood that drunk drivers will be arrested and have their licenses suspended quickly. Its petition to the Federal Highway Administration for a ban on radar detectors in commercial vehicles in interstate travel was in alliance with the American Automobile Association,* the International Association of Chiefs of Police, Public Citizen,* and other groups.

FURTHER READING

Coburn, Karen Ann. 1993. "Licensing Miss Daisy: An Old-Age Problem." *Governing,* April, pp. 24–25.
Twenty Years. 1989. Arlington, VA: Insurance Institute for Highway Safety.
U.S. General Accounting Office. 1992. *Highway Safety: Safety Belt Use Laws Save Lives and Reduce Costs to Society.* Washington, DC: Government Printing Office.
The Year's Work. Annual. Arlington, VA: Insurance Institute for Highway Safety.

INTERFAITH CENTER ON CORPORATE RESPONSIBILITY (ICCR)
475 Riverside Drive, Room 566
New York, NY 10115
(212) 870–2936

ORGANIZATION AND RESOURCES

The Interfaith Center on Corporate Responsibility was founded in 1974 but traces its roots to 1971 with the creation of the Interfaith Committee on Social Responsibility in Investments; the latter merged with the Corporate Information Center to form ICCR in 1974. ICCR is an international coalition of approximately 250 Protestant and Roman Catholic orders, denominations, agencies, dioceses, health care corporations, and pension funds. It is committed to merging social values with investment decisions and is motivated by the belief that responsible stewards must achieve more than an acceptable financial return on their investments. ICCR challenges the powerful role played by multinational corporations in the use and misuse of the Earth's human and physical resources and works for peace, economic justice, and stewardship of the Earth.

Several levels of membership offer access not only to news and information services but also to staff consultation privileges and votes on the governing board. Full membership with voting privileges requires minimum annual dues of $1,750; subscription to *The Corporate Examiner* is $35 annually. Members include the American Friends Service Committee, the Protestant Episcopal Church in the U.S.A., the Evangelical Lutheran Church in America, the Jesuit Conference, the Presbyterian Church, the World Council of Churches, and many other organizations. ICCR is a tax-exempt, nonprofit organization. Its 1990 budget was approximately $580,000; member dues make up the largest single source of revenue (46 percent of the total), and subscription sales make up an additional 20 percent. Timothy Smith is executive director, and the total staff is comprised of ten persons (including women and ethnic and racial minorities).

POLICY CONCERNS

ICCR traces its roots to the highly publicized 1970 "Tame GM!" campaign when the Project on Corporate Responsibility and spokespersons for the United Church of Christ pressed a General Motors shareholder meeting for improvements in product safety, respectful treatment of the environment, equal employment opportunity and affirmative action, and withdrawal from South Africa. Four resolutions were sponsored by the churches, led by the Episcopal Church, in 1971, all focusing on business in South Africa. In the following two decades the number of resolutions, issues, and sponsors increased, as did the level of shareholder support for such resolutions. In 1991, religious investors sponsored 279 social responsibility resolutions, and more than 80 percent of them gained enough votes to be resubmitted for a second year (compared with 17 percent in 1973). While corporate management tended to treat these efforts as insignificant annoyances in the early 1970s, management now meets regularly to negotiate with corporate responsibility advocates. In 1991 about one-third of proposed shareholder resolutions were withdrawn after agreements were reached between sponsors and management.

In the area of energy and the environment, ICCR has been involved in energy pricing, toxic waste disposal, nuclear energy, conservation, food irradiation, and environmental protection. It continues to press companies to endorse the Valdez Principles on environmental protection, to reduce emission of greenhouse gases, to develop environmentally sustainable technologies, and to monitor cleanup efforts in Alaska and Bhopal, India. While some gains have been made with respect to South Africa, ICCR continues to press for the dismantling of apartheid with tactics such as boycotts of oil companies and blocking their contracts with states, and publicizing bank community reinvestment practices in Harlem along with their continued investments in South Africa.

Although ICCR claims some gains in corporate affirmative action efforts, portrayal of women and minorities in programming, advertising, and logos, and labor agreements, wages, and working conditions, it continues to work in this area. Getting companies to report equal employment opportunity data to shareholders, have more inclusive representation on boards of directors, do business with female- and minority-owned firms, and locate in poor and minority communities are among its current efforts. It also is developing strategies to address the conditions of workers on the Mexico–U.S. border, and to advocate standards of conduct for corporations with facilities there.

Opposition to war is one of the oldest ICCR programs. While it claims some success in persuading companies to plan alternatives to weapons production, it continues to pursue resolutions on nuclear testing, radioactive hazards, and damage to the environment. The persistence of General Electric Corporation in the nuclear weapons business and the continuation of the Strategic Defense Initiative are at the top of its current agenda.

Since the mid-1970s, ICCR has been involved in the effort to halt the aggressive marketing of infant formulas. Strategies including a World Health Organization code, Federal Trade Commission investigations, and boycott of Nestlé Corporation products have been used in this ongoing campaign. ICCR's International Health and Tobacco Issue Group focuses on medicines, medical devices, biotechnology developments, and tobacco. It supports the goal of a smokefree society by the year 2000 and is stepping up a campaign against both domestic and international sales and marketing of tobacco products. The role of international banks in world debt and fair employment practices in Northern Ireland continue to be issues for ICCR.

TACTICS

ICCR uses the power of persuasion backed by economic pressure from both consumers and investors. Its members proceed by sponsoring shareholder resolutions, discussing concerns with management, divesting stock, conducting public hearings and investigations, publishing special reports, and testifying at forums including the United Nations, the Securities and Exchange Commission, congressional committees, and state and local legislatures. Members sponsor direct actions such as letter-writing campaigns, consumer boycotts, and prayer vigils.

The ICCR staff coordinates member actions, helps develop strategy, conducts research, publicizes corporate responsibility action, and consults with members on direct action options. The ICCR also serves as a clearinghouse for information on socially responsible alternative investments and community development. The organization often builds alliances with public pension funds, unions, and antiapartheid, environmental, civil rights, women's, peace, community, and health groups.

FURTHER READING

The Corporate Examiner. Quarterly. New York, NY: Interfaith Center on Corporate Responsibility.

Interfaith Center on Corporate Responsibility. 1991. New York; Interfaith Center on Corporate Responsibility. Membership pamphlet.

Marlin, Alice Tepper, and Susan Young. 1983. "Prying Open the Clam: On Proxies, Secrecy, and Social Accountability." In Mark Green, ed., *The Big Business Reader: On Corporate America.* New York: Pilgrim Press.

Singer, Andrew W. 1992. "The Whistle Blower: Patriot or Bounty Hunter?" *Across the Board,* November, pp. 16–22.

Vogel, David. 1983. "Trends in Shareholder Activism: 1970–1980." In Mark Green, ed., *The Big Business Reader: On Corporate America.* New York: Pilgrim Press.

L

LEAGUE OF WOMEN VOTERS OF THE UNITED STATES (LWVUS)
1730 M Street N.W.
Washington, DC 20036
(202) 429–1965

ORGANIZATION AND RESOURCES

The League of Women Voters of the United States was founded by members of the women's suffrage movement in 1920. In the 1990s the League has 110,000 members led by a staff of 50 and is organized into 32 regional, 50 state, and 1,250 local groups. The organization's annual budget is $3.55 million. All members receive *The National Voter*. The League is a nonpartisan, nonprofit, advocacy organization that urges all citizens to participate in government and the making of public policy.

POLICY CONCERNS

The League is profiled here because of its national-level activity on such issues as clean air, campaign finance reform, abortion rights and reproductive health services, defense reconversion, and arms control. At various times the League has worked with some of the more specialized consumer organizations, such as Public Voice,* on issues of common concern.

The LWVUS has supported such health and safety initiatives as the Safe Drinking Water, Federal Water Pollution Control, and Resource Conservation and Recovery acts. Energy costs and conservation were major issues on which the League was active during the 1970s and early 1980s. It supports development of alternative energy resources and lessening dependence on nuclear power.

TACTICS

The League is best known for its interest in good government and helping citizens become knowledgeable on complex public issues. Thus, a major bundle of concerns on which the League plays a major role in its Washington lobbying and public information activities is "good government" issues. This posture leads the organization into common cause with consumer organizations on issues of public participation in regulatory decision making, campaign finance reform, public right-to-know, and other measures designed to lessen the dependence that policymakers feel on special (business and economic) interests.

FURTHER READING

Davis, Phillip A. 1992. "RCRA Bill Slogs Along, Faces Troubled Waters." *Congressional Quarterly Weekly Report,* May 2, pp. 1158–1159.

Hager, George. 1992. "Opponents Launch Campaign to Stop Budget Amendment." *Congressional Quarterly Weekly Report,* May 30, pp. 1520–1521.

Lee, Robert W. 1988. "Big League Trouble over Partisanship." *Conservative Digest,* January, pp. 111–118.

Ridings, Dorothy S. 1985. "Advocating the People's Interest in Washington." *Vital Speeches of the Day* 51: 485–490 (June 1).

Young, Louise M. 1989. *In the Public Interest: The League of Women Voters, 1920–1970.* Westport, CT: Greenwood Press.

M
/

MOTHERS AGAINST DRUNK DRIVING (MADD)

511 E. John Carpenter Freeway	1000 Vermont Avenue N.W.
Suite 700	Suite 400
Irving, TX 75062	Washington, DC 20005
Tel (214) 744–6233	Tel (202) 842–3460
Fax 214–869–2206	Fax 202–842–3321

ORGANIZATION AND RESOURCES

Mothers Against Drunk Driving was founded in 1980 to stop drunk driving and support victims of what it sees as a violent crime. MADD has been successful in changing public attitudes about a subject that combines consumers of alcohol and users of motor vehicles, both important consumer goods in American society. By 1993 this 501(c)(3) organization had a staff of over 200 and a budget of $6.3 million, and could claim almost 3 million members. Founded by Candy Lightner after the death of her daughter, Cari, the organization demonstrates how important individuals can be in American interest group politics. MADD publishes *MADD in Action* and is organized into 430 chapters in nearly 50 states.

POLICY CONCERNS

The organization's stated goal is to have a .08 blood alcohol level adopted nationwide as the legal definition of intoxication. Recent activities have drawn attention to the abuse of alcohol at sporting events and alcohol advertising on television that is directed at young audiences. MADD also hopes to expand the use of administrative license revocations, encourage personal accountability for alcohol use, and advance victim rights in law enforcement and judicial proceedings.

TACTICS

MADD members and officials make very effective spokespersons for the organization's cause in legislative hearings and with the media. The group is also adept at coalition formation, grass-roots organizing, and creating public awareness (e.g., by getting television scriptwriters to insert information about using designated drivers on popular TV shows). However, the organization's tactics are profoundly influenced—as are those of Handgun Control, Inc.*—by the federal nature of American government. Battles must be fought at the local, state, and national government levels. MADD must divide its time between the legislative and judicial arenas in order to achieve its objectives.

The ostensible targets of MADD's activities are those who drink and drive, but the organization has inevitably come up against the liquor industry and auto manufacturers, not to mention the hospitality industry (e.g., restaurants, bars, etc.) and television advertising. One tactical response to the political heat generated by this organization and its supporters is General Motors' decision to put a warning into its owner's manuals urging that drivers behave responsibly.

FURTHER READING

Brown, Elizabeth A. 1991. "Alcohol Industry Tries New Image." *Christian Science Monitor,* July 19, p. 12.

"Getting MADD About Boozy Greeting Cards." 1988. *Newsweek,* July 4, p. 29.

"Graphic Accident." 1990. *Newsweek,* March 5, p. 58.

Keenen, Connie. 1994. "The Company She Keeps." *Los Angeles Times,* January 26, p. E1.

Lightner, Candy. 1990 "The Other Side of Sorrow." *Ladies Home Journal,* September, pp. 158–159.

N

/

NATIONAL AGRICULTURAL CHEMICALS ASSOCIATION (NACA)
1155 15th Street N.W., Suite 900
Washington, DC 20005
(202) 296–1585

ORGANIZATION AND RESOURCES

As a trade association representing the interests of manufacturers of agricultural chemicals, the National Agricultural Chemicals Association has sought to promote the benefits these products bring to food consumers and agricultural producers, develop markets for the industry's products, and monitor governmental actions impinging on the livelihood of member companies since its founding in 1933. Currently, the Washington activities of NACA's 100 members are directed by a 29-person staff. The organization's $7 million budget comes from a sliding-scale fee system by which members make their contributions. Many companies that are members of NACA also belong to the Chemical Specialty Manufacturers Association. NACA periodically publishes a *Bulletin* as well as *This Week and Next* on a weekly basis.

POLICY CONCERNS

NACA's Washington role was profoundly affected by the interest that Rachel Carson and other environmental and consumer critics began taking in DDT and other pesticides in the 1960s. Before that, the main Washington audience for pesticide policy was the "iron triangle" of congressional and U.S. Department of Agriculture (USDA) officials specializing in agriculture policy and the nation's farm groups represented in Washington. Before critics of the effects of agricultural chemical usage succeeded in transferring regulatory authority to the Environmental Protection Agency, chief responsibility for registering pesticides and regulating their use under the Federal Insecticide, Fungicide, and Rodenticide Act was entrusted to industry supporters in the USDA.

Since then, NACA, its members, and supporters in the agricultural sector have been fighting defensive battles to ward off stricter legislative rules under that act and the titles of the Food, Drug, and Cosmetic Act, which regulates the use of cancer-causing substances in the food supply. NACA has fought deregistration of existing chemicals and advocates regulation of chemical usage at the state and local levels, especially after local governments won new rights in a landmark Supreme Court case in 1991.

Recent years have seen an upsurge in state regulatory initiatives as organizations such as the National Coalition Against Misuse of Pesticides,* Public Voice for Food and Health Policy,* and their consumer, health, and environmental allies have zeroed in on increasing dependence of farmers and other food producers on chemical agriculture. Related concerns that have been incorporated into legislative initiatives by the opponents of chemical agriculture include right-to-know laws, liability insurance issues, and groundwater protection.

TACTICS

NACA employs the full range of tactics open to trade associations in Washington and makes effective use of executives from member companies in contacts with legislators and regulators. NACA members also work on their own, for example, fighting deregistration of specific chemicals in administrative proceedings and in the courts. NACA participates in a range of coalition activities, often with farm groups and trade associations representing pesticide applicators and suppliers. As the opposition to pesticide usage has gathered strength, these coalitions have broadened.

An example is the Coalition for a Sensible Pesticide Policy, formed to overturn the Supreme Court's 1991 decision allowing cities and counties to ban pesticides and lawn chemicals. NACA and its members have shown an ability to sit down and negotiate with opponents when that seemed the best approach (e.g., with a coalition of conservation and labor groups, the Campaign for Pesticide Reform, in 1985).

NACA went on the offensive in managing the public relations crisis the industry faced in the wake of the "60 Minutes" broadcast in 1989 of charges brought against the growth regulator Alar by the Natural Resources Defense Council.* At that time manufacturers formed a coalition called Responsible Industry for a Sound Environment. At the same time, apple producers and other fruit and vegetable growers dependent on agricultural chemicals formed the Minor Crop Farmer Alliance to assure that their interests in specific agricultural chemicals would be protected in the ensuing national debate. This episode and others of a similar nature where the needs of agricultural producer groups and agribusiness companies have diverged, show the broadening of the agricultural policy network in the 1980s. Farm politics is not of interest only to farmers anymore.

FURTHER READING

Beeman, Perry. 1994. "House Set to Break Pesticide Impasse." *Des Moines Register,* January 19, p. 1.
Freese, Betsy. 1987. "Industry Comes Alive on Chemical Safety." *Successful Farming,* April, p. 18.
Kriz, Margaret E. 1991. "Resisting Pesticide Ban Rule." *National Journal,* August 8, p. 1989.
———. 1992a. "Poison Gamesmanship." *National Journal,* April 18, pp. 930–933.
———. 1992b. "Sagging Aggies." *National Journal,* February 22, pp. 452–455.
Lechner, Sheryl. 1992. "Pesticide Wars." *Audubon,* March/April, p. 32.
Palmer, Elizabeth A. 1992a. "Chemical Firms Run to Congress for Relief from Local Laws." *Congressional Quarterly Weekly Report,* May 16, pp. 1331–1332.
———. 1992b. "House Panel Approves Rewrite of Disputed Pesticide Law." *Congressional Quarterly Weekly Report,* May 23, pp. 1443–1445.
"Pesticide Bill Prompts Mixed Reviews." 1992. *Science News,* October 22, p. 270.

NATIONAL ASSOCIATION FOR THE ADVANCEMENT OF COLORED PEOPLE (NAACP)

4805 Mt. Hope Drive   1025 Vermont Avenue N.W.
Baltimore, MD 21215   Washington, DC 20036
Tel (301) 358–8900   Tel (202) 638–2269
Fax 301–358–2332   Fax 202–638–5936

ORGANIZATION AND RESOURCES

Founded in 1909 with equality for African-Americans in politics, economic life, and education as its goal, the National Association for the Advancement of Colored People is one of the oldest civil rights organizations in the United States. Recently, this 501(c)(3) organization passed over better-known candidates such as Reverend Jesse Jackson and instead entrusted direction of its 100 staffers, 6 regional branches, and $12 million budget to new leadership. Its choice reflects the importance of corporations and other economic institutions to the health and economic well-being of those living in minority communities. The organization publishes *Crisis* ten times a year.

The NAACP responded to a sense of unease and need for a new direction by selecting Reverend Benjamin Chavis as its new head in 1993. Chavis had made his mark with the National Council of Churches and as an activist leader in the movement to protect low- and moderate-income communities from the effects of the environmental impacts of pollution generated by manufacturing plants located in or near their neighborhoods, toxic dumps and incineration facilities, and toxic waste sites left behind when companies opened up new plants in other areas. Conflict over his handling of a sexual harassment allegation led to Chavis's ouster in August 1994.

POLICY CONCERNS

The part of the NAACP's mission highlighted here concerns what has been called the environmental justice movement, a term encompassing the activities of organizations like Citizens' Clearinghouse Against Hazardous Wastes,* Citizen Action Fund,* National Toxics Campaign,* National Coalition Against Misuse of Pesticides,* and local affiliates of national environmental and consumer organizations.

TACTICS

A new generation of civil rights activists has made common cause with church and civic groups to promote community and worker right-to-know laws, and has not hesitated to threaten product boycotts, shareholder activism, and other direct action techniques to prod companies and government to action on these issues. These issues have also drawn the attention of national consumer and environmental organizations that seek to provide information, lobbying know-how, and technical assistance to the many grass-roots groups involved in these issues.

FURTHER READING

"Benjamin Hooks Defends NAACP in Farewell Speech." 1993. *Jet,* July 27, pp. 4–5.
"Denny's Teams up with NAACP to Combat Bias." 1993. *Jet,* June 21, p. 55.
Holmes, Steven A. 1994. "NAACP Leader, Ousted by Board, Hints He Will Sue." *New York Times,* August 22, pp. 1, 7.
Newman, Maria. 1994. "NAACP Is Expected to Keep Role." *New York Times,* August 22, p. 7.
Norment, Lynn. 1993. "Ben Chavis: A New Director, a New Direction at the NAACP." *Ebony,* July, p. 76.
Scott, Matthew. 1993. "Chavis to Lead NAACP into New Era." *Black Enterprise,* July, p. 17.
Thornton, Jeannye. 1993. "Chavis's Story: Eyes on the Next Prize." *U.S. News and World Report,* August 30/September 6, pp. 34–35.

NATIONAL ASSOCIATION OF ATTORNEYS GENERAL (NAAG)

444 North Capitol Street, Suite 403
Washington, DC 20001
(202) 628–0435

ORGANIZATION AND RESOURCES

The National Association of Attorneys General was founded in 1907 to help attorneys general fulfill the responsibilities of their offices and to support high-quality legal services in their jurisdictions. The Association fosters interstate cooperation on legal and law enforcement issues, conducts policy research and analysis of issues, and facilitates communication between the members and other levels of government. The attorneys general of the fifty states and the chief legal officers of the District of Columbia, the Northern Mariana Islands, Puerto Rico, American Samoa, Guam, and the Virgin Islands are members; the U.S. attorney general is an honorary member.

Four officers are elected annually for one-year terms; a small executive committee oversees management of the Association. The thirty-five-person staff is directed by Christine T. Milliken, executive director and general counsel; the Association's annual budget is approximately $5 million. Members participate through seven standing committees and additional special committees and working groups that study issues and make recommendations for adoption by the membership. Full membership meetings are held three times a year.

NAAG operates six clearinghouse projects, staffed by attorneys expert in U.S. Supreme Court and state court practice, on state antitrust and consumer protection laws, environmental enforcement issues, Medicaid fraud, asbestos litigation, and the use of civil RICO laws to combat narcotics trafficking. The Association also maintains a network of state legal experts in criminal, insurance, civil rights, corrections, and tax law.

Continuing legal education seminars are provided annually for attorneys general and their staffs on ten to fifteen topics in the areas of antitrust, consumer protection, charities, corrections, environment, insurance, Supreme Court advocacy, and other substantive legal areas. Additional support for those arguing cases before the Supreme Court is offered in NAAG's moot court program, which annually assists an average of thirty-five to forty attorneys general in preparing for oral argument before the high court. NAAG also provides amicus curiae coordination and information clearinghouse services, and conducts a fellows program to offer senior state litigators hands-on experience with the Supreme Court.

A general organization newsletter, *AG Bulletin,* keeps members posted on activities, federal legislation, seminars, and meetings. Six specialized newsletters are devoted to consumer protection, antitrust issues, Medicaid fraud, national environmental law enforcement, civil remedies in drug enforcement, and state constitutional law issues. Additional publications serve a variety of purposes, as exemplified by *Public Information Officer Handbook, State Attorneys General Guide to Environmental Law,* and *Attorneys General and New Methods of Dispute Resolution,* which reviews the use of mediation, arbitration, and similar techniques.

POLICY CONCERNS

The long-run central policy concern of NAAG is to protect the independence, define the scope, and enhance the management of offices of attorneys general. As chief legal officers of the states, commonwealths, and territories, they serve as counselors for state government agencies and the legislature, and as the ''people's lawyer'' for all citizens. The origins of the office go back to fourteenth-century England; extensive common law powers have developed since then, as have numerous constitutional and statutory duties and responsibilities. Attorneys general occupy the intersection of law and public policy in areas as diverse as consumer protection, business regulation, and drug abuse. Attorneys general are popularly elected in forty-three states, and appointed by the governors in five states and six jurisdictions, by the state Supreme Court in Tennessee, and by the legislature in Maine. Typical powers of attorneys general include the authority to intervene in public utility rate cases, enforce open meetings and records laws, enforce air pollution, water pollution, and hazardous waste laws, enforce antitrust prohibitions against monopolistic enterprises, and challenge or defend the constitutionality of legislative and administrative actions.

NAAG seeks to increase citizen understanding of the law and of law enforcement's role in order to assure both protection of individual rights and compliance with the law. It endeavors to promote cooperation and coordination on interstate legal matters in order to foster more responsive and efficient legal systems for citizens. The Association works to influence the development of national and state legal policy in consumer protection, antitrust, civil rights, criminal law, energy and the environment, and insurance. Recent efforts exemplifying the scope of NAAG concerns include major consumer protection initiatives to protect the public from telemarketing frauds, false advertising, fraud aimed at the elderly, and abuses in adjustable-rate mortgage payment computations and escrow account overcharges.

TACTICS

NAAG serves to create and maintain a collegial network among the chief legal officers of the states and jurisdictions by providing a common forum for learning and cooperation. It is both a source of information and a coordinator of joint endeavors. Its staff identifies and disseminates information to help attorneys general and their staffs stay aware of significant developments and emerging trends in federal and state governments. NAAG also facilitates developing coordinated approaches to major interstate legal problems in both state and federal venues. Its services in support of federal suits argued before the Supreme Court are critical because attorney general offices argue a substantial share of the cases heard by the Supreme Court in any given term. Recent efforts reflecting NAAG support include settlement of a price-fixing suit by forty-nine states and the District of Columbia against a major consumer electronics firm, resulting in refunds to more than half a million consumers nationwide. Joint action by fifty states and four jurisdictions has aided in defending new car ''lemon laws'' from preemption by the federal government. In addition, NAAG coordination of state action in oil overcharge cases has resulted in more than $1 billion dollars being returned to the states thus far.

The Association encourages state/federal cooperation in legislation and law enforcement. NAAG staff monitors proposed laws for their potential impact on federal relations, maintains contact with members of Congress and their staffs, and coordinates congressional testimony of attorneys general. The Association joins with executive agencies such as the U.S. Department of Justice, the Federal Trade Commission, the Environmental Protection Agency, and the Office of National Drug Control Policy in formal working groups aimed at enhancing cooperative law enforcement efforts; for example, it recently coordinated a joint state–federal investigation of health care fraud.

NAAG sometimes works with other associations of elected officials or legal professionals, as it did recently in a task force with the National Governors' Association to review environmental contamination at federal facilities. A recent cooperative project with the American Bar Association explored creative dispute resolution techniques in the offices of attorneys general.

FURTHER READING

Harney, Kenneth. 1991. "Battle Rages to Stop Abuse over ARMs." *Washington Post,* March 17, p. 47.

NAAG Publications. Annual. Washington, DC: National Association of Attorneys General.

National Association of Attorneys General. Annual. Washington, DC: National Association of Attorneys General.

National Association of Attorneys General: General Information. 1987. Washington, DC: National Association of Attorneys General.

"Spire: State Role as Shield for Consumer Has Grown." 1989. *Omaha World-Herald,* January 3, p. 32.

NATIONAL ASSOCIATION OF INSURANCE COMMISSIONERS (NAIC)

120 West 12th Street, Suite 1100   Hall of the States, Suite 636
Kansas City, MO 64105–1925   444 N. Capitol Street
(816) 842–3600   Washington, DC 20001–1512
     (202) 624–7790

ORGANIZATION AND RESOURCES

The National Association of Insurance Commissioners is an organization of the chief insurance regulatory officials of the fifty states, the District of Columbia, and four U.S. territories. The business of insurance is primarily regulated by state governments, and the mission of the NAIC is to provide a forum for the exchange of ideas and the formulation of sound regulatory policy that will protect policyholders and help maintain the financial stability of the insurance industry. The fifty-five-member organization is governed by an elected three-person executive committee that serves one-year terms. The staff of 200 is directed by Executive Vice President David B. Simmons.

Members work on issues of common concern through five committees—on life insurance, accident and health insurance, personal lines of property and casualty insurance, commercial lines of property and casualty insurance, and special issues. More specialized subcommittees and task forces advise the main committees; state regulatory staff and insurance company experts serve on subcommittees and task forces.

NAIC's financial services division provides members with support in financial regulation, computer audit techniques, reinsurance, and international insurance issues. It publishes the *NAIC Financial Condition Examiners Handbook* and provides computer support for financial examinations through a network by which members can access its data base, including company statement filings. In 1990, the NAIC adopted a financial regulation standards and accreditation program under which nine states have subsequently been certified.

Using its data base of company financial statements, NAIC has developed procedures to identify companies that are outside acceptable solvency, liquidity, or profitability parameters. A special team of examiners spends several weeks each year examining data on at-risk companies that are identified for further attention by individual insurance departments.

The NAIC's research division prepares both standard and custom reports and analyses to support insurance regulators' financial surveillance, rate regulation, actuarial analysis, market analysis, and related needs. Standard statistical reports include Auto Insurance Data Base and Profitability by Line by State. Areas of particular recent interest include workers' compensation, medical malpractice, small group health rating, and credit insurance. A library of materials on insurance, regulation, management, computer technology, and related topics is available in print and nonprint format for members' use.

To help regulators monitor the financial condition of insurers' securities investment portfolios, the NAIC maintains a specialized Securities Valuation Office in New York City. It determines the uniform accounting values of insurers' securities investments for all NAIC members; each January it publishes the quality ratings and prices for some 185,000 securities owned by U.S. insurance companies.

Recommended policies and procedures for regulating company behavior in claims handling, advertising and promotion, producer licensing, forms and rates, company management, and direct consumer information and services are published in the *Market Conduct Examination Handbook.* Model laws, regulations, and measures to improve examination tracking are available to NAIC members; several data bases and information systems are part of this support. The names of insurance agents and companies that have been subject to formal regulatory or disciplinary action are available; searches of these data are available upon request to members of the public. In 1990 the NAIC staff began developing a centralized nationwide complaint data base; data from member jurisdictions continue to be added, but the complete network will take a number of years to develop.

The NAIC became involved in education and training in 1985; programs deal with insurance issues and regulation for commissioners, professional regulatory staffs, and other interested persons. The Commissioners Education Program orients new commissioners and senior staff to insurance and insurance regulation. The Financial Examiners Education Program, initiated in 1990, is designed for beginning financial examiners.

Since its founding in 1871, the NAIC has been involved in addressing issues affecting insurance consumers. Consumer guides to buying Medicare supplement, long-term care, and cancer insurance are available directly and through member departments; guides on auto insurance and solvency are forthcoming. NAIC staff provide assistance to members investigating insurance fraud cases, act as liaison with federal investigations, and serve as a clearinghouse for information about individuals who have been connected with insurance fraud.

POLICY CONCERNS

The most persistent and potentially powerful issue bringing the NAIC to the national policy arena is the McCarran–Ferguson Act, which establishes state (as opposed to federal) regulation of insurance. The NAIC's general position is that the industry is best regulated at the state level and McCarran–Ferguson should be protected as it is. Since the mid-1980s it has faced various attempts to amend this legislation and preempt state regulatory authority. Current congressional proposals would restrict the antitrust exemption for insurance provided in McCarran–Ferguson; NAIC argues that altering currently accepted collective data use would unsettle the marketplace, causing dramatic pricing variations, instability, and reduced availability of insurance. The practices that are described by the NAIC and insurers as accepted collective data use are described by some congressional adversaries as price-fixing and unlawful tying practices. International trade issues have posed recent risks to state regulators. The NAIC has assisted U.S. trade negotiators on the General Agreement on Tariffs and Trade in relation to trade in services and issues of preemption of state authority.

Other issues bringing the NAIC to national visibility in recent years are the sale of health insurance policies designed to supplement Medicare for senior citizens and the development of national financial regulation standards to strengthen the solvency surveillance of insurance companies. In the area of Medicare supplement, the NAIC has responded to federal legislative directives by revising its model regulations to encourage standardized policies, require a higher loss ratio (65 percent) for individual companies, increase reporting requirements, impose a mandatory certification program, and increase civil and criminal monetary penalties for violators.

Federal restructuring of financial services, particularly the possibility of allowing banks to move into insurance, continues to be an issue of concern to the NAIC. It is reluctant to see the upheaval in the industry it regulates that would follow federal permission for banks to underwrite and sell insurance. The 1974 federal Employee Retirement Income Security Act (ERISA), with its complex provisions and amendments, involves NAIC attention and input. Most recently, NAIC has expressed doubt that ERISA provides sufficient protection to workers covered by self-funded, multiple employer welfare arrangements. The NAIC opposes expansion of ERISA preemptions of state regulation to include small employers and favors reform efforts to decrease regulatory fragmentation and broaden risk sharing in the health insurance marketplace for small employers.

While the usual posture of the organization is to oppose federal interference, there are areas in which the NAIC seeks federal action. It strongly supports efforts to make insurance fraud a federal offense and has worked with Congress to adopt legislation with the strongest possible penalties. It also is active in protecting those provisions of the federal Racketeer Influenced and Corrupt Organizations Act which allow state insurance regulators to sue when acting as receivers or liquidators of financially impaired insurers.

TACTICS

The NAIC develops and adopts model laws and regulations its members may propose for their individual jurisdictions to enact. Numbering over 200, these are published as the *NAIC Model Laws, Regulations, and Guidelines.* NAIC staff monitors jurisdictions considering these in order to provide support materials that may aid in getting the models adopted. In some cases, enactment of the model laws is required for the insurance department to be accredited by the NAIC. For example, model laws on managing general agents, reinsurance intermediaries, and financial examinations are required for departments to be accredited in financial regulation.

NAIC's Washington office staff monitors federal legislative proposals, hearings, and administrative activity relating to state insurance regulation. NAIC's unique expertise is called upon for testimony before congressional hearings and in rulemaking proceedings. NAIC staff members work with members of Congress and their staffs and with agency officials in developing proposals and planning strategy. Members of NAIC are kept informed about federal events with the monthly *Legislative Update,* news releases, and special alerts. Using the judiciary is another tactic available to the NAIC; its legal staff files amicus curiae briefs in cases of general interest to state insurance regulators.

Media relations on federal issues are handled by NAIC staff. They respond to journalists' inquiries, provide background information, and put reporters in contact with appropriate state regulators for interviews.

In 1991, the NAIC approved the use of up to $50,000 to fund consumer participation at NAIC meetings. Qualified applicants are selected by a board appointed by the NAIC officers and include two consumer representatives; consumer participants are reimbursed for travel expenses.

FURTHER READING

Barnes, Don. 1992. ''The Self-Destruction of State Supervision?'' *National Underwriter,* April 27, p. 47.

Brostoff, Steven. 1991. ''Dingell to NAIC: States Need Federal Oversight.'' *National Underwriter,* February 25, pp. 5–6.

Claybrook, Joan. 1988. "Ensuring Fair Insurance Practices." *Public Citizen,* May/June, p. 20.

Crenshaw, Albert B. 1991. "When the Security Blanket Begins to Unravel." *Washington Post,* national weekly edition, July 29–August 4, p. 20.

Fisher, Mary Jane. 1992. "Uncertainty on Insurance Issues Is in the Air." *National Underwriter,* April 13, p. 20.

Issues 1992. 1992. Kansas City, Mo.: National Association of Insurance Commissioners.

Meier, Kenneth J. 1988. *The Political Economy of Regulation: The Case of Insurance.* Albany: State University of New York Press.

"The NAIC in the 80s: Changing with the Times." 1988. *Council Review* (American Council of Life Insurance), June, pp. 2–3.

Services to NAIC Members. 1992. Kansas City, Mo.: National Association of Insurance Commissioners.

NATIONAL ASSOCIATION OF MANUFACTURERS (NAM)
1331 Pennsylvania Ave. N.W., Suite 1500
Washington, DC 20004–1703
(202) 637–3000

ORGANIZATION AND RESOURCES

The National Association of Manufacturers considers itself to be the most important "voice for manufacturing" in Washington, D.C. This 501(c)(6) organization, with a 1990 budget of $15 million, received most of its funding from its 12,500 member companies and their subsidiaries. Challenged by the lobbying role claimed by specialist manufacturing trade associations and the increased number of governmental and public affairs activities undertaken in Washington by individual companies, NAM has had to develop a working relationship with these voices for segments of American manufacturing. NAM was founded in 1895 and has a staff of almost 200.

POLICY CONCERNS

NAM moved its headquarters to Washington, D.C., in 1974 in order to deal with governmental regulation. Concerns focused on taxes, welfare, the role of agencies like the U.S. Federal Trade Commission, development of new energy sources, and concerns about the cost of energy to businesses. Subjects added in the 1980s included corporate takeover tactics, clean air, and clean water. Other subjects of concern reflect the importance of governmental action in relationship to trucking deregulation, employee drug testing, health care, campaign finance reform, product liability, and trade and competitiveness (e.g., the European Union and the North American Free Trade Agreement). The organization's goal in the general area of trade and competitiveness is what NAM officials call a national "pro-manufacturing" policy.

TACTICS

NAM publications acknowledge the existence of government affairs activities of member firms; NAM stresses that its activities on the Washington scene can reinforce those other efforts. Thus, member services are stressed. These include issue briefs, newsletters, and information for corporate public action committee managers, such as congressional scorecards. The organization also produces NamNet, an on-line public policy information system, which makes available computerized status reports on key legislation pending in Congress.

Besides congressional and executive branch lobbying on its own, NAM has headed coalitions on civil rights, global climate change, energy, occupational safety, and other topics when these issues have come before Congress in recent years.

FURTHER READING

Cowan, Alison Leigh. 1993. "A Long-silent Pritzker Speaks Up." *New York Times,* December 1, p. D6.

Hoerr, John P. 1990. "The Strange Bedfellows Backing Workplace Reform." *Business Week,* April 30, p. 57.

Pear, Robert. 1993. "Business Group Assails Scope and Cost of Clinton Health Plan." *New York Times,* October 21, p. A20.

NATIONAL ASSOCIATION OF RAILROAD PASSENGERS (NARP)

900 Second Street N.E., Suite 308
Washington, DC 20002
(202) 408–8362

ORGANIZATION AND RESOURCES

The National Association of Railroad Passengers speaks on behalf of consumers interested in expanded and improved passenger train service through AMTRAK, the government corporation created to operate the nation's passenger train system. Membership dues are $20 yearly, and half that for those over sixty-five. Part of a member's dues go to support *NARP News,* which is published monthly. In addition, NARP has a 900 phone number service to provide breaking news to interested members.

POLICY CONCERNS

NARP alerts rail passengers to changes in AMTRAK policies, reports on new routes and equipment, and on state rail transportation initiatives when they are operationalized or under consideration. NARP wants to see less use of automobiles in the context of a national transportation policy that relies more on the use of mass transit, intercity passenger rail, and ride sharing. These and other, more energy efficient and environmentally sound transportation alternatives constitute what the organization calls its Campaign for New Transportation Priorities. In this it is often joined by lobbyists for rail unions and opposed by organizations, like the American Association of State Highway and Transportation Officials, that argue the case for building more highways and upgrading existing parts of the highway system.

NARP monitors AMTRAK authorization bills, congressional actions concerning the Department of Transportations budget for AMTRAK operations, and rail line improvement projects (e.g., the Northeast Corridor Improvement Project). Although generally supportive of AMTRAK, the organization does sometimes fault the agency's operations, especially when they have brought passenger complaints (e.g., standees on unreserved seating trains and substandard food service). Thus, the organization supported much that went into the Intermodal Surface Transportation and Efficiency Act (ISTEA) and is working to ensure its implementation by the federal government and the states.

NARP also monitors state legislation, especially actions that provide logistical and budget aid for mass transportation. In turn, that has brought it to support expanded allowable uses for gas tax revenue at the federal and state levels. Many NARP members serve on advisory boards for state commuter rail and mass transit lines and bring a dual perspective on the usefulness of rail transportation.

TACTICS

A range of lobbying, public information, and research activities supports these policy concerns. NARP studies are widely distributed on Capitol Hill and to other organizations (e.g., environmental groups such as the Sierra Club,* regional councils with state transportation responsibilities, etc.). NARP and its supporters in Congress would like the organization and/or its members to be officially recognized as consumer representatives on boards associated with mass transportation policy-making for AMTRAK, ISTEA, and similar areas.

State organizations of rail consumers work with NARP. Examples cited in the organization's literature include the Arizona Rail Passengers Association, similar groups in Georgia and Iowa, Train Riders Northeast, the Wisconsin Rail Coalition, and the Citizens Transportation Action Campaign.

FURTHER READING

NARP News. Monthly. Washington, DC: National Association of Railroad Passengers.

NATIONAL ASSOCIATION OF REALTORS (NAR)

430 N. Michigan Avenue   777 14th Street N.W.
Chicago, IL 60611–4087   Washington, DC 20005–3271
(312) 329–8417   (202) 383–1289

ORGANIZATION AND RESOURCES

The National Association of Realtors calls itself the largest trade and professional association in the United States. Founded in 1908, NAR now claims over 805,000 members across the country. Members, who belong to one or more local real estate boards, consider themselves the eyes and ears of the home-buying public. NAR's total expenses in 1991 were $90,377,924. The association, a federation of fifty state associations and over 1,800 local real estate boards, publishes *Realtor News* and *Briefing Papers* for its members.

POLICY CONCERNS

NAR's policy concerns have mirrored, to some extent, the changes that have taken place in the national economy. For example, in the late 1970s NAR's Washington staff monitored issues connected with energy conservation and the development of new sources of energy such as solar power. Another major NAR emphasis is on housing and credit policies. Because NAR's members operate small businesses all over the United States, the organization is concerned about changes in laws governing labor–management relations, tax policy, and other small-business requirements.

TACTICS

In the 1990s, the organization took up national policy concerns under the following general headings, each of which corresponds to an association sub-committee: (1) energy, environment, and development; (2) housing and community development; (3) federal taxation; and (4) financial institutions and federal budget. That means NAR focuses on actions by the Federal Reserve System, the U.S. Treasury, and the Department of Housing and Urban Development. Officials at NAR also need to follow issues brought by governmental regulatory agencies, such as the Federal Trade Commission and the Federal Communications Commission, concerning sales and marketing issues.

The early 1990s saw a revival of concern about discrimination by sellers and mortgage lenders against women, people with disabilities, African-Americans, and other minority group members. Discrimination concerns mean increased scrutiny by the U.S. Justice Department. Finally, in addition to all that is going on nationally, realtors must attend to state and local government officials on issues ranging from zoning to appraisal rules.

FURTHER READING

Giese, William. 1990. "Home Buyer Quarrel Clinic." *Changing Times,* January, p. 20.

Lesley, Elizabeth. 1990. "In Real Estate." *Washington Monthly,* November, pp. 34–39.

———. 1992a. "Break for Black Realtors?" *Black Enterprise,* June, p. 48.

———. 1992b. "The Lawsuit That Could Cut Home Prices." *Business Week,* January 20, p. 78.

Razzi, Elizabeth. 1993. "The Fight for Agent Disclosure Spawns a Surprising Alliance." *Kiplinger's Personal Finance Magazine,* April, p. 101.

NATIONAL ASSOCIATION OF REGULATORY UTILITY COMMISSIONERS (NARUC)

1102 Interstate Commerce Commission Building
Constitution Avenue and 12th Street N.W.
Washington, DC 20423

Mailing Address:
P.O. Box 684
Washington, DC 20044–0684
(202) 898–2200

ORGANIZATION AND RESOURCES

The National Association of Regulatory Utility Commissioners is a quasi-governmental, nonprofit corporation composed of governmental agencies engaged in the regulation of public utilities and carriers. Its mission is to serve the consumer interest by improving the quality and effectiveness of public regulation in America. NARUC defines the essence of the regulatory process as the search for truth, the careful weighing of competing claims, and just decisions calculated to advance the public interest.

The call for the 1889 meeting that led to the founding of the Association was issued by the Interstate Commerce Commission to the state commissions for the purpose of promoting greater uniformity and expertise in regulating the railroads. Judge Thomas M. Cooley of Michigan, prominent jurist, author, and professor, is regarded as the "founding father" for his vigorous promotion of the idea that state and federal regulators need to cooperate. The focus on cooperation and uniformity has remained while other carriers and utilities have been added as subjects of regulation over the years.

Voting membership in NARUC is restricted to members of state, federal, and territorial commissions engaged in the regulation of public utilities or carriers. Staff members and commissioners and staff of other regulatory bodies are allowed to join as associate, nonvoting members. The present membership of 377 includes the Federal Communications Commission, the Federal Energy Regulatory Commission, the Interstate Commerce Commission, the National Telecommunications and Information Administration, the Nuclear Regulatory Commission, the Postal Rate Commission, the Rural Electrification Administration, the Securities and Exchange Commission, the U.S. Departments of Energy, Labor, and Transportation, sixty-two state agencies drawn from every state, the District of Columbia, Guam, Puerto Rico, the Virgin Islands, the cities of Houston and New Orleans, and fourteen Canadian agencies. Although federal agencies are members, NARUC is recognized as representing the state viewpoint in its advocacy work.

Officials of the association are elected annually for one-year terms; by tradition federal members are not elected to offices and the five regional affiliates rotate the nominees for offices among their members. Thus the second vice president, who moves up to first vice president, then to president, will be from the Mid-America, then Southeastern, Western, Great Lakes, and New England affiliates in turn. All voting members are expected to serve on one of the eight standing committees on administration, communications, electricity, energy conservation, finance and technology, gas, transportation, and water. An effort is made to achieve regional balance on committees. The standing committees of commissioners are supported by twenty-three more specialized staff subcommittees whose members are appointed for one-year terms and are balanced among the various regions. Committees and subcommittees meet at least three times a year to initiate and complete studies that may result in policy recommendations to the executive committee or to the membership meeting at its annual convention. A Washington staff of fifteen is under the direction of Paul Rodgers, administrative director and general counsel. The Association's budget is approximately $1 million annually.

Since the 1950s NARUC has sponsored education and training for regulatory commissioners and staff. Annual two-week seminars are conducted at Michigan State University, and training programs are included with three annual meetings and at additional times and locations. Specialized conferences for state transportation staff, engineering staff, attorneys, water specialists in the East and West, and on regulatory information are sponsored by NARUC. In 1976, NARUC authorized the establishment of the National Regulatory Research Institute at Ohio State University in Columbus to provide member commissions with technical assistance and timely, high-level policy research on regulatory issues. The Institute includes faculty in economics, engineering, finance, accounting, law, and public administration.

NARUC provides members a weekly bulletin that reports on regulatory agency and court decisions, congressional action, and other regulatory issues. An annual report that includes state commission regulations and statistics is published, as are the proceedings of the annual conventions of the association.

POLICY CONCERNS

NARUC is devoted to advancing commission regulation, and promoting uniformity of regulation by the commissions, coordinated regulation by the state commissions, and cooperation of the state commissions with each other and with the federal regulatory commissions. It emphasizes that the basic obligation of a regulatory agency is to assure the establishment and maintenance of such public utility and carrier services and facilities as may be required by the public interest, and to see that they are operated safely and provided at rates that are just and reasonable. NARUC maintains that rates should be fixed at the lowest reasonable level necessary to maintain the economic stability of the utility or carrier to render safe and adequate service.

The Association attempts to protect commission jurisdictions from encroachment. It argues that legislatures should not bind regulatory agencies to particular ratemaking and accounting theories, thereby depriving them of flexibility. It also is concerned to protect the exercise of independent judgment in commissioners' exercise of their statutory authority; to that end it advocates fixed terms of six years or more, comparable compensation between state and federal agencies, and other insulation from political influence. NARUC takes the position that regulatory agencies should render decisions expeditiously after public proceedings open to access by all interested parties; transcripts of proceedings should be provided at or below cost.

NARUC advocates the protection of state regulation of utilities and carriers because it keeps government close to the governed and stimulates prompt and responsive protection of the consumer interest. It argues that state agencies are best equipped to determine the justness and reasonableness of proposed rates and to discern the individual requirements of differing localities for safe and adequate service and facilities. State regulation also is said to best facilitate innovation and experimentation that allow the states to be testing grounds for the nation. Accordingly, NARUC takes the position that the federal government should regulate only the interstate aspects of utility and carrier operations that are beyond the ability of the states to effectively regulate because of geographic limitations. Intrastate aspects and interstate aspects of primarily local concern should be preserved for state regulation. Where Congress decides to enact new legislation that will impact state regulation, NARUC argues that it should stimulate cooperation by including joint federal–state boards for decision making, state advisory committees, minimum federal standards for state adoption and enforcement, federal matching grants-in-aid to state participants, and similar provisions. NARUC also asks that the federal government pay the travel, food, and lodging expenses of state representatives participating in such cooperative activities because of the national benefit that results.

NARUC advocates promotion of energy conservation and efficiency by regulatory agencies and takes the position that government should encourage the optimum development and use of domestic energy supplies from both conventional and unconventional sources. The Association maintains that states should continue to license energy-generating plants; federal participation should not interfere with the right of a state to prevent the construction of unwanted facilities within its borders. Neither federal nor state governments should levy excise or sales taxes on utility or carrier services that are essential to the public welfare.

The Association takes the position that utilities and carriers should not diversify into unrelated operations, so that full management resources are devoted to public service. Where both publicly owned and privately owned utilities compete in a service area, NARUC advocates that they be treated so that neither is favored. Also, where government is a customer, it should pay its fair share of the cost so that other consumers do not subsidize government users.

Finally, NARUC argues that review of regulatory decisions should be by courts of general jurisdiction rather than by courts whose jurisdiction is limited to regulatory decisions. It maintains that the latter have a tendency to assume a regulatory role instead of performing the conventional role of judicial review. Furthermore, federal courts should abstain from exercising jurisdiction until utilities and carriers have exhausted state administrative and judicial remedies.

TACTICS

By promoting the study and discussion of regulation, NARUC seeks to increase the uniformity of regulation, promote cooperation, and advance the quality of regulation. Its implicit argument is that the failure of a state to respond to public needs invites federal intervention.

The Washington staff monitors developments of regulatory interest in Congress, federal agencies, and the courts, and furnishes information to members through a weekly newsletter, special reports, and other supporting material. As the organizational spokesperson for state utility regulation, NARUC's expertise is regularly called upon for congressional testimony and regulatory comment. Legal and financial analysis of developing issues is conducted by staff to support the interests of state regulators. NARUC maintains liaison with other organizations, both public and private, that have an interest in utilities, energy, and transportation. It appoints state members to federal–state joint boards in communications and advisory committee members of the Electric Power Research Institute, the Gas Research Institute, and the Nuclear Electric Insurance Limited.

FURTHER READING

Crew, Michael A., ed. 1992. *Economic Innovations in Public Utility Regulation.* Norwell, MA: Kluwer Academic Publishing Group.
Derthick, Martha, and Paul J. Quirk. 1985. *The Politics of Deregulation.* Washington, DC: Brookings Institution.
Gormley, William T., Jr. 1983. *The Politics of Public Utility Regulation.* Pittsburgh: University of Pittsburgh Press.
The NARUC and the Quest for Excellence. 1991. Washington, DC: National Association of Regulatory Utility Commissioners.
National Association of Regulatory Utility Commissioners: Members, Committees, Policy. Annual. Washington, DC: National Association of Regulatory Utility Commissioners.

NATIONAL ASSOCIATION OF STATE UTILITY CONSUMER ADVOCATES (NASUCA)
1133 15th Street N.W., Suite 575
Washington, DC 20005
(202) 727–3908

ORGANIZATION AND RESOURCES

The National Association of State Utility Consumer Advocates illustrates the broadened Washington presence of organizations of government officials from the state and local levels since consumer protection issues took on added importance in the 1960s. NASUCA represents officials in thirty-seven states and the District of Columbia who advocate the consumer position on utility issues such as the availability and pricing of electrical power, natural gas, and telephone service. The organization publishes *NASUCA News* every other month.

POLICY CONCERNS

NASUCA represents its members' interests in Washington public policy debates about energy regulation, federal–state energy policy, and the like.

TACTICS

Like other organizations of state and local government officials involved in consumer protection activities (e.g., the National Association of Medicaid Directors, Association of Food and Drug Officials, etc.), NASUCA can speak to the scientific and technical issues that come up in debates about governmental regulation. Establishing an office charged to advocate for consumer interests in state and national utility regulatory decision making was a goal of consumer activists that took on greater urgency during the oil shocks of the 1970s and the debates about decontrol of energy prices in the early 1980s.

FURTHER READING

Geddes, R. Richard. 1992. "A Historical Perspective on Electric Utility Regulation." *Regulation,* Winter, pp. 75–82.
Gormley, William T. 1983. *The Politics of Public Utility Regulation.* Pittsburgh: University of Pittsburgh Press.
"Misreading Meters." 1985. *Consumer's Research Magazine,* November, p. 38.

NATIONAL AUDUBON SOCIETY (NAS)

666 Pennsylvania Avenue N.W.   950 Third Avenue
Washington, DC 20003   New York, NY 10022
Tel (202) 547–9009   (212) 832–3200
Fax 202–547–9022

ORGANIZATION AND RESOURCES

By virtue of its incorporation in 1905, the National Audubon Society is one of the oldest environmental organizations in the United States. In fact, NAS can trace its roots back even further, to organizations formed to promote bird-watching in several states before that date. One of the original reasons for the creation of a national organization in 1895 was protests by women who sought to protect wild birds from Florida hunters seeking feathers for hats. Such attempts by ornithologists, naturalists, and other conservationists to influence consumer buying habits should strike a sympathetic chord with the generation of "green" and concerned consumers that has developed in the 1990s.

Today the National Audubon Society claims about 600,000 members and publishes *Audubon* and *American Birds* bimonthly. With a budget of $44 million, the NAS operates nature sanctuaries around the country and provides a range of services to its members, who are organized into 40 state and 500 local groups.

POLICY CONCERNS

Almost a century after its founding, the NAS is still concerned about the preservation of birds and other wildlife in the United States and worldwide, as can be seen in its activities on issues such as wetlands protection. NAS has always opposed hunting; its members split on this issue at one time, and some left to form the National Wildlife Federation. However, the two organizations put these differences aside to work together to advance issues concerning the need for increased governmental protection of wildlife habitat.

Concern about the effects of toxins on people, wildlife, and the habitats of both have brought NAS members into a wide variety of health and environmental issues where they often find common cause with consumer advocates. In the 1960s many Audubon members became concerned about the use of DDT and other chemicals after reading Rachel Carson's *Silent Spring*. Besides a continuing concern about agricultural policy (e.g., water pollution, soil erosion, and agricultural chemicals), NAS has focused organizational resources on the creation and strengthening of such legislation as the Resource Conservation and Recovery Act, clean air and water legislation, Superfund, and the Toxic Substances Control Act.

TACTICS

On a range of agro-environmental issues—from pesticide use to wetlands— NAS and its usual consumer allies, such as Public Voice for Food and Health Policy,* Community Nutrition Institute, National Coalition Against Misuse of Pesticides,* and Public Citizen,* often encounter opposition from farm groups such as the American Farm Bureau Federation, the National Agricultural Chemicals Association,* and lobbyists representing other agribusiness organizations. Environmental and consumer organizations have joined with sustainable agriculture advocates, organizations representing family farmers, and others since 1985 to improve the conservation practices required when farm bills are considered by Congress.

The Audubon Society also pushes for increased protections for wetlands in discussions of the Clean Water Act. Opponents on these issues include real estate developers, oil interests, and timber lobbyists. During the Bush administration the issue was posed when proposed rules for identifying new wetlands became a controversial issue. At this time, NAS got information out to its members through *Wetlands Newsline,* which provided legislative updates and advised how to contact members of Congress. NAS is seen as one of the mainstream environmental organizations by Washington insiders.

FURTHER READING

Palmer, Elizabeth A. 1992a. "Chemical Firms Run to Congress for Relief from Local Laws." *Congressional Quarterly Weekly Report,* May 16, pp. 1331–1332.
———. 1992b. "House Panel Approves Rewrite of Disputed Pesticide Law." *Congressional Quarterly Weekly Report,* May 23, pp. 1443–1445.

NATIONAL CATTLEMEN'S ASSOCIATION (NCA)

1301 Pennsylvania Avenue N.W.	5420 S. Quebec Street
Suite 300	P.O. Box 3469
Washington, DC 20004	Englewood, CO 80155
(202) 347–0225	(303) 694-0305

ORGANIZATION AND RESOURCES

The National Cattlemen's Association is the chief voice in Washington, D.C., for the nation's cattle industry. It was founded in 1977, replacing several livestock organizations including the National Cattle and Horse Growers Association, founded in 1894. NCA, which claims that raising cattle now is American agriculture's largest industry, has forty-seven state organizations and twenty-nine national breed groups (e.g., Hereford, Charolais). The organization's staff numbers about 40 and there are approximately 230,000 members, mostly farmers, ranchers, breeders, and feeders. The NCA has offices in Englewood, Colorado, and Washington, D.C., and publishes *Cattlemen's News & Views* and *Regulatory Update.*

POLICY CONCERNS

In the 1990s the National Cattlemen's Association faces several important challenges. After more than two decades of accumulating information about the links between diet and health, the cattle industry has had to find ways to show that eating beef is compatible with a healthy lifestyle. Consumers also want to know more about how cattle are raised—what the effects are of the use of animal drugs, whether the industry is paying for the natural resources used to bring cattle to market—and whether taxpayers are getting their money's worth from government agriculture programs that cattle producers have come to expect.

Leaders of NCA's predecessors in Washington battled New Deal programs for agriculture but benefited from the increased governmental activism in the economy that resulted. And although the NCA still opposes governmental activism, cattlemen and cattlewomen pushed for and benefited from the Meat Import Act, passed by Congress in 1968. In the 1970s the organization's leaders and members became convinced that NCA needed to closely monitor what was going on in Washington as governmental actions and adverse economic conditions increased, leading the organization to open an office in the nation's capital in the mid-1970s.

Current topics, in addition to a continuing effort to overcome concerns about the healthfulness of beef, include government's interest—and that of the public—in water, wetlands, erodible land, animal drugs, and other topics. Issues that are drawing more public attention include animal welfare, grazing fees, clean air and water, and food safety. The latter came to the fore in the public mind with the deaths in 1993 of children who had eaten undercooked hamburgers bought at Jack-in-the-Box outlets in the Northwest. Finally, NCA officials have an agenda that involves issues of international trade, especially questions about bans on U.S. exports by the European Community.

TACTICS

Several themes visible in recent legislative battles suggest that NCA is on the defensive in the 1990s. Sometimes it works hard to preserve the status quo. Wherever possible—keeping grazing fees low and fighting off the urban and taxpayer claims for renegotiation of existing water rights legislation are good examples—NCA representatives in Washington are fighting to keep benefits already in place. Second, NCA tries to hold other issues off the agenda altogether or, failing that, to contain them. Charges made by consumer advocates like the Foundation on Economic Trends'* Jeremy Rifkin fall into that category. NCA also has expended a lot of energy to meet critics' charges about the dangers of a high-fat diet.

In the process, the NCA has had to broaden its focus in Washington beyond the U.S. Department of Agriculture and its Food Safety and Inspection Service and Forest Service. It has had to attend to the departments of the Interior (e.g., Secretary Bruce Babbitt's attempts to raise grazing fees by legislation or regulation) and Treasury (e.g., tax issues), and the Environmental Protection Agency. Criticism from Rifkin's Foundation on Economic Trends* (FET) and the Beyond Beef campaign was countered by touting comments from the American Heart Association and American Dietetic Association that lean meat could indeed be part of a recommended diet.

NCA tries to counter assertions by FET and other consumer (e.g., Center for Science in the Public Interest,* Public Voice for Food and Health Policy,* etc.) and environmentalist critics with messages about cattle growers' commitment to environmental stewardship and to food safety. On those issues, NCA touts its quality assurance programs, work with veterinarians on medication, and commitment to federal meat inspection and animal welfare.

FURTHER READING

Browning, Graeme. 1991. "Farming Without Toxics." *National Journal,* June 29, p. 1656.

12 Myths & Facts About Beef Production. n.d. Washington, DC: National Cattlemen's Association.

NATIONAL COALITION AGAINST PORNOGRAPHY (NCAP)
800 Compton Road, Suite 9224
Cincinnati, OH 45231
Tel (513) 521–6227
Fax 513 521–6337

ORGANIZATION AND RESOURCES

The National Coalition Against Pornography, which was founded in 1983, has as its objective to assist concerned members of the religious community and anti-pornography groups around the country.

POLICY CONCERNS

Like Action on Smoking and Health* and other anti-smoking advocates, parents and others concerned about the deleterious effects of rock music lyrics on minors such as the Parents' Music Resource Center,* and groups upset at the effects of drunk drivers such as Mothers Against Drunk Driving,* the National Coalition Against Pornography is interested in restricting the sale of a particular kind of consumer product that its members consider a danger to the health and/or well-being of the community.

TACTICS

NCAP's objective inevitably draws the attention of organized producer and industry interests and often brings into the ensuing political controversies a variety of third parties who seek to voice other public interests. Thus, anti-pornography organizations like NCAP draw criticism from organizations representing publishers and others concerned about protecting more "artistic" (i.e., serious) products and attract support from conservative organizations.

Recently, some women's groups concerned that pornography may lead to rape and other violent acts against women have found themselves on the same side as anti-pornography activists like NCAP in some of these debates. Organizations like the American Civil Liberties Union and watchdog groups monitoring conservative organizations like People for the American Way may also get involved. Participation in national policy debates by organizations representing state and local officials and the law enforcement community is likely when legislation restricting the sale of these products is debated.

Besides participating in national debates, NCAP helps groups active in local campaigns to eliminate obscene and/or pornographic materials and media judged harmful to minors by providing information about conducting petition drives, organizing workshops, producing and disseminating research, and operating a speakers' bureau.

FURTHER READING

Stetson, Dorothy McBride. 1991. *Women's Rights in the U.S.A.: Policy Debates & Gender Roles.* Pacific Grove, CA: Brooks/Cole.

NATIONAL COALITION AGAINST THE MISUSE OF PESTICIDES (NCAMP)
530 7th Street S.E.
Washington, DC 20003
(202) 543–5450

ORGANIZATION AND RESOURCES

The National Coalition Against the Misuse of Pesticides (NCAMP), founded in 1981, calls itself a grass-roots network. It has a five-person staff headed by Jay Feldman, who came to this job from Rural America, where he headed that organization's health programs. The organization is a 501(c)(3) organization claiming a membership of 300,000. It is concerned about the dangers that consumers face from the chemicals they purchase to use in their homes, and on their lawns and gardens, as well as the chemicals agricultural producers and manufacturers use in the production of food and other necessities that people buy and use every day.

Like Citizens' Clearinghouse for Hazardous Wastes, NCAMP considers itself a service organization for local groups all over the country. Accordingly, it provides information through two newsletters, *Pesticides and You* and *NCAMP's Technical Report,* so that consumers can put pressure on government and business for the production and use of safer alternatives. In 1991 about 80 percent of NCAMP's budget came from grants and the rest from contributions (8.7 percent), publication sales (3.7 percent), membership dues (2.8 percent), and small, miscellaneous sources. Members, including individuals and organizations, elect a fifteen-member board of directors, which hires the organization's staff.

POLICY CONCERNS

NCAMP's principal policy objectives are to enforce and strengthen existing procedures to remove dangerous pesticides from the market and to promote development and implementation of alternative pest management programs. That means strengthening the Federal Insecticide, Fungicide, and Rodenticide Act and the Federal Food, Drug, and Cosmetic Act (FFDCA). Other objectives are necessitated from nearly half a century of experience with these products, including indoor air decontamination, notification of residential populations of pesticide usage, and protections for people with multiple chemical sensitivity.

NCAMP is seeking to uphold and expand local authority to regulate pesticide usage (especially lawn and garden pesticides), notification, and reporting. Therefore it opposes legislation introduced into Congress since 1991 that, if enacted, would preempt local authority to regulate pesticides. Other current legislative initiatives include "circle of poison" legislation, which would put greater restrictions on exports to other countries of pesticides banned in the United States, out of fear that they would be used on produce that could then be imported into the United States.

TACTICS

As the only organization working on pesticide policy full time, NCAMP is engaged in a wide range of efforts in Washington, in the state capitals, and at the grass-roots level. NCAMP has an interesting position on pesticide legislation pending in Congress, preferring parts of the legislative status quo in the FFDCA's Delaney clause, which bars from processed food any chemical known to be carcinogenic. Many environmental and consumer groups take a middle position on this issue. Along with some influential liberals on the congressional health committees, many other groups are willing to abandon this zero-risk policy in exchange for a negligible-risk policy that would apply to foods (e.g., fresh fruits and vegetables) currently outside the ambit of the FFDCA's Delaney clause.

Since 1991 NCAMP and other pesticide critics have expanded the pesticide "wars" at the local level in order to take advantage of the Supreme Court decision in *Wisconsin Public Intervenor* v. *Mortier,* which allows local governments to enact stricter standards than the federal government does. At the same time, opponents, including the chemical industry and chemical user groups (e.g., the National Agricultural Chemicals Association,* the Chemical Manufacturers Association, the American Farm Bureau Federation, the Grocery Manufacturers of America,* the National Pest Control Association, the National Food Processors' Association, and the Professional Lawn Care Association) seek less stringent but uniform federal standards.

NCAMP provides technical assistance to localities seeking to enact pesticide control legislation and/or hold off industry lobbying efforts. The organization also distributes information on the effects of different pesticides and how to get help for pesticide poisoning, and holds an annual National Pesticide Forum where people can exchange information and share organizing strategies. Officials participate in public policy debates in Washington, including testifying before congressional hearings and working with the media (e.g., staff members appear on television public affairs shows, place articles about pesticides in newspapers, and try to get media attention for speeches and meetings).

FURTHER READING

Kriz, Margaret E. 1990. "Shades of Green." *National Journal,* July 28, pp. 1826–1831.
———. 1992. "Poison Gamesmanship." *National Journal,* April 18, pp. 930–933.
"Pesticide Bill Prompts Mixed Reviews." *Science News,* October 22, p. 270.
Safety at Home: A Guide to the Hazards of Lawn and Garden Pesticides and Safer Ways to Manage Pests. 1991. Washington, D.C.: NCAMP.

NATIONAL COALITION ON TELEVISION VIOLENCE (NCTV)

P.O. Box 2157
Champaign, IL 61825
(310) 248–5433

ORGANIZATION AND RESOURCES

The National Coalition on Television Violence was founded in 1980 with the objective of reducing the glamorized violence on broadcast television. Carole Lieberman, M.D., is chairperson and research director. An eight-member board of directors and a large number of associated endorsers include researchers and activists on the issue of aggression. NCTV is a nonprofit organization funded by membership dues and contributions; over 3,500 persons are members. Its budget is approximately $100,000 annually and it has a staff of five.

NCTV publishes a bimonthly newsletter, regular reports on aggression research for members and media writers, weekly TV monitoring reports, and numerous research reports, bibliographies, and educational materials. These include reports on TV cartoons and violent video games, bibliographies on war toys, boxing, and sports violence, and educational materials on monitoring music videos, movies, and prime time television.

POLICY CONCERNS

NCTV's primary concern is to focus attention on the harmfulness of glorified violence depicted in the media and to inform consumers about how much violence is on television. It also studies and draws attention to the violence in other entertainment media, such as films, music videos, and video games. Glamorization of alcohol, tobacco, and illicit drug use, and degrading sexual portrayals also are topics of concern. NCTV supports programming that depicts the harmful consequences of violence, drinking, and smoking. It advocates programs that stress problem resolution through nonviolence, break down divisive stereotypes, promote strong family and social bonding, and have high educational content. NCTV supports and calls for more warm, challenging, and thought-provoking programming for all ages.

TACTICS

NCTV has developed and uses a set of systematic guidelines to define and clarify those acts which are counted as interpersonal physical violence. It monitors prime time and Saturday morning television and films on a systematic basis, tallying and weighting the identified violent acts, and putting them into context by analyzing the message presented in the material. Its contextual guidelines consider these questions: (1) Are violent resolutions shown as the only way to solve problems? (2) Do characters succeed through the use of violence? (3) Are harmful consequences of violence clearly depicted? (4) Are characters portrayed as consistently evil without any good qualities? Account is also taken of the portrayal of alcohol, tobacco, and illicit drug use and degrading sexual situations. This research is the basis for publishing lists of the best and worst shows on prime time and Saturday morning television. The most violent shows are targeted by encouraging members to contact, monitor, and boycott advertisers and television stations. NCTV coalesces with other media watchdog and advocacy groups in efforts such as National Turn off the TV Day.

Gandhi Awards are conferred on pro-social films, actresses, and actors. Public glorification of violence is met with NCTV objections such as its protest of the appointment of Arnold Schwarzenegger as chairman of President Bush's Council on Physical Fitness. NCTV monitors the Federal Communications Commission and the Federal Trade Commission and advocates more consumer-sensitive decision making from those agencies.

Reports of scholarly research supportive of NCTV's mission are included in the newsletter, providing members with additional persuasive data for contacting policymakers or taking direct action of other kinds. NCTV reaches out to a wider audience through its relationship with the media; press releases, guest editorials, and interviews with broadcast and print journalists spread the message.

Research findings assembled by NCTV accompanied introduction of the Television Violence Act, sponsored by Senator Paul Simon (D–IL) in 1990. The bill encouraged, but did not require, the three major broadcast networks to set common standards on the level of violence in their programming. ABC, NBC, CBS, and the American Civil Liberties Union opposed the measure as a threat to First Amendment rights. NCTV regards the provision as insufficient and advocates public service announcements to warn viewers of the harmful effects of watching violence.

FURTHER READING

About the National Coalition on Television Violence. 1992. Champaign, IL: NCTV.
"Agency Poses Stiffer Tests for Kids' TV." 1993. *Omaha World-Herald,* March 4, p. 3.
Cannon, Carl. 1989. "Evidence from Studies Confirms TV's Connection with Violence."
		Omaha World-Herald, May 30, p. 11.
"Increased Violence Is Reported in Children's TV Programming." 1990. *Los Angeles Times,* January 26, p. 8.
Mills, Mike. 1994. "New Bills Make Waves for Broadcasters: Industry Prepares to Fight Calls to Curb TV Violence." *Congressional Quarterly Weekly Report,* January 29, pp. 161–63.
NCTV News. Bimonthly. Champaign, IL: National Coalition on Television Violence.
Siano, Brian. 1994. "Frankenstein Must Be Destroyed: Chasing the Monster of TV Violence." *Humanist,* January/February, pp. 20–25.
"Talks on TV Violence Encouraged." 1991. *Congressional Quarterly Almanac 1990.* Washington, DC: Congressional Quarterly, p. 374.

NATIONAL CONSUMER LAW CENTER (NCLC)

11 Beacon Street	1875 Connecticut Avenue N.W.
Boston, MA 02108	Washington, D.C. 20009
(617) 523–8010	(202) 986–6060

ORGANIZATION AND RESOURCES

The National Consumer Law Center was founded in 1969 for the purpose of making consumer law work for the interests of low-income people. NCLC has established itself as the nation's consumer law specialist, acting to bring understanding of complex consumer rights within the reach of less specialized practitioners. Even though consumers have many more rights now than they did in the 1970s, claiming those rights is still a major challenge upon which NCLC focuses.

The Center provides case assistance, legal research, and technical advocacy training in consumer and energy law for neighborhood Legal Services programs, private attorneys involved in *pro bono* work, lay advocates of the poor, and leaders of community organizations. For private attorneys and law firms, NCLC provides fee-for-service consultation.

Willard Ogburn is executive director of the NCLC. Support for the budget of approximately $1 million comes from foundation donors and federal and state grants to the tax-exempt organization. The Center's periodical publications include *NCLC Energy Update,* a bimonthly newsletter containing current information on energy and policy developments with particular focus on their impact on the poor. *NCLC Reports* is a quarterly newsletter covering new developments in the practice of consumer law for attorneys who represent low-income clients. NCLC also publishes an eleven-volume Consumer Credit and Sales Legal Practices series that provides technical assistance in all major aspects of consumer law.

POLICY CONCERNS

NCLC is motivated by the understanding that low-income consumers are particularly vulnerable to unscrupulous merchants and companies that cause auto repossessions, home foreclosures, utility disconnections, and other such crises. In areas such as energy, usury, credit, and debt harassment, NCLC acts to extend available consumer protections to those with ordinarily less access to legal help. Among its concerns are consumer bankruptcy and foreclosure laws, consumer credit provisions and usury standards, debt collection and repossession practices, deceptive sales practices and warranties, odometer law, truth in lending, and equal credit opportunity requirements and reporting.

TACTICS

NCLC works primarily by making its resources available to low-income clients, their attorneys, and community leaders. The Center's utility specialists in Boston and Washington closely monitor developments in utility and energy law to improve services for low-income consumers. NCLC provides analysis of highly technical information and specialized litigation support that local attorneys can use for their clients. The organization's expertise in credit law and work with Legal Aid attorneys was exemplified by its intervention in a Virginia case that saved 500 low-income and elderly homeowners from foreclosure. It intervened in the 1985 bankruptcy of the Landbank Equity Mortgage Company of Virginia, filing a class action suit to protect borrowers. NCLC persisted until the lenders settled, resulting in a savings to consumers of between $2.5 and $3 million.

By helping neighborhood attorneys to spot the issues and select legal arguments, authoring state-of-the-art legal practice manuals, representing consumers in local utility rate hearings, and litigating precedent-setting cases before the Supreme Court, NCLC shapes consumer law. The Center provides expert testimony and empirical research and analysis for public agencies such as state energy offices, attorneys general, and public utility commissions. Its work with state energy agencies is exemplified by the development and implementation of a utility payment plan for low-income consumers in Rhode Island that reduced the percentage of income consumers spent on heating costs and gained them assurance of continued service. In a federal lawsuit concerning energy company price overcharges during the oil crisis, NCLC negotiated a settlement accepted by the court which specified that low-income consumers will receive an equitable share of the funds. The Center continues to monitor the states' compliance with this agreement.

FURTHER READING

"Living Without Lawyers." 1993. *Public Utilities Fortnightly,* January 15, pp. 17–28.
The Nation's Consumer Law Expert: National Consumer Law Center. n.d. Boston: National Consumer Law Center.

NATIONAL CONSUMERS LEAGUE (NCL)
815 Fifteenth Street N.W., Suite 928
Washington, DC 20005
(202) 639–8140

ORGANIZATION AND RESOURCES

The National Consumers League (NCL) is a tax-exempt, nonprofit membership organization representing consumer and worker interests to government and business decision makers. It works to win and maintain health and safety protections and to promote fairness in the marketplace and workplace. Founded in 1899, it is the oldest consumer group in existence. Although originally intended to rally consumers to improve conditions for workers by supporting minimum wages, maximum hours, and social insurance, it soon moved into consumer protection issues, supporting the original federal pure food and drug legislation. NCL continues to play a key role in basic labor and consumer issues as both an educator and an advocate.

NCL is governed by a forty-five-member board of directors that includes such prominent individuals as Alan Bosch of the AFL–CIO* and Jacob Clayman of the National Council of Senior Citizens.* Members also represent statewide consumer groups, special populations such as minorities, rural communities, and cooperative programs. Linda Golodner is president of the board and executive director of the eleven-person staff. An annual budget of approximately $750,000 is supported by contributions, income from conferences and fundraisers, memberships, and the sale of publications. Membership numbers 8,000 individuals and 100 organizations. An annual survey of the membership solicits input on what programs and priorities the organization should pursue.

NCL Bulletin, a bimonthly newsletter published continuously by NCL since the 1930s, reports on and analyzes consumer issues. The Alliance Against Fraud in Telemarketing, coordinated by NCL, publishes *Quarterly,* a newsletter that informs readers about new fraudulent schemes, consumer education initiatives, and legislative and regulatory developments. The Alliance publishes a comprehensive desktop reference manual on telemarketing fraud for consumer protection agency staff members and other professionals who handle consumer complaints; it also is an official contributor to the Federal Trade Commission–National Association of Attorneys General Telemarketing Complaint System Database.

NCL provides consumers with useful information through brochures, guides, and booklets on a wide range of topics. Among items currently available are five guides on health care services such as hospice, home health care, ambulatory care services, health maintenance organizations, and life care communities; a primer on long-term care; and brochures on how to take medications safely. *The Earth's Future Is in Your Grocery Cart* is a guide to environmentally friendly choices in the grocery store; also available are brochures on auto insurance, recycling, women and AIDS, Pap tests, and over-the-counter medications.

Sponsoring conferences on specific topics is another way NCL reaches the public and interested parties. Issues addressed in this sort of forum in recent years include long-term health care, drug classification, privacy, and the use of 900 telephone numbers. NCL-sponsored conferences are sometimes international in scope; an example is experts from Great Britain, the Netherlands, Canada, and Australia coming together to discuss drug classification in their countries, drawing participants including representatives from congressional offices and committees, public interest groups, health care professionals, trade associations, business, and labor. NCL often sponsors conferences jointly with other entities, such as the conference on privacy issues sponsored in cooperation with the U.S. Office of Consumer Affairs.

NCL offers respected expertise in developing community-based consumer education. In Philadelphia the League developed and conducted a model education program for the elderly, their advocates, family members, and service providers on Medicare and private supplemental health insurance from 1983 to 1985.

Volunteers trained by the League then trained their peers through workshops and direct counseling in hospitals, senior citizen clubs, and church groups. The Health Care Financing Administration of the Department of Health and Human Services awarded the League its Beneficiary Services Award for its work on this program. In 1990 and 1991, NCL received grants from the Food and Drug Administration to develop consumer education materials for low-literacy consumers and to create new models for distributing health care materials in minority neighborhoods. More recently, NCL and the American Nurses' Association and Foundation received a grant from the W. K. Kellogg Foundation to improve access to community-based health care. New and existing coalitions of nurses, public interest groups, labor unions, businesses, community leaders, and other health care providers will be mobilized to strengthen access to health care for underserved populations.

POLICY CONCERNS

Issues of current concern to NCL include child labor, the minmum wage, meat, poultry, and seafood inspection, food and drug product labeling, telemarketing, consumer fraud, funeral industry practices, and health care. It works as part of a coalition to educate the public about child labor exploitation, strengthen existing protections against it, and work for better enforcement of protective laws and regulations. The League further opposes importation of goods made with child labor. NCL supports mandatory seafood inspection, including whistle-blower protection for workers; it worked to prevent implementation of the Streamlined Inspection System for cattle and poultry and continues to be part of the coalition monitoring its implementation.

The League cooperates in educational efforts to alert the public to the high incidence of telemarketing fraud and to steps that can be taken to protect potential victims. It supported passage of the Nutrition Labeling and Education Act that set guidelines for food labels on calories, fat, and other nutrients, and joined with other groups opposed to Bush administration delays in implementation. It supports stronger Food and Drug Administration (FDA) enforcement powers, including giving the FDA recall authority, subpoena powers, record inspection authority, embargo authority, and authority to exact civil penalties. The League supports strong Federal Trade Commission requirements for disclosure of prices of goods and services in the funeral industry.

NCL advocates stronger protection of nursing home residents. It also supports the standardization of ''medigap'' insurance policies and has surveyed state insurance regulators to document their failure to provide detailed consumer information on such coverage. NCL supports federal regulation of long-term care insurance but prefers comprehensive federal health care legislation including nursing home care. Attempts to cut Medicare benefits in order to balance the federal budget are staunchly opposed by NCL; at the same time, it supports requiring prescription drug manufacturers to give discounts to state Medicaid programs.

Workplace safety has long been of concern to NCL. It monitors administration releases of new regulations limiting worker exposure to hazardous wastes in construction, maritime, and agricultural industries. NCL has been involved in financial services issues as an advocate of truth-in-lending requirements. Tax reform opportunities have brought the group before Congress among those seeking a more progressive distribution of tax burdens. Motor vehicle safety, alcohol consumption, cigarette smoking, indoor air pollution, and AIDS are among other consumer health and safety topics NCL is working on.

Looking toward the future, issues about which NCL is raising attention include privacy in the workplace and parental leave. It believes that the right to privacy is one of the most important consumer and worker issues of the 1990s. Workplace decisions, medical and health records, financial and credit records, telecommunications, and direct marketing are among the threats to privacy being explored by NCL. New technology such as debit cards and electronic benefit cards, and what they will mean for consumers, is also on the NCL front line.

TACTICS

NCL approaches policy with a three-pronged strategy of research, education, and advocacy. Members of Congress and state legislatures look to the League for information about the consumer perspective on proposed legislation. It is frequently invited to testify before congressional committees and state legislatures. NCL staff members help write legislation and plan hearings on issues; in a recent year staff worked in these ways with the House Government Operations Committee, House Education and Labor Committee, Senate Labor Committee, and Select Committee on Youth and Families joint hearings.

The League is often called upon by federal and state government agencies for advice and written comments on proposed regulatory changes that affect consumers. The Food and Drug Administration, the Federal Trade Commission, the Department of Labor, and the U.S. Office of Consumer Affairs are the federal executive agencies it works with most frequently.

NCL has institutionalized access to executive branch agencies through its position on numerous advisory committees. These include the U.S. Health and Human Services Managed Care Council and National Committee for Quality Assurance, the National Institutes of Health Consensus Development Conferences on osteoporosis and dental anesthesia and sedation, the Food and Drug Administration's Consumer Consortium, and the Environmental Protection Agency's Clean Air Act Advisory Committee. It chairs the Department of Labor's Child Labor Advisory Committee.

Relationships with the mass media are carefully cultivated, and NCL is frequently interviewed for its commentary on the consumer impact of issues. Coalescing on issues is another frequent practice for NCL; it ordinarily allies with groups representing consumers, labor, and the elderly but also is open to joint projects with business and trade associations. NCL coordinates a coalition of consumer groups, federal agencies, representatives of state government, consumer protection offices, trade associations, labor unions, and businesses called the Alliance Against Fraud in Telemarketing. The League cochairs the Child Labor Coalition with the American Youth Work Center and the International Labor Rights Education and Research Fund; its purpose is to curb child labor abuses in the United States and abroad. Individual consumers coming to NCL with specific product or service complaints are helped in getting them resolved. NCL staff members refer complainants to local government agencies and organizations specializing in those problems.

FURTHER READING

The Alliance Against Fraud in Telemarketing. n.d. Washington, DC: National Consumers League.
Health Care Agenda. n.d. Washington, DC: National Consumers League.
Mills, Mike. 1993. "Bills to Free up Airwave Space, Fight Phone Fraud Advance." Congressional Quarterly Weekly Report, February 27, p. 456.
Nadel, Mark V. 1971. The Politics of Consumer Protection. Indianapolis: Bobbs-Merrill.
NCL Bulletin. Bi-monthly. Washington, D.C.: National Consumers League.
NCL Fact Sheet. Annual. Washington, DC: National Consumers League.
Publications. Annual. Washington, DC: National Consumers League.
Vose, Clement E. 1957. "The National Consumers League and the Brandeis Brief," Midwest Journal of Political Science 1: 177–190.

NATIONAL COUNCIL OF SENIOR CITIZENS (NCSC)
1331 F Street N.W.
Washington, DC 20004–1171
(202) 347–8800

ORGANIZATION AND RESOURCES

The National Council of Senior Citizens is an advocacy organization dedicated to the belief that America's elderly are worthy of the best the nation can give. NCSC was founded in 1961 by the AFL–CIO* during the struggle for Medicare. It now includes 5,000 senior citizen clubs and 36 area and state council affiliates, with a total membership of 5 million people. Members are recruited by direct mail to the general public and by union retiree directors who help organize clubs for retired workers. The National Council is governed by an eight-member executive committee of the board of directors, which is comprised of thirty-five regional members and eighty-six members at large. Lawrence T. Smedley, executive director, holds a Ph.D. in economics from American University and came to the NCSC from the Occupational Safety, Health, and Social Security Department of the AFL–CIO. The NCSC staff numbers 120; the budget is $62 million, including approximately $55 million in government grants and contracts. Of the revenue not restricted by government projects, about half comes from member dues and contributions; housing project fees represent a smaller but substantial portion of unrestricted revenue.

NCSC nurtures its grass-roots strength through field operations that train senior citizen activists in grass-roots lobbying techniques and running effective issue campaigns. An annual convention and regional conferences where activists discuss issues and lobbying strategies, and enhance their skills help keep the NCSC network connected. *Senior Citizens News,* published monthly for all members, reports on organization activities and issues of concern to senior citizens. It includes a ''Congressional Voting Record'' as a special annual supplement. *The Retirement Newsletter* is a monthly, four-page bulletin supplied in bulk to pension funds and international unions for distribution to their retirees; in many cases it is mailed out with monthly pension checks. The newsletter provides information on federal and state programs including housing, transportation, legal services, nutrition, and consumer issues.

The National Senior Citizens Education and Research Center is a nonprofit 501(c)(3) corporation established by the NCSC. It publishes *The Retirement Newsletter* and operates the Nursing Home Information Service, which was founded in 1974 as a clearinghouse for consumers interested in long-term care. The service maintains and shares a data base on facilities and literature on how to find, choose, and evaluate appropriate services and facilities, and on how to find advocacy when care is below standard. It publishes a newsletter, the *Nursing Home Patients Bill of Rights,* and *How to Choose a Good Nursing Home.* The Education and Research Center is working with the Resolution Trust Corporation in an effort to expand housing for the elderly by purchasing properties from failed savings and loans. Also on its agenda is the expansion of services for residents in existing properties managed by the NCSC Housing Management Corporation.

Since 1968 the NCSC has administered the Senior AIDES Program on behalf of the U.S. Department of Labor. The project is funded by Title V of the Older Americans Act, the Senior Community Services Employment Program. Senior AIDES provides part-time employment for persons fifty-five years of age and older who have limited incomes; in 1990 there were 10,300 persons enrolled in 150 AIDES projects in 27 states and the District of Columbia. Participants receive training to improve their job skills and work in a variety of community service jobs, such as providing food service at nutrition sites, day care for children and older adults, victim assistance, and home health care, and as teachers' aides. Since 1986, NCSC has joined with the Environmental Protection Agency to conduct the Senior Environmental Employment Program, which is authorized under the Environmental Programs Assistance Act of 1984. Senior citizens work at EPA regional offices and laboratories around the country and as native environmental liaisons with Indian tribes.

The NCSC Housing Management Corporation manages 30 buildings throughout the country, comprising more than 3,300 units of housing for the elderly and disabled. Additional projects with construction value of more than $20 million are in various stages of development under NCSC applications for low-interest loans from the U.S. Department of Housing and Urban Development.

POLICY CONCERNS

Maintaining the integrity of Social Security, and Medicare in particular, is the top policy priority for NCSC. Regressive taxation of the poor and the middle class and declining capital gains tax rates are firmly opposed by the NCSC; these concerns have brought it into federal budget debates for more than a decade. It was involved in separating the Social Security Trust Fund from the budget deficit calculation. Termination of pension plans or capture of their "excess assets" by employers has been on NCSC's agenda; it supported legislation to curb these practices, citing evidence that almost 2,000 pension plans have been terminated since 1981, with $20 billion in assets taken from the plans by employers.

Insurance issues affecting senior citizens are of concern to NCSC as well. Increased federal regulation of "medigap" insurance policies, including mandatory loss ratios and prohibitions against selling such policies to those who already have them or are covered by Medicaid, was successfully supported by NCSC in 1990. It is also among the advocates for national health care and has worked to dissuade the American Medical Association* from its previous refusal to back national care.

NCSC was part of the broad coalition supporting family and medical leave legislation. It advocated emergency leave for employees to care for sick parents, a spouse, or a newborn infant, or for personal illness. Legislation was vetoed by President Bush in 1990 but passed by Congress and signed by President Clinton in 1993.

Guaranteeing all Americans the right to decent housing is one of NCSC's goals; it is especially focused on affordable, secure, and decent housing for the elderly. It oversees reauthorization of legislative provisions for low-income elderly housing and has an ongoing interest in appropriations. The 1990 Cranston–Gonzalez National Affordable Housing Act included provisions NCSC and other allies had sought for eight years. However, NCSC continues to point out that the average time an applicant spends on a waiting list for elderly housing is three to five years.

NCSC advocates for residents of nursing homes by working with community groups and government agencies to secure laws and regulations that protect nursing home residents from physical or mental abuse and ensure greater oversight of long-term care facilities. It also seeks to provide increased access to alternatives such as home health care services.

TACTICS

NCSC adheres to its labor heritage with strong participation in voter registration drives and get-out-the-vote campaigns, working phone banks, and attending candidate forums and rallies. The latter events are sometimes attended by "senior truth squads" who come armed with information and pointed questions; candidates whose records are more favorable may have press conferences held on their behalf. NCSC has a political action committee that contributed approximately $115,000 to candidates in 1990, a majority of whom were elected. NCSC support was important in the victories of Lawton Chiles in the Florida gubernatorial race and of Tom Harkin, Paul Simon, and Carl Levin in Senate races.

Grass-roots lobbying tactics are well rehearsed by the nationwide NCSC organization; periodic "Legislative Updates," fast-action "Seniorgrams," and a legislative hotline service are used to target key leaders in selected states and congressional districts. Wide distribution of the annual NCSC Congressional Voting Record helps inform grass-roots activists.

NCSC maintains an active presence on Capitol Hill, taking a leading role on Medicare, Social Security, and pensions, and coalescing with labor, consumer, and civil rights groups on many issues. Activist NCSC members occasionally take to the streets to demonstrate, as they did to call attention to the American Medical Association's position against national health care. It also uses pledge or petition campaigns, gathering signatures to present to Congress in support of its position.

FURTHER READING

Cigler, Allan J., and Burdett A. Loomis, eds. 1991. *Interest Group Politics,* 3rd ed. Washington, DC: CQ Press.

Edsall, Thomas Byrne. 1984. *The New Politics of Inequality.* New York: W. W. Norton.

Pratt, Henry J. 1993. *Grey Agendas: Interest Groups and Public Pensions in Canada, Britain, and the United States.* Ann Arbor, MI: University of Michigan Press.

Progress Report. Annual. Washington, DC: National Council of Senior Citizens.

Public Interest Profiles 1988–1989. 1988. Washington, D.C.: Congressional Quarterly, Foundation for Public Affairs.

Senior Citizen News. Monthly. Washington, DC: National Council of Senior Citizens.

NATIONAL FEDERATION OF INDEPENDENT BUSINESS (NFIB)

600 Maryland Avenue S.W., Suite 700
Washington, DC 20024
Tel (202) 554–9000
Fax 202–554–0496

ORGANIZATION AND RESOURCES

The National Federation of Independent Business, which was created in 1943, styles itself in its 1991 *Annual Report* "*the* advocate for small and independent business owners." With a membership of over half a million, the organization draws support from small businesses in the fields of retail sales, services, construction, and manufacturing. Most are quite small, with over half having five or fewer employees and almost three-fourths employing fewer than ten employees. The organization deploys a fifty-person Washington staff to monitor legislative and regulatory issues, produce research, and engage in other public affairs activities. NFIB publishes *IB Magazine* for its members bimonthly.

POLICY CONCERNS

Early in the 1990s an NFIB survey showed that the most important problem for small business was the cost of health insurance. Also important were labor-management issues, including subjects like parental leave, which was being pushed by labor and its liberal allies in Washington, D.C., and in the states. During the Bush administration the organization opposed the civil rights bill that was finally passed. Other issues of perennial concern include taxes, the federal budget and governmental fiscal responsibility generally, banking, legal reform, the effect of environmental laws on small businesses, and related issues.

TACTICS

The NFIB is often cited for its extensive grass-roots network, which reaches into the district of nearly every elected official in Washington. The organization sometimes works with other business groups but differentiates its members' interests from those of the U.S. Chamber of Commerce* and the National Association of Manufacturers,* which NFIB officials consider spokespersons for big business. NFIB supplements its lobbying and monitoring of regulatory activities affecting its constituency with an active political action committee. It also pursues public affairs initiatives through the media.

The organization works in coalitions with other groups when necessary, as can be seen in the activities of the Healthcare Equity Action League, a coalition NFIB participated in with insurers, hospitals, and other health care providers. Altogether, the organization claimed to represent 1 million employers and 35 million workers. NFIB also was a member of the Carlton Group, formed in 1975. This group of corporate tax specialists, which regularly met for breakfast in a well-known Washington hotel and included the U.S. Chamber of Commerce,* the Business Roundtable,* the Committee for Effective Capital Recovery, and the American Business Conference, claimed considerable success in gaining favorable tax changes in 1980.

Finally, on health care and other issues, NFIB is active at the state level, where it presents the opinions of small, independent businesses to policymakers and is certain to be a major player when Congress takes up health care reform during the Clinton administration.

FURTHER READING

Dennis, William J., Jr. n.d. *Small Business Problems and Priorities.* Washington, DC:
    NFIB Foundation.
Victor, Kirk. 1993. "Swing Time." *National Journal,* June 12, pp. 1402–6.
Vogel, David. 1989. *Fluctuating Fortunes.* New York: Basic Books.

NATIONAL FUNERAL DIRECTORS ASSOCIATION (NFDA)
11121 West Oklahoma Avenue
Milwaukee, WI 53227–0641
(414) 541–2500

ORGANIZATION AND RESOURCES

The National Funeral Directors Association is a federation of state associations with 18,000 members in the 50 states and the District of Columbia. Founded in 1882, it is the largest association of funeral directors in the United States. NFDA represents members that occupy a unique niche in American communities but are also small businesses and share some common small business interests. The typical NFDA member represents a family-operated firm that has been in business for fifty-nine years; many firms represent second-, third-, or fourth-generation family operations. The average number of funeral services members hold per year is 160, although one-third of the members handle fewer than 100 per year. Nearly half of the members serve communities with less than 10,000 population; 80 percent hold an associate or four-year college degree. NFDA has twenty-five staff members under the direction of Robert E. Harden; the annual budget is approximately $5 million.

The Association works to improve relations between funeral directors and other professional groups like clergy, doctors, psychologists, and death and bereavement educators. It has also joined with other professional associations, including those of medical examiners, coroners, and pathologists, in an organized effort at multiple-death disaster management.

NFDA compiles statistics and information, such as an annual survey, available to members to allow them to measure their business against others across the country. Its learning resource center makes available books, videotapes, and home study materials on topics such as embalming and business management, as well as consumer brochures on grief, prearrangement of funerals, and other topics. Seminars and convention programs offer members opportunities to learn about trends and techniques. Tools to enhance member skills in public relations include speech kits, a community relations handbook, and press releases for submission to local media.

Membership benefits available through NFDA include a negotiated music licensing contract with BMI/ASCAP. Materials to help members comply with federal regulations are provided by the Association; compliance manuals are available on the Federal Trade Commission Funeral Rule, the Americans with Disabilities Act, and the Occupational Safety and Health Administration's rule on exposure to bloodborne pathogens. In addition to using the compliance manual on price information disclosure, members may send their general price lists to NFDA for a compliance evaluation.

Members receive *The Director,* a monthly magazine with articles on funeral service and compliance issues. *State Officer's Bulletin* is sent periodically to officers of the state-level associations. Information is available over a news hotline from NFDA headquarters. Other services to members include property and casualty insurance for member businesses, retail and merchant credit card programs, and negotiated discounts.

POLICY CONCERNS

The NFDA is concerned with the impact on members of the Federal Trade Commission rule on funeral industry practices that became effective in 1984. The rule is intended to provide consumers with price disclosures and other accurate information; NFDA's role has been to advocate for making the rule more manageable for its members.

Funeral homes are covered by Occupational Safety and Health Administration (OSHA) regulations. NFDA's concern is that OSHA's regulations are not formulated with consideration of funeral homes' unique characteristics, and its inspectors often are unfamiliar with funeral home operations. The Association advocates making it easier and less costly for its members to comply with OSHA regulations. Environmental regulations on medical wastes apply to funeral businesses, and NFDA monitors both Environmental Protection Agency and congressional initiatives on these issues.

The treatment of prepaid funeral contracts in determining eligibility for Supplemental Security Income is a recent concern for NFDA. While the value of such contracts is fully or partially excluded from income in deciding eligibility, proposals to eliminate these exclusions have come under consideration. Such a change would leave holders of these contracts ineligible for SSI but not able to access the funds held for their funeral. It also would make the purchase of these contracts less attractive for potential buyers.

NFDA is concerned about recent decreases in death benefits available under Social Security and from the Department of Veterans Affairs. Funeral directors are often involved in helping families understand and claim these benefits. Among other policies that impact funeral homes as small businesses are requirements of the Americans with Disabilities Act, the Civil Rights Act, and other employment legislation. Federal legislation to mandate employer-provided benefits such as family leave and health insurance are opposed by NFDA on the grounds of cost as well as other negative impacts.

TACTICS

The staff of NFDA monitors policy directions, collects data from member businesses, testifies before congressional committees and subcommittees and regulatory agencies, works informally with congressional and executive branch staff, and uses grass-roots techniques. NFDA also uses the judiciary, filing petitions, amicus curiae briefs, or test cases.

NFDA's government relations division maintains a political action committee, a political education committee, and a political action network. The political education committee brings in speakers for association meetings, supports the development of special compliance workshops and materials, finances direct mailings to members for rapid mobilization of letter and phone responses to members of Congress, and brings funeral directors to Washington to meet with legislators and regulators. It sponsors an annual Legislative and Leadership Conference in the capital as an organized opportunity for members to visit officials and communicate their concerns. Members of the political action network are called upon to communicate directly with members of Congress, especially those with whom they have a special relationship.

The Association's public relations program is committed to developing a favorable image for funeral service throughout the nation. Through media contacts, press releases, and informational mailings, it works to turn media attention from costs to the caring, professional service of funeral directors.

FURTHER READING

Compliance Manual for the Funeral Industry Practices Rule. 1990. Milwaukee, WI: National Funeral Directors Association.
Join Us. 1991. Milwaukee, WI: National Funeral Directors Association.
Membership Profile and Federal Mandates on Funeral Service. 1992. Milwaukee, WI: National Funeral Directors Association.
Political Action Committee. 1992. Milwaukee, WI: National Funeral Directors Association.
Political Action Network. 1992. Milwaukee, WI: National Funeral Directors Association.
Political Education Committee. 1992. Milwaukee, WI: National Funeral Directors Association.
Pertschuk, Michael. 1982. *Revolt Against Regulation: The Rise and Pause of the Consumer Movement.* Berkeley: University of California Press.
Tolchin, Susan J., and Martin Tolchin. 1983. *Dismantling America: The Rush to Deregulate.* Boston: Houghton Mifflin.

NATIONAL INSURANCE CONSUMER ORGANIZATION (NICO)
PO Box 15492
Alexandria, VA 22309
(703) 549–8050

ORGANIZATION AND RESOURCES

The National Insurance Consumer Organization was founded in 1980 by J. Robert Hunter and Ralph Nader, after the insurance industry lobbied Congress to pass legislation preventing the Federal Trade Commission (FTC) from investigating the insurance business. Curbing the FTC cut consumers off from a potentially important source of information, which NICO seeks to provide. NICO received funding assistance from Nader and maintains a working relationship with the Nader family of organizations. J. Robert Hunter, was president of NICO until 1994 when he became insurance commissioner for the State of Texas. He is a former administrator of the Federal Insurance Administration

(FIA); his best-known achievement there was his decision to have the FIA take over administration of the federal flood insurance program, eliminating the role of private insurance companies. Kathleen O'Reilly succeeded Hunter as NICO president. Former state insurance commissioners James Hunt of Vermont and Howard Clark of South Carolina serve on the NICO board of directors. Membership of NICO is approximately 2,000 persons; memberships and contributions account for about one-quarter of the $200,000 budget, half is from foundation grants, and an additional one-quarter from the sale of publications. The staff numbers four persons.

NICO is the only national organization devoted solely to insurance issues, and it takes positions on the consumer impact of all types of insurance. In spite of its small size, it strives to be a significant player on consumer education and insurance reform issues at state and national levels. It collects data, produces reports that receive wide publicity, and publishes consumer guides such as *Taking the Bite out of Insurance: How to Save Money on Life Insurance* and *Buyer's Guide to Insurance*. It also publishes a bimonthly newsletter and offers a computer service that will analyze a member's life insurance coverage and recommend better alternatives.

POLICY CONCERNS

NICO describes itself as protection for consumers against one of the strongest and richest industries in the American economy with the most powerful lobbying forces at both state and federal levels. Consistent policy themes raised by NICO are that insurers are unscrupulous, state regulation is inadequate, and federal intervention is necessary. NICO publications describe rate-setting practices by insurers as anti-competitive price-fixing, allowing the companies to make unlimited profits. State regulators and the industry are said to have a revolving door relationship, with half of state regulators coming from the industry and moving back into industry jobs when they leave public employment.

The organization advocates that state regulators consider investment income to insurance companies in reviewing and establishing premium rates. Describing the insurance industry as a monopoly, NICO seeks to have the 1946 McCarran–Ferguson Act repealed to make it clear that insurance is wholly subject to federal antitrust standards. Other means of enhancing competition in the industry, such as additional detailed price disclosure and comparison standards, are among NICO's recommendations. The group challenges insurance industry explanations for rising premiums of liability, auto, and health insurance. For example, NICO points out that auto insurance rates have risen four times faster than inflation over a period in which autos are safer and litigation, claim frequency, and auto-related deaths and injuries have decreased. It opposes efforts to change the tort law system, which it describes as motivated by insurers seeking to divert attention from the real source of the problem—greedy, inefficient liability insurers. Proposals advanced by women's groups, such as the National Organization for Women, to outlaw the use of gender as a rating variable in insurance are supported by NICO.

TACTICS

NICO monitors state and federal legislation and rulemaking affecting insurance consumers and data on insurance and insurers. Its analyses and studies usually offer an interpretation that differs dramatically from that presented by insurance providers. Its publications attempt to educate consumers to be more prudent buyers of insurance coverage. The sole consumer voice on insurance, NICO is often asked to testify before congressional and state legislative hearings and to provide expertise in regulatory proceedings. The organization cultivates a warm relationship with the press, and its position statements often receive good news coverage.

Working in coalitions with other consumer groups is common for NICO; Public Citizen* and the Consumer Federation of America* are frequently among its allies. It has recently worked as part of a coalition to evaluate consumer services provided by state insurance departments, devise a model for improvement, and promote that model through the National Association of Insurance Commissioners.* It also takes part in direct state-level efforts such as promoting California's Proposition 103, calling for a major rollback of auto insurance rates. A favorite tactic is to call attention to how much money the insurance industry spends on lobbying—$70 million in an unsuccessful effort to defeat Proposition 103, for example.

FURTHER READING

Brostoff, Steven. 1991. "Industry Slams NICO Life Insurance Book." *National Underwriter,* March 18, p. 25.

Bykerk, Loree. 1989. "Gender in Insurance: Organized Interests and the Displacement of Conflict." *Policy Studies Journal,* 17:2, pp. 261–275.

———. 1992. "Business Power in Washington: The Insurance Exception." *Policy Studies Review,* 11: 3/4, pp. 259–279 (Autumn/Winter).

Meier, Kenneth J. 1988. *The Political Economy of Regulation: The Case of Insurance.* Albany: State University of New York Press.

National Insurance Consumer Organization. 1992. Membership solitication information.

NATIONAL LEAGUE OF CITIES (NLC)
1301 Pennsylvania Avenue N.W.
Washington, DC 20004
Tel (202) 626–3000
Fax 202–626–3043

ORGANIZATION AND RESOURCES

Founded in 1924, the National League of Cities represents the interests of small cities on a range of issues that impinge directly or indirectly on consumer protection policy. The League has almost 1,500 members, a staff of 75, and a budget of $8.5 million in the early 1990s. It is affiliated with a network of state leagues of cities. The organization publishes *Nation's Cities Weekly* for its members.

POLICY CONCERNS

The League and other members of the intergovernmental lobby, concerned about the health implications of industrial and residential waste, supported the reauthorization of the Resource Conservation and Recovery Act in 1987. On these and similar issues the cities can be expected to argue that the businesses involved and the national government bear the majority of the cleanup burden. Cities and states sometimes disagree about which of them should have responsibility to enforce environmental cleanup laws, as could be seen in the case of the Safe Drinking Water Act, another health and safety issue high on the agenda of consumer and environmental groups in the 1980s and 1990s.

Other issues of note have been the League's quality of life agenda, which has included energy conservation, noise abatement, and related issues.

TACTICS

Like other members of the intergovernmental lobby, the NLC may simultaneously be the target and ally of consumer advocacy groups on different issues. Members of Congress, many of them remembering their own start in elective politics, ordinarily will be sympathetic to claims of hardship from mayors and council people they know in their own districts. However, as budgets tightened in Washington in the 1980s, Congress and members of the intergovernmental lobby sometimes found themselves in conflict as federal policy turned from funding grants that provided income to local governments to mandates and requirements that local officials felt were onerous.

FURTHER READING

Anton, Thomas. 1989. *American Federalism and Public Policy.* Philadelphia: Temple University Press.

Merline, John W. 1991. "Cable Rates." *Consumers' Research Magazine,* June, p. 38.

Peterson, Paul, Barry Rabe, and Kenneth Wong. 1986. *When Federalism Works.* Washington, DC: Brookings Institution.

Thomas, John Clayton. 1992. "The Term Limitations Movement in U.S. Cities." *National Civic Review,* Spring/Summer, pp. 155–73.

NATIONAL TAXPAYERS UNION (NTU)

325 Pennsylvania Avenue S.E.
Washington, DC 20003
Tel (202) 543–1300
Fax 202–546–2086

ORGANIZATION AND RESOURCES

Founded in 1969, the National Taxpayers Union sees its chief role as a watchdog warning taxpayers about excessive and wasteful government spending. For NTU's Washington-based staff and some 200,000 members, that does not mean the organization will take a predictable path—supporting conservative causes and opposing governmental initiatives that liberals favor. NTU has a 501(c)(4) tax designation, an affiliated political action committee called the State Victory Fund, and an affiliated foundation. The organization is almost entirely supported by individual donations. NTU publishes *Dollars and Sense* for its members every other month.

POLICY CONCERNS

To see that both government and business are the targets of NTU action, consider the positions the organization has taken against waste by the Pentagon and as a critic of government's role in the savings and loan crisis. NTU's maverick status in the Washington conservative community is further seen in its first victory against government and industry plans for a supersonic airplane, on which issue the organization found itself in agreement with "good government" groups and the fledgling environmental lobby.

Other projects NTU has opposed as government/industry boondoggles include the Clinch River breeder reactor, New York City's Westway highway project, and the federal government's synfuels program. Other recent examples are the organization's alliance with Ralph Nader's Public Citizen* on the issue of congressional and executive branch pay (in particular, "double-dipping").

However, NTU has parted company with consumer and other liberal public interest groups on issues such as its support for a balanced budget constitutional amendment, health care, and state property tax limitation initiatives like Proposition 13 in California and Massachusetts' Proposition 2½. It also confronts the American Association of Retired Persons* and other senior citizen advocates in their preference for repealing the Social Security benefit cuts for retirees under 70 who earn more than $10,000 per year.

TACTICS

Besides entering into coalitions to pursue lobbying strategies in policy debates in Washington and the states, the National Taxpayers Union seeks to influence public and elite opinion through its reports and studies. It also is active in getting its policies accepted through state petition drives. The push, dating back to 1975, for a balanced budget amendment to the U.S. Constitution is a good example of how the organization uses both state and national policy arenas.

FURTHER READING

Dumas, Kitty. 1992. "Budget-Buster Hot Potato: The Earnings Test." *Congressional Quarterly Weekly Report*, January 11, pp. 52–54.

Hager, George. 1992. "Opponents Launch Campaign to Stop Budget Amendment." *Congressional Quarterly Weekly Report,* May 30, pp. 1520–1521.

Herman, Tom. 1994. "Making a Deal with the IRS Grows Easier but May Depend on Where You Live." *Wall Street Journal,* January 26, p. A1.

Hewitt, Paul S. 1994. "A Congressional Report Card." *Wall Street Journal,* January 25, p. A14.

Idelson, Holly. 1992. "Johnston Works to Clear Path for Revamped Energy Bill." *Congressional Quarterly Weekly Report,* February 8, pp. 297–299.

Leuchter, Miriam A. 1990. "How to Protest Your State's Rising Taxes." *Money,* October, p. 28.

McWilliams, Rita. 1988. "The Best and Worst of Public Interest Groups." *Washington Monthly,* March, pp. 19–22.

NATIONAL TOXICS CAMPAIGN (NTC)
1168 Commonwealth Avenue
Boston, MA 02134
Tel (617) 232–0327
Fax 617–232–3945

ORGANIZATION AND RESOURCES

The National Toxics Campaign is a Boston-based organization supporting the activities of grass-roots groups around the country that are concerned about the effects on communities, workers, and consumers of the use, transportation, and storage of toxic materials. Supported by a staff of 1,935, 10 regional offices, and a $1.2 million yearly budget at the beginning of the 1990s, the NTC is an example of the new breed of organizations that straddle the line between consumer and environmental politics. Its members include 1,400 local and national labor, environmental, and citizen groups. The NTC has 501(c)(4) tax status and is affiliated with a 501(c)(3) organization, the National Toxic Campaign Fund. The NTC publishes *Toxic Times* on a quarterly basis. Its current national coordinator, John O'Connor, wrote a book, *Fighting Toxics,* that describes the scope of the problem the group faces and his experience using right-to-know legislation to fight toxics issues as an activist in Massachusetts.

POLICY CONCERNS

The National Toxics Campaign is chiefly concerned with the effective enforcement of federal and state laws governing toxic materials, including pesticides and toxic waste sites. Laws placed on the books on these subjects include the Resource Conservation and Recovery Act, various Superfund statutes, and laws governing treatment and disposal at military sites. The NTC was part of the consumer coalition that opposed the North American Free Trade Agreement in 1993, in part because of what the groups saw as inadequate environmental requirements placed on Mexican factories, and especially the effects of environmental degradation on both sides of the U.S. border.

TACTICS

The activities of the National Toxics Campaign illustrate an emerging reality of consumer and citizen group tactics as it operates at the grass-roots level in the United States. In order to chip away at broad problems, it targets both business and government. In 1989, for example, the NTC succeeded in negotiating an agreement with five supermarket chains that they would require disclosure of pesticide usage on food products they sell. This small step was fiercely fought by several food industry trade associations, the National Agricultural Chemicals Association,* and the Republican leadership at the Environmental Protection Agency.

Like other grass-roots groups, the NTC conducts canvassing and petition drives, presents information to the public on toxics issues, and works closely with local groups concerned about problems with toxics in their neighborhoods and communities. The NTC published a book, *Shadow on the Land,* and worked with the National Family Farm Coalition on getting provisions reducing chemical usage in farming and supporting sustainable agriculture during the farm policy debate in 1990.

FURTHER READING

Kriz, Margaret. 1990. "Shades of Green." *National Journal,* July 28, pp. 1826–1831.
Schwab, Jim. 1989. "The Attraction Is Chemical." *The Nation,* October 16, p. 416.

NATIONAL TRAINING AND INFORMATION CENTER (NTIC) NATIONAL PEOPLE'S ACTION (NPA)
810 North Milwaukee Avenue
Chicago, IL 60622
Tel (312) 243–3035 (NTIC)
Tel (312) 243–3038 (NPA)
Fax 312–243–7044

ORGANIZATION AND RESOURCES

The National Training and Information Center and National People's Action reflect the style of their founder, veteran community activist Gale Cincotta, who is executive director of NTIC, a 501(c)(3) organization, and chair of NPA, an affiliate group that has 501(c)(4) tax status. NTIC, with a staff of 14 and a budget of $612,000 in 1990, serves as the training arm for the 300 community affiliates whose members make up NPA's grass-roots base.

POLICY CONCERNS

NPA is best known for its work seeking to influence corporations, especially banks and other lending institutions, to take a more active role in community development and housing for low- and moderate-income people in Chicago and other cities around the nation. Over the years, the organization has expanded its concerns beyond community reinvestment and redlining issues to organize residents on issues of the costs of such necessities as energy and health care. Recent activities also reflect the effects of federal budget cuts in housing, community development, welfare, and food assistance during the 1980s, and the growing crime and drug crises affecting urban America in the 1990s.

TACTICS

In addition to testifying before Congress about the effects of redlining and community reinvestment policies, NPA's targets in Washington have included the agencies (e.g., Department of Justice, Department of Housing and Urban Development, the Federal Reserve System, Department of Energy, the White House Office on Drug Policy, etc.) that are charged with implementing federal legislation of concern to the organization. The group's corporate targets have included the National Association of Manufacturers,* the American Bankers Association,* and the insurance industry.

In Chicago, the group is noted both for its highly visible protests ("street hits") and for other forms of direct action that get the organization on television and force its targets to pay attention. These confrontations or threats of them sometimes lead to agreements being worked out with banks and other major economic institutions. A salient example of such a resolution was the creation of the Community Reinvestment Alliance to channel reinvestment funds to Chicago's poorer neighborhoods. It is the organization and the "stick" provided by requirements in federal legislation that help push companies to develop such financial "carrots."

FURTHER READING

Buone, Anthony F., and George A. Hachey. 1993. "Ethical Gaps in Financial Services Networks: Lessons from the Mortgage Banking Industry." *Business and the Contemporary World*, Autumn, pp. 140–52.
Garland, Anne Witte. 1985. "Gale Cincotta." *Ms.*, January, pp. 50–51.

NATIONAL WOMEN'S HEALTH NETWORK (NWHN)
1325 G Street N.W.
Washington, DC 20005
(202) 347-1140

ORGANIZATION AND RESOURCES

The National Women's Health Network is the only national public interest organization devoted solely to women and health. It was formed in 1976 by a group of women activists, both laypersons and doctors, who wanted to emphasize health awareness and prevention rather than drugs, surgery, and hospitalization. Prominent individuals such as Olivia Cousins and Judy Norisigian are among those serving on its board of directors. Beverly Baker is executive director of the ten-person staff that includes four interns. More than 10,000 individuals and 500 organizations are members; dues are $25 per year, and members receive a bimonthly newsletter.

POLICY CONCERNS

Issues to which the Network currently devotes attention include drugs and medical devices, menopause and drug therapy, reproductive rights, AIDS, breast cancer, maternal and child health, occupational health, research on women's health, and national health care reform. The Network seeks to ensure that women are not harmed by the marketing of unsafe drugs and mechanical devices; it has been part of the campaigns to require uniform tampon absorbency labeling, to protect consumers' rights to sue because of harm from drugs or devices even though approved by the FDA, and to make some medications available without prescription.

NWHN promotes the view that menopause is a normal part of women's lives and that women have the right to information in order to make their own decisions about drugs. In pursuit of this goal, the Network has been a source of expertise for pamphlets, the "MacNeil Lehrer News Hour," and other efforts to enhance understanding of the effects and side effects of estrogen and other replacement therapy drugs. With respect to reproductive rights, NWHN seeks to enable all women to choose when, where, and with whom they bear children, to support the rights of women who choose to use birth control and abortion, and to be free from coercion in deciding. It is active in pro-choice coalitions, has petitioned the FDA to revise its requirements for approval of new methods of barrier contraception, and supports the effort to get RU-486 into the United States. It also has helped block attempts to withdraw federal funding from family planning centers that offer information about abortion.

NWHN has been a leader in developing and distributing information on women and AIDS. Its goal is to inform women about the necessity of preventive measures, to educate the public about the importance of women's roles as caretakers of people with AIDS and special issues for women with AIDS, and to lead the way in opposing discrimination against people with AIDS.

In promoting good breast care and a reduction in the number of women who are diagnosed with breast cancer, NWHN has championed serious research and funding attention to breast cancer. It has pressured the National Cancer Institute to study dietary prevention of breast cancer, advocates study of a possible connection between cancer and oral contraceptives, and has been part of the effort to make screening mammograms eligible for Medicare coverage. It also works to ensure that other women-specific health issues are addressed and to remedy the underrepresentation of women in clinical research studies.

NWHN also is committed to working for a health care system more appropriate for all women as consumers and providers, and to improve access to health care services for poor women, older women, women of color, lesbians, rural women, and disabled women. It is part of the Committee for a National Health

Program and is providing input on what childbearing policy should be under a national health program, calling for the inclusion of childbearing centers and midwifery-centered care.

TACTICS

Since its founding, NWHN has moved from an outsider organization whose members had to "break into Food and Drug Administration hearings to question the safety of contraceptive pills," to a recognized source of expertise that is invited to testify at such hearings.

The strategy of NWHN is to provide women with reliable, concise information so that they can make informed decisions about health care. Such information is distributed to members, to the media through a national information clearinghouse that answers specific requests, and to national policymakers. For example, the Network conducted the first survey on women and AIDS in all fifty states, territories, and the military.

The Network forms coalitions with other public interest organizations to lobby Congress, regulatory agencies, and particularly the Food and Drug Administration; it will also use the courts. The Network was one of the organizations that used the courts to advocate for Dalkon Shield users to be compensated for their injuries.

FURTHER READING

Hartmann, Susan M. 1989. *From Margin to Mainstream: American Women and Politics Since 1960.* New York: Alfred A. Knopf.

1990 Achievements. 1991. Washington, D.C.: National Women's Health Network.

National Women's Health Network. 1991. Membership recruitment letter.

The Network News. Bimonthly. Washington, DC: National Women's Health Network.

Stetson, Dorothy McBride. 1991. *Women's Rights in the U.S.A.* Pacific Grove, CA: Brooks/Cole.

U.S. Congress. House Select Committee on Aging Subcommittee on Housing and Consumer Interests. 1993. *Hearing on Consumer Health Information for Women: Assessing the Role of the Federal Government.* Washington, DC: Government Printing Office.

NATURAL RESOURCES DEFENSE COUNCIL (NRDC)

40 West 20th Street
New York, NY 10011
Tel (212) 727–2700
Fax 212 727–1773

ORGANIZATION AND RESOURCES

The Natural Resources Defense Council has been an active environmental policy presence in Washington and state government since its founding in 1970. A nonprofit organization claiming 170,000 members, it operates on a budget derived from members' dues, grants from foundations, attorneys' fees, and other sources. Members receive a subscription to *NRDC Newsline* and *Amicus* as part of the yearly dues benefits. They also receive information on environmental issues, related public policy concerns, and the activities of the paid and unpaid scientists, lawyers, and environmental specialists on NRDC's staff.

POLICY CONCERNS

NRDC, along with the Environmental Defense Fund,* constitutes the wing of the environmental movement that first sought out expertise from scientists—and later economists—to bolster attempts to enforce environmental statutes through the courts. For over twenty years, NRDC staffers have provided expert testimony to congressional panels and participated in rulemaking and other administrative forums held by the Environmental Protection Agency and other executive branch agencies.

Throughout its life, the organization has been concerned with a wide variety of issues including nuclear power costs, pesticide regulation, and farm policy. NRDC officials have been involved in regulatory policy and were among those critical of Vice President Quayle's Council on Competitiveness for what they saw as a tendency to circumvent the legislative mandates Congress had placed on regulatory agencies like the Environmental Protection Agency.

In the early 1990s, NRDC attracted national attention when a report the organization produced about the growth retardant Alar, used on the nation's apple crop, highlighted public concerns about food safety and questioned the adequacy of congressional and executive branch decisions about the effects of dangerous chemicals on human health. NRDC's report raised the issue of whether scientific determinations built into law and regulatory policy on the effects of pesticide exposure to the average person should apply to children and others who might be more susceptible to the chemicals found to cause certain cancers in laboratory animals.

TACTICS

The Alar concern, which attracted national attention when the NRDC report served as the basis for an investigation by the popular television news magazine "60 Minutes," is part of a broader agenda for pesticide reform that has been pushed by an environmental and consumer coalition, of which NRDC is a member, since the mid-1980s. The consumer coalition has met with strong opposition from the agrichemical industry (represented in Washington by trade organizations such as the National Agricultural Chemicals Association*) and its allies, as well as agricultural producer groups concerned with narrowing the range of choices that farmers have to control pests and weeds.

The furor that erupted over Alar prompted increased activism by consumer organizations concerned about the effects of chemicals on human health and drew criticism of NRDC's scientific claims from Bush administration officials at the Environmental Protection Agency and from conservative consumer watch-dog groups such as the American Council for Science and Health.*

The Alar controversy briefly concentrated the attention of consumers on food safety issues, led to a sharp drop in apple sales, prompted increased activity regarding food safety by federal agencies, and contributed to the announcement that the manufacturer was voluntarily withdrawing Alar from the market. NRDC remains at the forefront of the environmental community concerned about pesticide policy and, as a result, of agricultural policy generally because of the success of its lawsuits in the early 1990s challenging the Bush administration's interpretation of the Federal Food, Drug, and Cosmetic Act's Delaney clause.

Like other environmental and consumer groups, NRDC sees state government action as crucially important in the 1990s to supplement and improve upon the parts of its policy agenda that can be acheived in Washington. The state focus can be seen in the work on Proposition 128 in California in 1990. Although this referendum, which would have enacted stricter standards on pesticide usage, failed, the strategy of seeking other means to achieve the general objective of obtaining reform legislation from Congress remains in force.

FURTHER READING

Arrandale, Tom. 1992. "The Mid-Life Crisis of the Environmental Lobby." *Governing,*
    April, pp. 32–36.
Browning, Graeme. 1991. "Taking Some Risks." *National Journal,* June 1, pp. 1279–
    1282.
Kriz, Margaret. 1990. "Shades of Green." *National Journal,* July 28, pp. 1826–1831.
———. 1992. "Poison Gamesmanship." *National Journal,* April 18, pp. 930–934.
McWilliams, Rita. 1988. "The Best and Worst of Public Interest Groups." *Washington
    Monthly,* March, pp. 19–22.
Rubin, Alissa J. 1992. "Congress May Break Deadlock on Food Safety Laws." *Con-
    gressional Quarterly Weekly Report,* February 15, pp. 354–356.
Shute, Nancy. 1991. "Unfair Competition." *Amicus Journal,* Summer, pp. 31–34.

O
/

OMB WATCH
1742 Connecticut Avenue N.W.
Washington, DC 20009–1171
(202) 234–8494

ORGANIZATION AND RESOURCES

OMB Watch is a nonprofit research, educational, and advocacy organization that monitors federal executive branch activities affecting nonprofit, public interest, and community groups. Its main focus is the Office of Management and Budget (OMB). Its goal is to encourage broad public participation in government decision making in order to promote a more open and accountable government.

OMB Watch was founded in 1983 during increasing concern over the Reagan administration's use of OMB to control the regulatory process. Gary Bass, PhD., is executive director of a staff of six persons. Approximately 85 percent of the organization's income is from foundations, and the remainder from membership, publication sales, technical assistance, and other activities. Basic membership for individuals, community groups, and public libraries costs $35 annually; membership for national groups, governments, and businesses costs $100. Members receive *Government Information Insider,* a bimonthly magazine on regulation issues, and *OMB Watcher,* a bimonthly newsletter about OMB activities; special alerts and in-depth reports are issued as needed. OMB Watch describes its service as an early warning system for both sophisticated national groups and grass-roots community activist groups serving vulnerable populations.

POLICY CONCERNS

Because of the wide reach of OMB's influence, this watchdog organization has become involved in a variety of policy issues. It has been a source of expertise for labor unions, senior citizen groups, environmental groups, animal rights advocates, and others in specific efforts to understand and influence the role of OMB in shaping the timing and content of regulations. OMB attempts to eliminate housing questions from the 1990 census were blocked by a coalition of research organizations, trade associations, and public interest groups working in response to an OMB Watch alert.

Its publications provide regular updates of issues affected by OMB. Recent salient topics for OMB Watch have included the role of Vice President Quayle's Council on Competitiveness, the power of "executive privilege" against Freedom of Information Act claims, child care regulations, food labeling regulations, nursing home reform regulations, and the administrative costs of the U.S. health care system compared with Canada's.

TACTICS

The organization engages in four primary tactics: information policy, nonprofit education, administrative advocacy, and media relations. Its information strategy consists of monitoring information and regulatory submissions to OMB, advancing policies to increase public access to government information and protect the public's right to know, and encouraging the use of computers in the public interest. Its nonprofit education strategy includes offering technical assistance and training on the budget and on policies that restrict citizens' abilities to express their views, such as Internal Revenue Service restrictions on advocacy and grant administration rules. Administrative advocacy consists of informing the public about executive branch implementation of legislation and disseminating information about how to influence the process. Finally, OMB Watch serves as a resource for policy and technical analysis for the media, provides background information on government processes, and suggests story ideas for contacts in the press.

Among OMB Watch's more visible tactics are its federal budget "road shows" to discuss the deficit and the impact of federal spending on state and local governments. It also serves as a resource for congressional committee efforts to deal with the role of OMB in clearing agency testimony before Congress, privatizing government operations, reviewing proposed regulations, and other financial management initiatives.

FURTHER READING

Blackley, Paul R., and Larry DeBoes. 1993. "Bias in OMB's Economic Forecasts and Budget Proposals." *Public Choice,* July, pp. 215–32.

Dumas, Kitty. 1990. "Congress or the White House: Who Controls the Agencies?" *Congressional Quarterly Weekly Report,* April 14, pp. 1130–1135.

Government Information Insider. Bimonthly. Washington, DC: OMB Watch.
Idelson, Holly. 1991. "Glenn Trying to Shed Light on Rule-Making Process." *Congressional Quarterly Weekly Report,* November 23, p. 3449.
The OMB Watcher. Bimonthly. Washington, DC: OMB Watch.
OMB Watch: Serving as a Catalyst. 1991. Washington, DC: OMB Watch. Pamphlet.
Priest, Dana. 1991. "The Secret (Maybe Illegal) Life of the Competitiveness Council." *Washington Post,* national weekly edition, November 25–December 1, p. 33.
U.S. Congress. House Committee on Government Operations; Government Information, Justice and Agriculture Subcommittee. 1993. *Hearing on the Regulatory Sunshine Act of 1992.* Washington, DC: Government Printing Office.
What Is OMB Watch? 1991. Washington, DC: OMB Watch. Pamphlet.
Woodward, Bob, and David Broder. 1992. "The Super, Secret Deregulator." *Washington Post,* national weekly edition, January 20–26, pp. 8–10.

OPERATION PUSH

930 East 50th Street
Chicago, IL 60615
Tel (312) 373–3366
Fax 312–924–3571

ORGANIZATION AND RESOURCES

Based in Chicago since it was founded in 1971 by Jesse Jackson, People United to Save Humanity, or Operation PUSH, was one of the second generation of civil rights organizations created after the death of Dr. Martin Luther King, Jr. PUSH deserves mention in a volume dedicated to consumer policy because of the pressure its leaders were able to place on major corporations to advance its civil rights agenda and as an example of the interest that religious and civil rights organizations have sometimes taken in consumer policy.

POLICY CONCERNS

People interested in researching the impact of minority consumers in the retail marketplace will find numerous references to PUSH in the African-American press and articles in the national weekly newsmagazines. PUSH has been trying to achieve economic equality for minorities in major institutions of American life. In the early 1990s, PUSH was reorganized to put it on a sounder financial footing and broadened its attention from corporate social responsibility and economic development issues to include campaigns to improve inner city education.

TACTICS

Most visible of PUSH's tactics are boycotts directed at prominent corporations such as the athletic shoe manufacturer Nike, retailers, and fast food chains such as Kentucky Fried Chicken. It also uses other direct action techniques, combined with behind-the-scenes negotiations with corporate leaders. The success of some of these campaigns in getting corporations to increase the number of minority managers, franchisees, and other midlevel officials brought PUSH considerable media attention in the 1980s.

FURTHER READING

Barrett, Todd. 1990. "When Games Turn Nasty." *Newsweek,* August 27, pp. 44–45.
"PUSH Confab Focuses on Economic Development and Education Advancement."
        1990. *Jet,* August 20, pp. 24–31.
" 'PUSH Is Not Dead,' Says New President." 1991. *Jet,* July 15, p. 12.
"PUSH Lays off Entire Staff After Financial Shortfall." 1991. *Jet,* February 11, p. 5.

P

PARENTS' MUSIC RESOURCE CENTER (PMRC)
1500 Arlington Boulevard, Suite 300
Arlington, VA 22209
Tel (703) 527–9466
Fax 703–527–9468

ORGANIZATION AND RESOURCES

The Parents' Music Resource Center was founded in 1985 to increase awareness by parents and others of the effect that music lyrics promoting violence were having on the nation's children and to explore strategies to deal with this problem. The organization has a small staff and 501(c)(3) tax status; in 1990 it had a budget of just over $500,000. It publishes *The Record* six times a year to update supporters—there are no branches or formal members—about the issues that the organization is pursuing. Quickly gaining attention through the congressional testimony and other press coverage generated by prominent founding members—Tipper Gore, wife of the vice president, for example—the organization is reacting to the spread of the consumer society in the last half of the twentieth century to a new category of consumers.

POLICY CONCERNS

In the United States, millions of children spend billions of dollars annually on a range of consumer goods from clothes to fast food to personal care products to entertainment. That industry has noticed this phenomenon can be seen in the design of products like movies and television shows as well as the content of advertisements in media that children and teens read and watch. The larger problem articulated by the Parents' Music Resource Center and a range of other parents', civic, and religious groups is how the larger society has contributed to an erosion of parental authority in the process. The main goal of the PMRC has been to convince the recording industry to voluntarily label its music products.

TACTICS

The group's main tactics to date include coalition formation (e.g., with the national PTA), conferences, outreach to the media, and related means. The principal target has been the trade organization for the nation's music industry, the Recording Industry Association of America, some of whose members have voluntarily "stickered" their records with the warning: "Parental Advisory—Explicit Lyrics" as a result of the publicity the news media have given to the PMRC campaign.

FURTHER READING

Anderson, Jack, and Michael Binstein. 1992. "Baker Zaps Rocker Critical of His Wife."
    Washington Post, February 6, p. B11.
Bruning, Fred. 1985. "The Devilish Soul of Rock 'n' Roll." Maclean's, October 21, p.
    13.
Cocks, Jay. 1985. "Rock Is a Four-Letter Word." Time, September 30, pp. 70–71.
Gowen, Anne. 1993. "Tipper Gore Quits PMRC." Rolling Stone, April 15, p. 20.
Hentoff, Nat. 1985. "The Disc Washers." The Progressive, November, pp. 29–31.
Hoyt, Mary Finch. 1985. "How Parents Can Stop Obscene Rock Songs." Good House-
    keeping, November, pp. 120ff.
Menehan, Kelsey. 1985. "Parents Group Wants Labels on Explicit Rock Records."
    Christianity Today, November 22, pp. 68–69.

PEOPLE FOR THE ETHICAL TREATMENT OF ANIMALS (PETA)
P.O. Box 42516
Washington, DC 20015
(202) 770–PETA

ORGANIZATION AND RESOURCES

People for the Ethical Treatment of Animals was formed in 1980 by two animal activists, Alex Pacheco and Ingrid Newkirk, concerned about the treatment of monkeys in an animal research laboratory. Its goal is to advance public awareness of issues associated with animal protection. As a national nonprofit animal protection organization, it qualifies for tax-exempt status under Section 501(c)(3) of the Internal Revenue Code. In the year ending July 1992, PETA received the bulk of its total operating revenues ($9,024,295) from contributions and donations from members and other interested persons. Other sources of funding included revenue generated by sales of "cruelty-free merchandise," rentals, and investments. Its leaders claim a membership of 400,000 and consider PETA to be part of a larger national and worldwide animal rights movement. PETA's activities are devoted to changing public attitudes toward the use of animal products in the consumer marketplace and the way animals are treated in the course of medical, governmental, and other research.

PETA publishes *Action Alerts* on specific issues and provides information to members four times a year in *PETA NEWS* and *Compassion Corps*. The organization also sponsors an internship program at its Washington headquarters that involves work in various PETA departments (e.g., mail room, outreach, communications, research and investigations) and with other organizations in the Washington, D.C., area, such as the Physicians Committee for Responsible Medicine, the Animal Legal Defense Fund, the National Alliance for Animal Legislation, and the Washington Humane Society.

POLICY CONCERNS

Since its founding, PETA has been concerned about the use of animals in governmental and private medical laboratories. Besides trying to completely stop animal testing, PETA seeks to promote humane trapping standards, protect endangered species, protect animals on the farm and in the food production process, opposes the wearing of fur products, seeks to end cruelty to animals in sports and entertainment, and promotes a meatfree diet. These objectives have met with strong resistance from important industries and professional groups whose economic livelihood is threatened by these objectives. Prominent industries that have felt the brunt of PETA campaigns include beef, pork, and fur producers and the cosmetic and medical testing industries. In addition, PETA has targeted specific fast food corporations such as Burger King and Kentucky Fried Chicken, cosmetic companies such as L'Oreal, and department store chains such as Nordstrom's.

TACTICS

Members and others concerned about issues that PETA considers to be animal cruelty are urged to engage in a variety of protest tactics aimed at companies and those involved in the production and sale of animal products. PETA tries to organize letter-writing campaigns aimed at government decision makers with responsibility for regulating the conditions under which animals are cared for, such as officials at the U.S. Department of Health and Human Services, which has responsibility for labs conducting research for the National Institutes of Health. PETA seeks to extend existing protection to animals through enactment of new legislation, such as the Downed Animal Protection Act, which would give new responsibility to the U.S. Department of Agriculture.

PETA conducts public campaigns based on its investigations of complaints of cruelty to animals and seeks to get consumers to boycott firms and products of which it disapproves and to adopt what the organization calls a "cruelty-free lifestyle." Many of its activities are controversial and draw sharp fire from industry critics. Hovever, PETA has demonstrated skill in attracting publicity from the mass media through inventive protest actions that have included activists dressed as blind bunnies and as vegetables.

FURTHER READING

PETA Guide to Compassionate Living. n.d. Washington, DC: PETA.
Singer, Peter. 1989. "Animal Liberators." *New York Review of Books,* February 2, pp. 36–38.

PUBLIC CITIZEN
2000 P Street N.W.
Washington, DC 20036
(202) 833–3000

ORGANIZATION AND RESOURCES

Public Citizen was founded in 1971 by Ralph Nader as a nonprofit citizen research, lobbying, and litigation organization. It now serves as an umbrella for five ongoing subsections that have their own identities: Buyers Up,* Congress Watch,* Critical Mass Energy Project,* Health Research Group,* and Litigation Group.* The umbrella responsibilities include overall administrative and financial management, fund-raising and development, coordination, and special projects not included in the activities of the subsections. Joan Claybrook is president of Public Citizen, the separate staff of which numbers twenty-three persons in the Washington office; there is a single staff person for Public Citizen California, and a two-person staff for Public Citizen Texas. The five subsections have a total staff of sixty-eight people.

The mission of Public Citizen is to fight for consumer rights in the marketplace, safe products, a healthy environment, safe and healthy workplaces, clean and safe energy sources, and corporate and government accountability. The organization makes a point of not accepting government or corporate grants. Its principal sources of income are subscriptions and publications sales (53 percent), contributions and membership fees (19 percent), grants from Public Citizen Foundation (10 percent), income from Buyers Up (8 percent), rental income (5 percent), court awards (2 percent), and royalty, interest, and other sources (3 percent). Revenues and support for calendar 1991 were reported to be $6,364,000. Annual membership is a $20 contribution or more; this is not tax deductible, but tax-deductible contributions may be made to Public Citizen Foundation, which supports education, litigation, research, and public information activities. Public Citizen membership grew from approximately 40,000 in 1988 to 60,000 in 1989, 100,000 in 1990, and 140,000 in 1991. Members receive *Public Citizen,* a bimonthly magazine published by the foundation, and information on special publications and reports of the organization.

POLICY CONCERNS

Public Citizen has been involved in every major national consumer or government reform issue since its founding. Among these are product safety, truth in packaging, truth in lending, food safety, motor vehicle and highway safety, proposals for a federal agency for consumer advocacy, advertising standards, product liability, shareholder democracy, handling of consumer complaints, funeral industry practices, health care, white-collar crime, whistle-blowing, freedom of information, campaign financing, and congressional salaries. Public Citizen found itself on the defensive during the 1980s, usually seeking to protect gains won before the rise of the Reagan era. Its president, Joan Claybrook, describes that decade as one during which problems of social injustice, abuse of corporate power, and corruption in government were allowed to fester and the system of regulations meant to protect consumers, workers, and the environment was allowed to deteriorate. Public Citizen's strategy during the Reagan era was exemplified by its lengthy but successful lawsuit, with the United Steelworkers of America, against the Office of Management and Budget's use of the Paperwork Reduction Act to block regulations requiring companies to provide health, consumer, and worker information warnings.

Recent issues in which Public Citizen has been involved include the savings and loan industry bailout, particularly the cost, the incidence of the cost, management of the bailout, evidence of regulatory misconduct, and the treatment of white-collar crime by savings and loan executives. It has blocked efforts to narrow and weaken the civil provisions of the Racketeer Influenced and Corrupt Organizations Act. Nuclear waste policy has also been on Public Citizen's agenda; it helped organize a nationwide grass-roots effort to oppose an attempt by the Nuclear Regulatory Commission to deregulate low-level radioactive waste and allow it to be disposed of as ordinary waste. The need for $100 billion to clean up the Pentagon's nuclear facilities also came under Public Citizen fire.

Although Public Citizen supported trucking deregulation, it is now raising safety concerns about the use of larger, multiple-unit trucks on the nation's highways. The cost and quality of insurance has been one of the group's concerns, and it promoted a California ballot measure, Proposition 103, to roll back auto insurance rates. It has opposed efforts to limit product liability suits with arguments that the victims of defective products have the right to recover full damages from the manufacturers. Affordable, accessible health care for Americans promises to be one of the largest issues in Public Citizen's immediate future advocacy. It supports a single payer system like Canada's so that every U.S. resident would be able to choose his or her own doctor or hospital without any copayments or deductibles, and the funding would come through the federal government.

TACTICS

Public Citizen is active in every public forum—Congress, executive agencies, the courts, and the media. Its staff does research, publishing reports, periodicals, and books that are released with well-cultivated media attention. Information from this research forms the basis of testimony before congressional committees, petitioning of regulatory agencies, and special topical policy conferences that it sponsors. Its grass-roots efforts depend on extensive media coverage, the stature and image of Ralph Nader, and mass direct mailings to members. It also uses tactics aimed at both the media and policymakers, as it did in fighting product liability restrictions by bringing in twenty-eight survivors of defective products. These individuals held a dramatic news conference at the National Press Club and then spent two days visiting members of Congress. Their tragic stories were credited with turning the Senate's focus away from lawyers to the people injured by faulty products and services.

Public Citizen not only facilitates coordination among its own subgroups but also arranges alliances with other organizations, such as Citizens for Tax Justice,* Center for Auto Safety,* Consumer Federation of America,* and the American Association of Retired Persons.* The organization also uses the courts, often to prod federal agencies to perform their duties more responsibly, as in the suit against the Consumer Product Safety Commission over its failure to ban the sale of all-terrain vehicles to children under sixteen.

FURTHER READING

Annual Report. Annual. Washington, DC: Public Citizen.

Babbitt, Wendy. 1991. "The Funeral Industry: A Business You'd Rather Ignore—But Shouldn't." *Public Citizen,* July/August, pp. 24–26.

Biskupic, Joan. 1990. "Accord on RICO Revision Is Shaping up in House." *Congressional Quarterly Weekly Report,* March 17, p. 841.

Claybrook, Joan. 1994. "Campaign Finance Reform Needs Grass Roots Push." *Public Citizen,* Summer, p. 2.

Creighton, Lucy Black. 1976. *Pretenders to the Throne: The Consumer Movement in the United States.* Lexington, Mass.: Lexington Books, D. C. Heath.

Crosier, Louis. 1994. "Home Equity Scams Foreclose on the American Dream." *Public Citizen,* Summer, pp. 10–13.

Harris, Richard A., and Sidney M. Milkis. 1989. *The Politics of Regulatory Change.* New York: Oxford University Press.

Nader, Ralph. 1992. "Shopping for Innovation: the Government as Smart Consumer." *American Prospect,* Fall, pp. 71–78.

———. 1994. "GATT Threatens U.S. Environment. Consumer Protection Laws." *Public Citizen,* May/June, pp. 18–21.

Public Citizen. Bimonthly. Washington, DC: Public Citizen.

Schlozman, Kay Lehman, and John T. Tierney. 1986. *Organized Interests and American Democracy.* New York: Harper & Row.

Schwartz, John. 1994. "Smoking Under Siege." *Washington Post,* national weekly edition, June 27–July 3, pp. 6–7.

Victor, Kirk. 1994. "Clinton and Consumers." *National Journal,* January 15, p. 145.

Vogel, David. 1989. *Fluctuating Fortunes: The Political Power of Business in America.* New York: Basic Books.

PUBLIC CITIZEN CONGRESS WATCH (PCCW)
215 Pennsylvania Avenue S. E.
Washington, D.C. 20003
(202) 546–4996

ORGANIZATION AND RESOURCES

Congress Watch is the legislative advocacy arm of Public Citizen,* the consumer organization founded by Ralph Nader in 1971. Pamela Gilbert is the executive director of a staff of twenty with an annual budget of about $770,000, making it one of the two largest segments of the organization. Fund-raising, membership support, and other maintenance issues are handled by the Public Citizen umbrella whose president is Joan Claybrook. The mission of Congress Watch is to investigate and publicize scandal, corrpution, and wrongheaded or anti-consumer policies in both the legislative and executive branches of government.

POLICY CONCERNS

Although the broad assignment of Congress Watch takes it into many issues, a number of themes appear more often than others on its agenda—campaign finance, financial services, white-collar crime, and food and product safety. Reforming campaign finance to limit the role of special interest money has long been a Congress Watch cause; it supports banning or sharply limiting political action committee contributions, limiting campaign expenditures, and funding campaigns with public funds raised by a voluntary income tax checkoff.

Savings and loan deregulation, failures, scandals, and the federal bailout have been prime recent topics in the financial services arena. Congress Watch advocates more efficient handling of the bailout, funding from wealthy institutions rather than middle- and low-income taxpayers, and stronger efforts to punish the fraudulent behavior of wealthy savings and loan executives. Pro-consumer insurance reform proposals find Congress Watch lobbyists on Capitol Hill. It has worked for repeal of the insurance industry's exemption from federal antitrust laws, with the aim of fostering more competition in the insurance marketplace. It also advocates federal oversight of insurer solvency based on its studies of long-term trends in property and casualty insurance.

Protection and empowerment of whistle-blowers is a perennial Congress Watch issue; most recently its lobbyists have advocated allowing whistle-blowers to bring suit on behalf of the government. Defending civil racketeering laws that can be used against white-collar crime such as that in the accounting, securities, and savings and loan industries has been a recent concern for Congress Watch. It has led a coalition of prosecutors, local government officials, plaintiffs' attorneys, and fraud victims against a recent drive by the financial industry to weaken civil racketeering laws.

Recent food safety efforts have focused on higher standards and enforcement of fish inspection laws and proposals to bar the export of pesticides banned for use in the United States. Congress Watch helped persuade Congress to reauthorize the Consumer Product Safety Commission and grant it expanded enforcement authority. It has also been active in the long-standing battle with manufacturing interests over product liability laws; Congress Watch takes the position that existing standards and procedures allow consumers to recover damages from producers of unsafe products.

Congress Watch has been part of the debate over the effects of international trade agreements on domestic health, safety, and the environment. Its position has been that the North American Free Trade Agreement and the General Agreement on Trade and Tariffs include harmful provisions that have been hidden from the public, and it sought to compel the Office of the U.S. Trade Representative to issue environmental impact statements for both agreements.

TACTICS

Congress Watch uses multiple influence strategies: it frequently presents testimony before congressional committees, it publishes reports that it disseminates directly and through the media, it coalesces with other organizations, and it mobilizes citizens through grass-roots organizing. Campaign finance reform has been the subject of a major "Clean Up Congress" campaign pursued with both direct and grass-roots lobbying strategies in alliance with other citizen groups including Citizen Action Fund* and Common Cause.* This campaign has involved building grass-roots coalitions in seventy-five congressional districts, working closely with newspaper editors and local radio talk show hosts, and contacting hundreds of members of Congress and their staffs.

Congress Watch led a coalition of labor, community, religious, and housing groups that worked with Representative Joseph Kennedy in an unsuccessful but well-publicized effort to shift the cost of the savings and loan bailout onto corporations and the wealthy. Michael Waldman (then executive director) and the staff of Congress Watch wrote the Random House publication *Who Robbed America: A Citizens' Guide to the S&L Scandal,* intended to mobilize citizens' anger over the bailout. This was followed by a report titled *The Botched Bailout: Restructuring the Resolution Trust Company,* documenting how the Resolution Trust Corporation has mismanaged the bailout. Congress Watch is poised to press its recommendations each time the administration comes to Congress for additional infusions of funds. Financial consumer associations, to allow citizen input in financial services policy-making, are proposed by Congress Watch as a constructive and protective remedy.

FURTHER READING

Annual Reports. Washington, D.C.: Public Citizen.
Gilbert, Pam. 1991. "Ruckus over RICO." *Public Citizen,* July/August, p. 30.
Kaplan, Robert B. 1990. "New Empowerment Tools." *Public Citizen,* September/October, p. 30.

Pertschuk, Michael. 1986. *Giant Killers.* New York: W. W. Norton.

Radalat, Ana. 1990. "Congress Ducks: Campaign Finance Reform." *Public Citizen,* September/October, p. 11.

———. 1991. "An Embarrassment of Riches." *Public Citizen,* July/August, pp. 9–11.

Schiff, Robert. 1994. "Public Citizen Pushes Reluctant Senate to Pass Gift Ban." *Public Citizen,* Summer, p. 27.

Victor, Kirk. 1994. "Clinton and Consumers." *National Journal,* January 15, p. 145.

Woodall, Patrick. 1993. "Indecent Proposals." *Public Citizen,* September/October, pp. 10–15.

PUBLIC CITIZEN HEALTH RESEARCH GROUP (PCHRG)

2000 P Street N.W., Suite 708
Washington, DC 20036
(202) 872–0320

ORGANIZATION AND RESOURCES

The Health Research Group was founded in 1971 by Ralph Nader and Sidney M. Wolfe, M.D., who continues as its executive director. Its expressed goal is to fight for the public's health and to give consumers more control over decisions that affect their health. Health Research Group is one of five subdivisions under the Public Citizen* umbrella organization and has a current annual budget of about $580,000. It has a staff of 14 and sends its *Health Letter* to 80,000 subscribers for a contribution of $35 or more per year. Within Public Citizen, Health Research Group is the source for information about the safety of drugs and medical devices, public health issues, the delivery of health care, and the quality of doctors and hospitals.

POLICY CONCERNS

Health Research Group considers itself a watchdog of the drug industry and its regulation; it gathers data on drug effectiveness, costs, safety, labeling, and prescription and marketing abuses. It was an advocate for the 1990 Medical Device Amendments that strengthened reporting requirements and recall authority for defective products such as heart valves and pacemakers. Restrictions on use of the silicone gel breast implant have also been a target of the organization's research, publicity, and lobbying.

Health Research Group has been a significant part of the campaign for a smokefree environment. Its research and lobbying resulted in the passage of 1986 legislation requiring health warnings on the labels of snuff and chewing tobacco. More recently, it has protested R.J. Reynolds' advertising targeting of young smokers and the Philip Morris agreement with the National Archives to commemorate the bicentennial of the Bill of Rights that skirts a nineteen-year ban on cigarette promotion on television. It has also worked to expose the links between tobacco industry interests and members of Congress and the executive branch.

Health Research Group expects to be part of the national debate over health care delivery; it is developing strategy for a comprehensive national health program modeled after the Canadian single-payer system. It plans a long-term campaign to replace private health insurers with a universal, federally funded health program. Working with Public Citizen Congress Watch* and Physicians for a National Health Program, it released an analysis of census data highlighting the number of Americans who lose their health insurance in a year. More specific studies related to health care reported abuses in the frequency of Cesarean section births, patient access to medical records, and treatment of the mentally ill. It has been involved in the debate over the potential impact of international trade changes under the North American Free Trade Agreement; its position is that the agreement as submitted for ratification will endanger public health achievements in the United States.

TACTICS

Health Research Group draws on a wide range of strategies, including providing testimony before Congress, publicizing abuses through the media and its own publications, petitioning regulatory agencies (particularly the Food and Drug Administration), and working with state health regulatory agencies. For example, it has recently petitioned the FDA to revise labeling on a common sleeping pill to include information about additional side effects, in order to alert both doctors and patients to the risks involved. It also has testified before Congress and turned over information to the inspector general of health and human services about the practice of pharmaceutical companies' giving doctors cash or free airline tickets to persuade them to prescribe one drug rather than another.

A major recent effort by Health Research Group was the publication of *6,892 Questionable Doctors,* based on data from state medical boards, the Department of Health and Human Services, Medicare, and the Drug Enforcement Administration. Its 1,100 pages list doctors disciplined for overprescribing or misprescribing drugs, criminal convictions, drug and alcohol abuse, substandard care or negligence, and sexual abuse of patients. Its newsletter reports on medical practice abuses such as "patient dumping" and federal efforts to deter the practice.

Working jointly with the National Alliance for the Mentally Ill, it publishes *Care of the Seriously Mentally Ill,* which rates each state's programs for treating seriously mentally ill residents. Ratings are based on the quality of their hospitals, outpatient/community support, vocational rehabilitation, housing, and children's services. It also reported abuses of the Community Mental Health Center program administered by the National Institute of Mental Health, using data obtained through the Freedom of Information Act.

Health Research Group has allied with organized labor to pursue workplace safety issues. For example, it allied with the International Chemical Workers Union to petition and subsequently file a lawsuit over the presence of cadmium in the workplace and treatment of exposed workers. It was joined by five prominent House of Representatives committee chairmen in a 1985 lawsuit against the Occupational Safety and Health Administration for its failure to promulgate regulations governing the short-term exposure of hospital workers to the carcinogen ethylene oxide.

FURTHER READING

Annual Report. Annual. Washington, DC: Public Citizen.

Atkinson, Carla. 1991. "A National Health Plan." *Public Citizen,* July/August, pp. 20–21.

Clinard, Marshall B. 1990. *Corporate Corruption: The Abuse of Power.* New York: Praeger.

Dye, Michael. 1994. "Silent Danger of Medical Malpractice." *Public Citizen,* May/June, pp. 10–13.

Fugh-Berman, Adriane. 1994. "Training Doctors to Care for Women." *Technology Review,* February/March, pp. 34–40.

Goodman, Marshall R., and Margaret T. Wrightson. 1987. *Managing Regulatory Reform: The Reagan Strategy and Its Impact.* New York: Praeger.

Health Letter. Monthly, Washington, DC: Public Citizen Health Research Group.

Schwartz, John. 1994. "Smoking Under Siege." *Washington Post,* national weekly edition, June 27–July 3, pp. 6–7.

PUBLIC CITIZEN LITIGATION GROUP
2000 P Street N.W.
Washington, DC 20036
(202) 785–3704

ORGANIZATION AND RESOURCES

Public Citizen Litigation Group is one of the five subsections functioning under the larger Public Citizen* organization. It was founded in 1972 by Ralph Nader; Alan B. Morrison was the original director and continued in that role until the early 1990s when David Vladeck assumed the job. He directs a staff of eleven, ten of whom are attorneys. Approximately $728,000 of the 1991 Public Citizen expenses were reported for the Litigation Group, making it one of the two largest of the Public Citizen subsections in terms of expenditures.

The multifaceted mission of the Litigation Group is to defend consumer rights, fight for meaningful health, safety, and environmental standards, defend citizens' freedoms and insist on officials' accountability under separation of powers, battle for open government and elimination of excessive secrecy in the executive branch and the courts, act as a watchdog of the professions, protect employees against their employers, and protect the democratic rights of workers within unions.

POLICY CONCERNS

General public interest concerns pursued by Litigation Group include antitrust law, privacy issues, shareholders' rights, and abuses of the franking privilege by members of Congress. Pursuing open government standards has included litigation over the electronic mail system used at the White House, seeking release of tapes from the Nixon White House, and numerous cases involving the unsealing of court records or pursuit of documents under the Freedom of Information Act. Challenging regulators includes oversight of agencies charged with protecting consumers' health, safety, and environment. Litigation Group has been involved in efforts to protect the Delaney clause, to ban the use of methylene chloride in decaffeinating coffee, to communicate the hazards of smokeless tobacco, and to ban the pesticide Alar. Efforts to speed up the installation of passenger-side air bags in autos, to require the Nuclear Regulatory Commission to institute training rules for nuclear plant workers, to enforce rules requiring employers to warn employees about dangerous chemicals in the workplace, and to gain more stringent rules on flammable grain dust have been part of Litigation Group's work.

Recent Litigation Group successes in the area of union democracy and workers' rights have established that union members have the right to a mailing list in advance of the officially scheduled election, in order to effectively campaign for opposition candidates, that union members are entitled to the full set of contract materials and the right to communicate with other members before they have to vote on the contract, and that the Teamsters Union is required to reveal its investment records to see whether there are conflicts of interest. Litigation Group has also blocked efforts to gerrymander union electorates and has protected members' rights to sue employers directly for violations of federal and state law instead of having to rely exclusively on union officers for such protection.

Litigation Group polices the professions and has invested in an ongoing effort to fight restrictions on information useful to consumers of legal, accounting, and other professional services. It has supported advertising of legal services, the availability from nonlawyers of reduced-cost assistance in filing for bankruptcy, and the disclosure of unethical practices and disciplinary proceedings against lawyers and other professionals.

TACTICS

Engaging in litigation is the primary strategy of Litigation Group, but the organization also monitors federal and state legislation and regulation, presents testimony before congressional committees, and participates in regulatory proceedings. In its twenty years, Litigation Group has filed hundreds of cases under the Freedom of Information Act. Among its recent cases were efforts to obtain Food and Drug Administration records showing whether silicone gel may be safely used for breast implants and safety analyses of accidents at nuclear plants. It also secured the release of thousands of pages of Colonel Oliver North's diaries during the Iran–Contra affair. Litigation Group has blocked efforts by the Food and Drug Administration to circumvent the Federal Advisory Committee Act requirements for open meetings by hiring a private consultant to select and conduct the advisory committee.

Among its more notable separation of powers cases were the Supreme Court ruling striking down the Gramm–Rudman–Hollings Act involvement of the comptroller general in federal spending decisions, and the challenge to the power of the president to defer spending money appropriated by the Congress. Litigation Group represented Public Citizen in its joint suit with the United Steelworkers of America against the Office of Management and Budget for blocking workers' disclosure rules on hazardous chemicals on the grounds of the paperwork cost. Most recently, it has been litigating to enforce laws that ensure federal employees are not unduly hindered in efforts to disclose illegal and improper activities in the executive branch to the public and to Congress.

In consumer health issues, Litigation Group used the courts to spur the Food and Drug Administration to proceed with tampon absorbency (linked to toxic shock syndrome) labeling requirements, to try to gain compensation for women injured by the A. H. Robins Dalkon Shield, and to defend the consumer position in the Robins bankruptcy reorganization. In 1988, Litigation Group persuaded a judge hearing a case brought by a smoker against Liggett and Myers to unseal documents exposing that the company knew about the hazards of cigarette smoking as early as the 1950s. More recently, it filed an amicus curiae brief in the Cipollone case against Liggett and Myers.

Litigation Group has added two additional tactic areas. It has launched an effort to provide help to lawyers in legal services programs and in small firms whose cases have reached the Supreme Court but who have little or no Supreme Court experience. Drawing upon its experience in scores of cases, including twenty-seven argued on the merits before the Supreme Court, Litigation Group locates important cases and offers advice and assistance. It also has moved into the area of preemption, which has become important in the wake of the Reagan years' allowance of the states to move into many regulatory issues. Cases here range from deceptive advertising to state privacy law claims challenged by business groups that argue weaker federal standards preclude the states from acting.

FURTHER READING

Annual Report. Annual. Washington, DC: Public Citizen.

Carroll, Andrew Silow. 1993. "The Medium Is the Message." Public Citizen, September/October, p. 28.

Kaltenheuser, Skip. 1994. "Pesticide Hazards Increased by Federal Preemptions of State Law." Public Citizen, Summer, pp. 20–23.

Nye, Peter. 1994. "Surge of SLAPP Suits Chills Public Debate." Public Citizen, Summer, pp. 14–19.

"Public Citizen Wins 22nd Case Before Supreme Court." 1994. Public Citizen, May/June, pp. 6–7.

Radelat, Ana. 1990. "Smoke Out: The Tobacco Industry Faces its Most Daunting Challenges." Public Citizen, September/October, pp. 12–15.

Tankersley, Mike. 1994. "The Medium Redux: Courts Order Preservation of Government's Electronic Records." Public Citizen, May/June, pp. 27–28.

PUBLIC INTEREST RESEARCH GROUPS (PIRGs)

Addresses of state offices are listed at the conclusion of this profile.

ORGANIZATION AND RESOURCES

PIRGs are student-run, student-funded nonpartisan organizations that conduct research, advocacy, organizing, lobbying, and educational and media campaigns on a wide range of issues. They originated through the work of Ralph Nader in the early 1970s. Nader and two of his associates, Donald Ross and Jim Welch, did speaking tours on university campuses, encouraging student activism in the public interest. Following such an address at the University of Oregon in 1970, the model for such groups was forged.

The organization is student run and student funded, and includes direct student activism, but it also hires lawyers, scientists, organizers, and other professionals to provide expertise and continuity. Following an organizing meeting, students publicize the idea and circulate petitions to gauge student support; students then vote to formally establish and fund a PIRG on their campus. The pattern worked out at Oregon and then Minnesota was detailed by Nader and his staff of organizers in *Action for a Change,* which has been followed on more than 175 campuses in 30 states and Canada. The campus-based groups elect members to a state board that hires an executive director, determines priorities for staff action, and coordinates projects with other state or national public interest groups. Over 1 million persons are members, and more than 350 professional staff are employed by PIRGs nationwide.

The student fee financial base of the PIRGs has been à target of conservative opposition since the late 1970s. The per-student fee is usually $2 to $5 per term. A group of eight students represented by the Mid-Atlantic Legal Foundation filed suit against Rutgers University and the New Jersey PIRG in 1979, on the grounds that the fee collection system violated their constitutional rights. The plaintiffs won at the appellate level, and in 1986 the U.S. Supreme Court declined to hear an appeal. The decision struck down the refundable fee method at public universities. Under this method fees were collected from all students, along with other student fees, and students who did not want to support PIRG could apply for a refund directly from PIRG. The decision did not implicate fees at private schools or other fee collection methods, and the New Jersey PIRG switched to the most common method among public universities: the waivable fee system. Under such a system, the PIRG fee is billed with other student fees, but students who do not want to pay may check a box on their registration form or tuition bill. Another method is funding through the regular student fee mechanism, with PIRG being treated like other student programs. This method is also under attack by the Mid-Atlantic Legal Foundation. College Republicans and Young Americans for Freedom have joined the effort to defund or disrupt the PIRGs by a variety of means.

POLICY CONCERNS

PIRG concerns include consumer rights, social justice, environmental protection, political reform, energy policy, and government responsibility. Specific projects, chosen by each PIRG, range from auto repair to dental health and toxic waste. Missouri PIRG wrote and lobbied into law provisions requiring banks to shorten their check-clearing periods. Vermont PIRG won legislation establishing the country's first public dental health program for children. New Jersey PIRG monitors water pollution and industrial discharges; New York PIRG has produced major reports on toxic chemical contamination that have been featured on "60 Minutes."

Oregon PIRG launched a citizen initiative to establish a citizens' utility board, which 53 percent of voters approved in spite of a million-dollar opposition campaign by utility companies. PIRGs also claim credit for protection of the Boundary Waters Canoe Area, requirements that political parties publicize caucus meeting times and places, and challenging the constitutionality of the requirement that draft registration-eligible students sign an oath that they have registered before they are eligible for federal financial aid.

TACTICS

The goal of PIRGs is to provide students the opportunity to learn that you can "fight city hall." Students select projects to work on, determine the strategies and tactics to use, do the research, and pursue the issue, in some cases earning academic credit as well as experience as active citizens. Several PIRGs use campus radio station facilities to produce syndicated radio shows on issues of student and community interest; others have had their own cable television shows. Some produce newsletters that are sent to students, community leaders, news media, and elected officials. Most PIRGs offer some sort of hotline or action center to assist with consumer complaints.

Some PIRGs conduct community organizing campaigns that may include petition drives or letter-writing campaigns, leaflets, rallies, or community meetings. PIRGs also intervene in regulatory hearings, for example, as consumer representatives in utility rate-setting proceedings. They have used the courts to address such issues as the protection of constitutional rights and the environment (Griffin 1987).

In selecting the projects on which to focus, PIRGs' state boards of directors observe several parameters: the amount of student involvement a project will offer, the importance of the issue and likelihood of its being affected by PIRG action, whether the PIRG's work would be duplicating rather than supporting the efforts of other groups, and whether the probable outcome is worth the effort required. Within these broad guidelines, one finds a wide array of specific projects.

FURTHER READING

Annual Report. Washington, DC: U.S. PIRG.

Bezold, Clement. 1987. "Beyond Technocracy: Anticipatory Democracy in Government and the Marketplace." In Jack DeSario and Stuart Langton, eds., *Citizen Participation in Public Decision Making.* Contributions in Political Science no. 158. New York: Greenwood Press.

Griffin, Kelley. 1987. *Ralph Nader Presents More Action for a Change.* New York: Dembner Books.

Nye, Peter. 1993. "Creative Accounting: How Audits Failed." *Public Citizen,* September/October, pp. 18–19.

Torry, Saundra. 1994. "Harvard Law Group Tackles Social Injustice." *Washington Post,* February 18, p. A3.

U.S. PIRG. n.d. Membership recruitment flyer.

ADDRESSES OF STATE PIRGs

Alaska PIRG
P.O. Box 1093
Anchorage, AK 99510 (907) 278–3661

California PIRG
1147 S. Robertson #202
Berkeley, CA 94704 (415) 642–9952

Colorado PIRG
1724 Gilpin Street
Denver CO 80218 (303) 355–1861

Connecticut PIRG
University of Connecticut, Box U-8
Storrs, CT 06268 (203) 486–5002

Florida PIRG
1441 E. Fletcher Avenue
Tampa, FL 33612 (813) 971–7564

Georgia PIRG
no current address available

Illinois PIRG
no current address available

Iowa PIRG
Iowa State University
Memorial Union, Room 36
Ames, IA 50011 (515) 294–8094

Maine PIRG
92 Bedford Street
Portland, ME 04103 (207) 780–4044

Maryland PIRG
3110 Main Dining Hall

University of Maryland
College Park, MD 20742 (301) 454–5601

Massachusetts PIRG
29 Temple Place
Boston, MA 02111 (617) 292–4800

Michigan PIRG
Box 4375
Ann Arbor, MI 48109 (313) 662–6597

Minnesota PIRG
2412 University Avenue SE
Minneapolis, MN 55414 (612) 376–7554

Missouri PIRG
4144 Lindell Boulevard
Suite 219
Saint Louis MO 63108 (314) 534–7474

Montana PIRG
356 Corbin Hall
University of Montana
Missoula, MT 59812 (406) 243–2907

New Jersey PIRG
84 Paterson Street
New Brunswick, NJ 08901 (201) 247–4606

New Mexico PIRG
University of New Mexico
Box 66 SUB
Albuquerque, NM 87131 (505) 277–2757

New York PIRG
9 Murray Street
New York, NY 10007 (212) 349–6460

North Carolina
no current address available

Ohio PIRG
Wilder Box 25
Oberlin College
Oberlin, OH 44074 (216) 775–8137

Oregon Student PIRG
1536 SE 11th
Portland, OR 97214 (503) 231–4181

Texas PIRG
no current address available

Vermont PIRG
43 State Street
Montpelier, VT 05602 (802) 223–5221

Washington PIRG
5628 University Way NE
Seattle, WA 98105 (206) 526–8843

Wisconsin PIRG
no current address available

PUBLIC VOICE FOR FOOD AND HEALTH POLICY
1001 Connecticut Avenue N.W., Suite 522
Washington, DC 20036
Tel (202) 659–5930
Fax 202 659–3683

ORGANIZATION AND RESOURCES

Public Voice for Food and Health Policy was founded in 1982 by Ellen Haas, a longtime consumer activist who had served as president of the Consumer Federation of America* and as director of the consumer division of the Community Nutrition Institute. Haas continued to head the organization until her appointment by President Bill Clinton to a senior post in the U.S. Department of Agriculture, where she would administer many of the same food and nutrition programs whose reach Public Voice has monitored.

Public Voice, a 501(c)(3) organization, is funded by foundations and revenues generated by conferences, contributions, sales of publications, and membership dues, in that order. Approximately 600 organizations, individuals, and coalitions are members of Public Voice.

POLICY CONCERNS

Public Voice aims to influence private and public decisions about food, agriculture, and related health issues. In the first category are the decisions made by food growers, agribusiness organizations, supermarkets, and other retail sales corporations serving the food consumer. Their decisions and those of consumers are influenced by available information and by government. For that reason Public Voice tries to shape the debate on food and agriculture policy to provide available, affordable, safe, and nutritious food. For example, Public Voice successfully petitioned USDA to change its meat grading system to reflect advice from doctors and health researchers that consumers should eat leaner cuts of meat.

Public Voice's main governmental targets in the executive branch of government are USDA, the Food and Drug Administration, and the Environmental Protection Agency. Also of importance are the congressional agriculture committees, Congress's watchdog committees and agencies (e.g., the House Government Operations and Senate Governmental Affairs Committees, the General Accounting Office, and the Office of Technology Assessment), and the committees that have jurisdiction over health and environmental issues.

Public Voice contributes information to the farm policy debate, paying particular attention to how the USDA's programs for low-income consumers operate (e.g., food stamps, school breakfast and lunch, WIC, etc.) whenever Congress takes up those issues. Finally, Public Voice is concerned about the influence of private interests, especially agribusiness, on decision making at the U.S.Department of Agriculture and the uses to which food processors and retailers put the food grown by agricultural producers.

TACTICS

A *Blueprint for Pesticide Policy,* a report issued in 1989 in cooperation with the League of Women Voters Education Fund, shows one way that Public Voice, working with other national organizations, tries to shape the public policy debate. This was a conscious attempt to have a consumer perspective in the policy stream during debate over pesticide policy by the executive and legislative branches of government. Along with *Agriculture Policy, Consumers and the Environment,* which was intended as a guide for the broader publics tuning in to food and agriculture policy during the 1990 farm policy debate, *Blueprint* represented a joint effort by Public Voice and the League of Women Voters' Food Forum Education Project, which in turn was funded by the W. K. Kellogg Foundation.

This project shows Public Voice's reach into diverse communities including grower, agribusiness, and rural advocacy organizations, consumer and environmental groups, land grant universities, the foundation world, and governmental agencies. When officials for Public Voice testify before congressional committees, they often find themselves on the same side of issues with consumer groups (e.g., Public Citizen,* Community Nutrition Institute, Consumer Federation of America,* etc.), antipoverty advocates, spokespersons for family farmers, sustainable agriculture organizations, liberal farm groups, and environmental organizations.

Frequently, but not always, opponents of issues on which Public Voice feels strongly include the National Agricultural Chemicals Association,* the American Farm Bureau Federation, and other agricultural producer organizations. Besides the Public Policy Forum, a good example of Public Voice's interest in working with other organizations came in the work the organization and its allies did to prepare for the 1990 farm policy debate. The organization joined with Citizens for a Sane Economy to oppose continuing the national sugar subsidy and has shown a willingness to work with conservative groups concerned about excessive government spending on a range of proposals to curb agricultural subsidies.

Public Voice recognizes members of Congress with a Golden Carrot award for special achievements in advancing food and health policy for the general population as well as low-income consumers. Getting new issues onto the public and governmental agenda for debate and discussion is also important, as can be seen in the reports issued on subjects such as seafood safety and the difficulties of shopping for food in rural America. Its work since the late 1980s on seafood safety with the National Fisheries Institute, the industry's largest trade association, shows that Public Voice can work with industry groups and mobilize consumer and health groups for a workable regulatory approach.

FURTHER READING

A Blueprint for Pesticide Policy. 1989. Washington, DC: Public Voice for Food and Health Policy.

Agriculture Policy, Consumers and the Environment. 1990. Washington, DC: Public Voice for Food and Health Policy.

Contaminated Catch: Holes in the Shellfish Safety Net. 1989. Washington, DC: Public Voice for Food and Health Policy.

Higher Prices, Fewer Choices: Shopping for Food in Rural America. 1990. Washington, DC: Public Voice for Food and Health Policy.

No License to Label: How Federal Standards Restrict Lower Fat Foods. 1991. Washington, DC: Public Voice for Food and Health Policy.

Off to a Poor Start: Infant Health in Rural America. 1988. Washington, DC: Public Voice for Food and Health Policy.

Smoking Them Out: Tobacco Dollars/Tobacco Votes. 1987. Washington, DC: Public Voice for Food and Health Policy.

What's for Lunch? II. A 1990 Survey of Options in the School Lunch Program. 1990. Washington, DC: Public Voice for Food and Health Policy.

R
/

RESOURCES FOR THE FUTURE (RFF)
1616 P Street N.W.
Washington, DC 20036
(202) 328–5000

ORGANIZATION AND RESOURCES

Founded in 1952 through a grant from the Ford Foundation, Resources for the Future has become an important voice in the Washington research community examining the economic impact of public policies involving the environment and development. Yearly expenses in 1991 of $8.1 million give a sense of the size of the organization and the scope of its activities. At first RFF's mission was to study whether the emerging superpower competition would deplete key U.S. natural resources needed for other national missions. An environmental focus was added later, and with the decline of the Eastern bloc, concern has shifted to whether the U.S. economy can accommodate the demands on natural resources to support a rise in the standard of living for the poor.

RFF publications invoke the standard role that economics has given to the consumer as the driving force in economic life but are increasingly preoccupied with attempting to clarify and evaluate externalities not captured in private markets. Recent research by RFF staff also is concerned with the design of public policy and governmental institutions.

POLICY CONCERNS

RFF's energy and natural resources division researchers have worked to develop and test a methodology to assess the economic and natural resource impacts of global climate change. Expressed views of natural resource management issues are changing to incorporate public concerns including clean air and water and viable ecosystems. Developing social cost estimates to reflect the effects of automobile exhaust emissions on human health is one of the projects of RFF's quality of the environment division.

As can be seen from these and other issues, RFF's researchers usually address not the general public but their peers in such professions as law, science, and economics who work in government, industry, public interest (e.g., consumer and environmental) groups, academia, and Washington-based think tanks. For example, RFF established the National Center for Food and Agriculture Policy (NCFAP) in 1984 with a grant from the W. K. Kellogg Foundation in order to conduct such a dialogue with specialists concerned about the multiple claims on natural resources in agriculture. With additional funding from foundations, industry, and government, NCFAP sought to advance knowledge on agriculture's role in the larger society, especially such issues as agriculture's role in trade policy, the environment, and food safety.

TACTICS

RFF has its chief impact on public policy through the use that others make of its research because the organization does not lobby or advocate positions on public issues or events. Researchers working in some of RFF's units are engaged in these debates, evaluating decision-making approaches, risk management, cost-benefit analysis, and the like. RFF presents public policy briefings, and individual researchers participate in the kinds of policy networks that are characteristic of contemporary Washington policymaking.

Despite the increased attention that economic issues were given in Washington public policy debates in the 1980s, RFF officials are not satisfied with the organization's impact on the practical decisions made all around them in Washington. RFF has not reached the point where decision makers automatically seek out what it has to contribute on an issue. Organization leaders are concerned that citizens and governments are making important economic development choices with too little information about economic and environmental issues.

FURTHER READING

Annual Report. Washington, DC: Resources for the Future.

Browne, William P., et al. 1991. *Sacred Cows and Hot Potatoes: Agrarian Myths in Agricultural Policy.* Boulder, CO: Westview Press.

Cropper, Maureen L., and Paul R. Portney. 1992. "Discounting Human Lives," *Resources* 108:1–4.

Toman, Michael A. 1992. "The Difficulty in Defining Sustainability." *Resources* 106: 3–6.

S /

SAVINGS & COMMUNITY BANKERS OF AMERICA (SCBA)
900 19th Street N.W., Suite 400
Washington, DC 20006
(202) 857–3100

ORGANIZATION AND RESOURCES

Savings & Community Bankers of America was created by the June 1992 merger of the United States League of Savings Institutions and the National Council of Community Bankers. The League dated from 1892; the National Council, formerly the National Council of Savings Institutions, was formed by a 1983 merger of the National Savings and Loan League and the National Association of Mutual Savings Banks. The merger and name change occurred in the wake of the savings and loan scandals and bailout, and was part of the League's effort to reform its tarnished image. SCBA has approximately 2,100 member institutions, including state and federally chartered savings and loan associations, savings bank, cooperative banks, and commercial banks with combined assets of more than $800 billion. It has members in all fifty states, Puerto Rico, Guam, and the Virgin Islands.

The board of directors includes forty-eight voting members, half from the League and half from the Council; beginning in 1994, directors will be elected without regard to their former affiliation. A sixteen-member executive committee of the board is responsible for governance of the organization; its president, Paul A. Schosberg, oversees a staff of 100. Schosberg came to the SCBA post from the New York League of Savings Institutions and previously served as chief of staff for two members of Congress from New York. Reporting to the president are the general counsel and seven functional areas—economics and research, finance and administration, government relations, member services, policy development, public affairs, and technical support and programs.

SCBA has five for-profit subsidiaries, based in Chicago, that provide professional investment products, credit card services, financial forms, real estate auction marketing programs, and endorsements for insurance programs. Its educational affiliate is the Center for Financial Studies, on the campus of Fairfield University in Connecticut, which conducts a wide range of courses to prepare managers for broader responsibilities in financial institutions and also sponsors the National School of Banking, a graduate-level program for high-potential managers. The American League of Financial Institutions is another SCBA affiliate. Its members are institutions owned and operated by African-Americans, Asian-Americans, Hispanic-Americans, and women; it provides educational and technical services to its members and promotes savings and home ownership among ethnic and inner-city communities.

A wide range of publications is provided by SCBA to its members. *Washington Perspective* is a weekly newsletter that informs members about developments in legislation and regulation. In-depth analyses on specific enactments are provided in publications such as *Regulatory Report, Special Management Bulletin, Corporate Finance Letter,* and *Tax Insight.* A monthly magazine, *Savings and Community Banker,* includes articles on operations and industry trends; *Economic Outlook* tracks economic forces that influence the industry's direction. References such as the *Federal Guide* and *Supervisory Service* provide tools for managers, attorneys, and others involved in the savings industry. SCBA's programs for directors and trustees include special training seminars as well as the *Trustees and Directors Handbook* and the monthly *Directors and Trustees Digest.*

POLICY CONCERNS

SCBA emphasizes that savings and community financial institutions are vital to economic stability and growth. Most of the investments that members make are in residential real estate loans, but an increasing number of institutions also provide commercial loans for local businesses, student and consumer loans, credit cards, and church loans. The services they provide include savings accounts, certificates of deposit, trust services, safety deposit boxes, and insurance.

SCBA intends to lead its members toward profitable strategic growth in real estate lending and community financial services by promoting freedom of choice of financial services offered by members. The organization supports the safety and soundness of the industry and the dual banking system through strong but reasonable and effective regulation. The association seeks to ensure that new legislation and regulations do not impose excessive operating burdens on institutions or reduce a stable, affordable flow of credit. It focuses in particular on the Federal Home Loan Bank System, the role of community institutions, holding company regulation, and mortgage finance policy.

Pointing out that the savings rate in the United States is far lower than that of other industrialized countries, SCBA supports policies to promote savings. Increased savings would provide funds for socially valuable activities such as home ownership and college education, support retirement and unanticipated medical expenses, and support business creation of jobs and community growth. Member institutions sponsor in-school savings programs for children, seminars for future homeowners, and workshops on the financial needs of retirees. SCBA specifically advocates that the federal government maintain current levels of insurance on savings deposits to promote increased savings by the population.

SCBA is committed to affordable housing for Americans, pointing out that 5 million low-income households in America are unable to obtain decent housing with one-third of their income, the recommended maximum ratio. The organization has undertaken initiatives to educate members about affordable housing opportunities and support the extension of credit to underserved neighborhoods. It focuses on fulfilling both the letter and the spirit of the Community Reinvestment Act and related federal laws that require institutions to extend credit to all segments of the community.

TACTICS

SCBA's mission is to provide effective and unified lobbying in Washington on all of the industry's legislative and regulatory issues. Its Washington staff monitors hundreds of proposed new laws and regulations each year, to determine whether they will have an impact on members. It collects members' reactions to proposals as the basis for its response to policymakers, the media, and the public. It offers technical expertise and information to its members, the media, educational institutions, government agencies and officials, and the public.

Executives of member financial institutions are supported in their direct contacts with officials by SCBA efforts. Through letters, phone calls, and personal visits, executives let policymakers know how proposals will affect local economies and the performance of their financial institutions. SCBA testifies at congressional committee and subcommittee hearings, submits letters and comments, and maintains ongoing contacts with regulators, members of Congress, and their staffs.

The government relations department of SCBA is responsible not only for legislative and regulatory activities and compliance issues but also for the political action committee, COMPAC. The organization also files amicus curiae briefs in selected industry court cases.

FURTHER READING

Day, Kathleen. 1989. "The Decline and Fall of a Powerful Lobby." *Washington Post*, national weekly edition, August 7–13, p. 19.

Savings & Community Bankers of America: The Association and the Industry. 1992. Washington, DC: Savings & Community Bankers of America.

Savings & Community Bankers of America: Fact Sheet. 1993. Washington, DC: Savings & Community Bankers of America.

U.S. Congress. House Committee on Banking, Finance, and Urban Affairs Subcommittee on General Oversight, Investigations, and the Resolution of Failed Financial Institutions. 1993. *Hearing on the Bank Enterprise Act's Ability to Catalyze Community Development Banking.* Washington, DC: Government Printing Office.

U.S. Congress. Senate Committee on Banking, Housing, and Urban Affairs. 1993. *Hearings on Problems in Community Development Banking, Mortgage Lending Discrimination, Reverse Redlining, and Home Equity Lending.* Washington, DC: Government Printing Office.

SIERRA CLUB

730 Polk Street
San Francisco, CA 94109
Tel (415) 776–2211
Fax 415 776–0350

ORGANIZATION AND RESOURCES

The Sierra Club was founded in San Francisco by John Muir in 1892, making it one of the oldest organizations in the United States committed to safeguarding and improving the nation's environment. In recent years its goals have broadened to encompass increased concern about international issues as well, but here we focus on the role that Sierra plays in American national politics. It has over 600,000 members who contribute to an annual budget in excess of $35 million through annual dues of $35 a year (less for senior citizens, students, and those on limited incomes). *Sierra,* published every other month, is its official magazine.

In addition, Sierra publishes a summary of public policy issues affecting the environment in *National News Report,* which is sent biweekly to subscribing local club officers and members of the public. Finally, like the National Audubon Society* and other groups with active local chapters, many of Sierra's more than 400 local organizations issue their own newsletters.

The organization maintains a separate public interest law firm, the Sierra Club Legal Defense Fund, which is active on matters where litigation is judged useful to protect the environment, and a separately funded political action committee, SCOPE.

POLICY CONCERNS

Sierra is best known for its work to protect and expand wilderness areas and its concern for endangered species, ancient forests, and the effects of development on these areas (e.g., campaigns to protect the Arctic National Wildlife Refuge from oil and gas development). Sierra has been involved in a wider range of concerns since the arrival of environmental politics on the national scene in the late 1960s, as can be seen in its work for passage of the National

Environmental Protection Act in 1970, its opposition to the supersonic transport in 1971, and more recently, its attempts to raise auto fuel efficiency standards and reorient the Highway Trust Fund via the Intermodal Surface Transportation and Efficiency Act of 1991.

The Club maintains a Washington, D.C., office to support the legislative and public policy agenda developed by its state and national leadership, which tries to influence legislative and administrative decisions at the national level. Emerging concerns include food and agriculture policy—Sierra worked in a coalition with consumer (Consumer Federation of America,* Public Voice*) and environmental (Natural Resources Defense Council,* National Wildlife Federation, and National Audubon Society*), and family farm/alternative agriculture (Institute of Alternative Agriculture, Soil and Water Conservation Society, Center for Resource Economics, etc.) organizations to influence the 1990 farm bill—especially on issues concerning groundwater pollution, natural resources, and pesticide risks.

TACTICS

Sierra is located somewhat to the left of center in the environmental community. Its members are more activist than those in the National Audubon Society* but much less so than people who belong to Greenpeace,* Sea Shepherds, and Earth First! On the other end of the spectrum lie membership organizations like the National Wildlife Federation, Nature Conservancy, and Conservation Foundation and smaller groups like National Resources Defense Council,* Resources for the Future,* and the Environmental Defense Fund.* Part of the difficulty of classifying this organization is the different kinds of activism shown by the national and state organizations, and differences over tactics and objectives within the organization, not to mention the overlap in memberships.

This crossover phenomenon can be seen in California Sierrans' involvement in the referendum campaign to enact "Big Green," Proposition 128 (the California Environmental Protection Act), in 1990 along with Natural Resources Defense Council and many other organizations. Spurred by dissatisfaction with the output of the California legislature, it combined individual bills (e.g., phasing out of agricultural pesticides and chlorofluoro-carbons, or CFCs) and a 20 percent reduction of global warming gases, including carbon dioxide, by the year 2000.

That measure, which did not succeed at the polls, attracted the attention and support of the national organizations of a range of groups profiled in this book because it showed a promising strategy to get around the gridlock that affected the national environmental movement's agenda in Washington during the Reagan-Bush years. That battle, and the ones that Sierra supports in Congress to strengthen national pesticide policy, illustrate the opposition that agricultural producers, agribusiness, chemical manufacturers, and other industry groups are able to mount.

Increasingly, Sierra and other environmental organizations are becoming active on issues before Congress like water subsidies to farmers and ranchers in the western states, where they are finding new allies in urban interests and even, occasionally, state business groups concerned about the water needs of urban areas (e.g., California's Business Roundtable). These issues are likely to take a larger share of attention from environmental groups such as Sierra as everyone looks for ways to cut the national budget in order to fund their priorities during the cash-strapped 1990s.

FURTHER READING

Arrandale, Tom. 1992. "The Mid-Life Crisis of the Environmental Lobby." *Governing,* April, pp. 32–36.
Davis, Phillip E. 1992a. "Congress Seeks to Rechannel Flow of Water in the West." *Congressional Quarterly Weekly Report,* March 7, pp. 527–532.
———. 1992b. "Water Bill Heads to Bush's Desk over Farm Interests' Protests." *Congressional Quarterly Weekly Report,* October 10, pp. 3150–3152.
Idelson, Holly. 1992. "Conferees at Last Find Harmony on National Energy Strategy." *Congressional Quarterly Weekly Report,* October 3, pp. 3030–3033.
Kriz, Margaret. 1990. "Shades of Green." *National Journal,* July 28, pp. 1826–1831.
Stokes, Bruce. 1991. "Greens Talk Trade." *National Journal,* April 13, pp. 862–866.

SMALL BUSINESS LEGISLATIVE COUNCIL (SBLC)
1156 15th Street N.W., Suite 510
Washington, DC 20005
(202) 296–5333

ORGANIZATION AND RESOURCES

The Small Business Legislative Council is an independent, long-term coalition of trade and professional associations that share a concern for small business. Its purpose is to consolidate the strength and maximize the influence of small business on federal policy issues of importance to the entire small business community. Founded in 1976, the Council has grown to include 106 association members representing nearly every segment of the economy, including manufacturing, retailing, distribution, professional and technical services, agriculture, and construction. Membership is open to associations whose members are predominantly small businesses or independent professionals, providing that at least 70 percent of the association's income is derived from independent operations not dominant in their field. The United Bus Owners of America, the National Tooling and Machining Association, the National Association of Home Builders, and the National Moving and Storage Association are among its members. SBLC dues are 0.90 percent of each association's dues income during the past fiscal year, with a minimum of $500 and a maximum of $2,000. Each member association has full voting rights in selecting the board of directors, chairman, and officers.

Issue committees of members develop policy proposals and monitor Council activities in areas including tax policy, government procurement, environment, and employment issues and pension laws. Each Council member is encouraged to propose new policies for consideration and to appear before the issue committees to discuss its proposals. Policy proposals adopted by the board of directors are submitted to the entire membership for approval.

SBLC is an extension of the capabilities and staffs of member associations, allowing them to increase their Washington profile by sharing expertise and resources. The Council staff of two is directed by John Satagaj, the president, and provides information and analysis of issues significant to small business operators. Members receive reports and news bulletins to keep them informed of recent developments, allowing them to conduct a more successful government affairs program. *SBLC Journal* is a monthly newsletter that reports Council activities to members. SBLC sponsors seminars and conferences on important issues and makes available support materials related to federal regulation, such as *Compliance Guide to the Americans with Disabilities Act.*

POLICY CONCERNS

SBLC is focused on issues that affect small businesses as a whole, including the economy, taxes, liability insurance, budget, antitrust enforcement, employment issues, government procurement, the environment, and venture capital and other financing mechanisms. The Council's perspective on the economy advocates attention to restoring both consumer and business confidence by reinstating investment tax credits, reducing capital gains taxes, and expanding government reliance on private-sector purchases of goods and services. It maintains that government-imposed additions to the cost of doing business must be controlled by comprehensive attention to the cumulative impact of regulatory initiatives.

SBLC's general position on environmental issues is that its members are willing to do what they can to operate in an environmentally responsible fashion, but that they do not have a clear idea how to do so because government requirements are so complex, redundant, and contradictory. The Council advocates simplification throughout this policy arena from statutes to compliance so small firms could, for example, keep a single data sheet on material safety.

SBLC is actively concerned with proposed legislation to prohibit an employer from hiring permanent replacement workers during a strike; its position is that the legislation would effectively require an employer to accede to union demands and, by removing any risk associated with a strike, dramatically increase unions' ability to organize new workers. Federal legislation requiring employers to allow family and medical leave is opposed by SBLC. It argues that such requirements encroach upon the flexibility of the employer and employee to tailor benefits to their specific needs. Furthermore, its analysis suggests that this establishes a new category of benefits that is likely to include paid leave requirements.

The Council has been among supporters of product liability reform legislation such as that championed by Senator Robert Kasten (R-WI). SBLC argues that the current system creates uncertainty for manufacturers, its standards no longer reflect the realities of the marketplace, and the civil justice system has "gone amok." A uniform national liability system, in SBLC's analysis, would protect both consumers and businesses by assuring prompt payment to legitimate liability claimants, protect against plant closings by reducing liability costs, and create a more even competition among American, Japanese, and European manufacturers.

SBLC is among the many organizations concerned with reform of health care. Here its focus is on the escalating costs of health care rather than on access to care or availability of insurance. In response to proposals to mandate employer coverage, the Council cautions that the nation cannot take business's ability to pay for granted. It supports providing a refundable tax credit for health expenses to help low- and middle-income Americans purchase health insurance and health services, reforming the small group insurance market, establishing a minimum benefit package exempt from state-imposed mandated benefits, creating a rigorous federal cost containment program including medical malpractice reform, and extending Medicaid to all those below the poverty line in order to reduce shifting costs to the private sector. To fund those components requiring additional revenue, SBLC suggests reducing defense outlays, establishing means tests for entitlement programs, and increasing individual tax rates for incomes over $250,000 per individual.

TACTICS

SBLC operates both by supporting member associations in their own government affairs efforts and by directly disseminating information about the impact of public policy on small business. It is careful to avoid issues that affect member associations or individual businesses differentially. It prepares and distributes position papers, articles, and videotapes to spread the small business message. It also uses contacts with Congress and the executive branch to open doors for members, arranging meetings with congressional staff, representatives, senators, White House staff, and federal agencies. SBLC provides testimony before congressional committees and subcommittees and regulatory agencies. The Council's Washington stature is such that its 1992 annual meeting in the capital was addressed by President Bush, who was introduced as a "true champion of small business." House and Senate Small Business Committee chairmen also addressed the meeting.

The National Federation of Independent Business,* the large major association of small businesses, is sometimes an ally of SBLC. For example, both recently worked with the Internal Revenue Service on proposed rules to simplify the payroll tax deposit system after having worked on the legislative effort to require such simplification.

FURTHER READING

The Economy—A Small Business Perspective. 1992. SBLC Issue Paper. Washington, DC: SBLC.

Elimination of Cap on Damages in Equal Employment Opportunity Cases. 1992. SBLC Issue Paper. Washington, DC: SBLC.

Family and Medical Leave Act. 1992. SBLC Issue Paper. Washington, DC: SBLC.

Health Care Costs. 1992. SBLC Issue Paper. Washington, DC: SBLC.

Insurance Industry Reform. 1992. SBLC Issue Paper. Washington, DC: SBLC.

Payroll Tax Deposit Reform. 1992. SBLC Issue Paper. Washington, DC: SBLC.

Product Liability Reform. 1992. SBLC Issue Paper. Washington, DC: SBLC.

SBLC Journal. Monthly. Washington, DC: Small Business Legislative Council.

Small Business Legislative Council. 1992. Washington, DC: SBLC.

Striker Replacement Legislation. 1992. SBLC Issue Paper. Washington, DC: SBLC.

Symposium: Deregulation in Retrospect. 1993. *Southern Economic Journal,* January, pp. 436–514.

T
/

TOBACCO INSTITUTE (TI)
1875 I Street N.W., Suite 800
Washington, DC 20006
(202) 457–4800

ORGANIZATION AND RESOURCES

Formed in 1958, the Tobacco Institute has been the principal voice in Washington for tobacco farmers, distributors, and retailers. As the noose around the tobacco industry has tightened with accumulated scientific evidence about the effects of smoking on the health of smokers and others who inhale the smoke in their immediate environments, the Tobacco Institute has also claimed to represent the interests of tobacco consumers. This trade group, which absorbed the Tobacco Tax Council in 1982, has twelve members and eighty-three staff persons. It has four regional offices and forty-nine state groups; its activities are largely funded by the two main tobacco manufacturers, R. J. Reynolds and Philip Morris.

POLICY CONCERNS

Over the years, the Tobacco Institute has been involved in campaigns to blunt a wide range of anti-smoking initiatives, including attempts to limit and/or eliminate tobacco advertising, to require health labels on cigarette packages, to limit smoking in public transportation (e.g., on AMTRAK, airlines, etc.), and to establish smokefree environments in restaurants, workplaces, and other facilities.

TACTICS

Prominent among the anti-smoking forces whose effects the Tobacco Institute seeks to counter have been Action on Smoking and Health* and health advocacy groups like the American Lung Association, American Heart Association, and American Cancer Society,* to mention just a few. It is also useful to note that 1994 marked the thirtieth anniversary of the first surgeon general's report advising about the negative health effects of smoking. Besides the activities of the Tobacco Institute, a considerable amount of lobbying in Washington in support of the tobacco industry is done by R. J. Reynolds and Philip Morris and their political action committees, and by lawmakers from tobacco-producing states, although the congressional agricultural lobby is not considered as influential as it once was.

FURTHER READING

Cloud, David S. 1994. "Tobacco Industry Losing Allies As Congress Eyes Health Tax." *Congressional Quarterly Weekly Report,* April 23, pp. 985–989.
Hilts, Philip J. 1994. "Way to Make Safer Cigarette Was Found in 60's, but Idea Was Shelved." *New York Times,* May 13, p. A10.
Janofsky, Michael. 1993. "The Tobacco Industry Seeks to Assure America That It's Against Underage Smoking, Too." *New York Times,* October 26, p. D21.
Levin, Myron. 1989. "Fighting Fire with P.R." *The Nation,* 55 (July 10)., pp. 52–55.

TRIAL LAWYERS FOR PUBLIC JUSTICE (TLPJ)
1625 Massachusetts Avenue N.W.
Washington, DC 20036
(202) 797–8600

ORGANIZATION AND RESOURCES

Trial Lawyers for Public Justice was formed in 1982 by a group of lawyers who litigate for plaintiffs in personal injury lawsuits, and consumer advocates Ralph Nader and Joan Claybrook. Members seek to help their clients recover monetary damages and, in the process, influence the litigation's targets, business and government, to discontinue unsafe practices. Attorneys also bring suits against government in whistle-blower cases and against companies in what they consider consumer rights cases. Member lawyers pay $1,000 a year; foundations can be patrons for a donation of $10,000. Cases supported by the organization must have important potential or actual public policy significance.

POLICY CONCERNS

Examples of the kinds of toxic torts, whistle-blower, and consumer rights cases brought by TLPJ include *Anderson* v. *W.R. Grace,* in which families of leukemia victims sued to recover damages they claimed resulted from the presence of toxic wastes in the drinking water. TLPJ also was involved in the cases that environmental groups brought against Exxon in the wake of the oil spill in Prince Edward Sound, Alaska.

TACTICS

Besides bringing cases, TLPJ seeks to influence congressional decision making on topics such as nuclear licensing procedures. The organization also seeks stronger and more extensive provisions for class action suits and private suits by attorneys general, and strict liability for companies. On the latter issue in particular, TLPJ has been criticized by lobbyists and other spokespersons for doctors, hospitals, and others seeking to reform medical malpractice and restrain product liability litigation.

FURTHER READING

Barr, Evan T. 1986. "Poisoned Well." *The New Republic,* March 17, pp. 18–20.
Kaltenheuser, Skip, 1994. "Pesticide Hazards Increased by Federal Preemptions of State Law." *Public Citizen,* Summer, pp. 20–23.
Kosterlitz, July. 1991. "Malpractice Morass." *National Journal,* February 6, pp. 1682–1686.

$$\frac{\qquad\qquad}{\qquad} \overset{\text{U}}{\Big/} \frac{\qquad\qquad\qquad}{}$$

UNION OF CONCERNED SCIENTISTS (UCS)
26 Church Street
Cambridge, MA 02238
Tel (617) 547–5552
Fax 617–864–9405

ORGANIZATION AND RESOURCES

The Union of Concerned Scientists was founded in 1969 by a group of scientists and academics at the Massachusetts Institute of Technology. It has grown to about 100,000 members. Besides its headquarters in Cambridge, a UCS staff of thirty-two works out of a Washington, D.C., office. The organization's quarterly publication *Nucleus* attests to its primary mission, which is to provide an alternative to governmental information about the dangers of nuclear confrontation with the former Soviet Union during the height of the Cold War.

POLICY CONCERNS

Usually about three-quarters of the organization's activity has been directed to issues of nuclear arms reduction and nuclear security policy. It is UCS's watchdog role on health, safety, and economic issues associated with domestic nuclear power and its relation to government regulators that brings it into the orbit of consumer policy. A recent related concern getting attention from the organization is global warming, its definition, causes, and consequences.

TACTICS

Drawing upon its unique identification with scientific expertise, UCS has established itself as a key source of public information about industry and government, as can be seen in the organization's publications and testimony before congressional and governmental panels over the years. The organization has a speakers' bureau, the Scientists' Action Network, which makes members and supporters available for public appearances and media presentations on topics for which UCS produces briefing papers.

FURTHER READING

Davis, Phillip A. 1992. "Environmental Protection, Costs Must Be Reconciled." *Congressional Quarterly Weekly Report,* September 26, pp. 2908–2910.

Holden, Constance. 1992. "Scientists' Campaign to Save Earth." *Science,* November 27, p. 1433.

Idelson, Holly. 1992. "Nuclear Weapons Complex Braces for Overhaul." *Congressional Quarterly Weekly Report,* April 25, pp. 1066–1073.

Lanouette, William. 1990. "The Boom in B-2 Bashing." *Bulletin of the Atomic Scientists,* September, pp. 8–9.

Schneider, Keith. 1993. "Science Group Urges a Delay in Selling Gene-Altered Feed." *New York Times,* October 6, p. A10.

UNITED AUTO WORKERS (UAW)

8000 E. Jefferson
Detroit, MI 48214
Tel (313) 926–5000
Fax 313–832–6016

ORGANIZATION AND RESOURCES

The United Auto Workers, founded in 1935 and led for many years by Walter Reuther, was in the forefront of a variety of liberal causes including civil rights and antipoverty legislation during the Kennedy/Johnson years. At the same time, Reuther and the leaders of other industrial unions got involved in policy debates in Washington on behalf of economic or consumer issues affecting workers and their families. Both the role that the 1.4 million-member UAW plays in the politics of minority and low-income communities and pocketbook issues affecting union members concern us here.

POLICY CONCERNS

Labor sometimes allies with business when the economic livelihood of a major sector of American society, such as the auto industry, is called into jeopardy. In the latter case, for example, concerns about the competitiveness of the American auto industry with its Japanese and European rivals may cause labor to side with management and disagree with organized consumer interests. In another example, the union has worked in recent years with the "big three" American auto manufacturers against an increase in the corporate average fuel economy (CAFE) standards, fearing that requiring the American companies' fleets to do better on gasoline consumption would cost jobs for union members.

Opposing legislation brought up in the Senate to raise CAFE standards was a diverse Coalition for Vehicle Choice, with consumer and environmental groups on the other side.

TACTICS

The UAW can deploy the full range of tactics available to labor unions, including meeting with members of Congress and their staffs, testifying at congressional hearings, PAC contributions, and so on. In addition, the UAW, especially in Reuther's time, had close ties with Democratic presidents and with the civil rights movement, from which vantage point officials worked financially and organizationally with others in the union community to support many of the more specialized consumer, human rights, and civil rights organizations (e.g., the Center for Community Change,* Children's Defense Fund,* American Association of Retired Persons,* Consumer Federation of America,* etc.).

FURTHER READING

Bennett, James. 1994. "UAW Wants Trade Payoff in Jobs." *New York Times.* January 1, p. 43.

Bernstein, Aaron. 1993. "Now Labor Can Be Part of the Solution." *Business Week,* March 1, p. 75.

Kriz, Margaret E. 1991. "Going the Extra Mile." *National Journal,* May 11, pp. 1894–1898.

"Labor's Love Lost?" 1992. *The Nation,* July 6, pp. 3–4.

U.S. CHAMBER OF COMMERCE (USCOFC)
1615 H Street N.W.
Washington, DC 20062
(202) 463–5427

ORGANIZATION AND RESOURCES

The Chamber of Commerce is a national federation of 180,000 businesses, 2,850 state and local chambers of commerce, and 1,400 trade and professional associations. Founded in 1912, its purpose is to articulate policy positions for the business community and influence public opinion and public policy. The organization is formally governed by a multitiered board of directors comprised of forty-one directors, four regional vice chairmen, a five-person senior council, and five other officers. Dr. Richard L. Lesher is president of the Chamber and directs the Washington office with a staff of 1,200 persons and an annual budget of more than $65 million. Approximately 70 percent of the group's income is from its membership, 15 percent from advertising, and 15 percent from publications, conferences, and other sources.

Members participate in developing policy positions by attending periodic regional forums and serving on topic committees. Topics getting attention include employee benefits, health care, energy, food and agriculture, labor relations, privacy, and taxation.

The Chamber conducts continuing education programs through its Center for Leadership Development. Institutes for Organization Management serves approximately 2,400 executives annually with its curriculum. The Corporate Executive Development Program conducts weeklong seminars on business interaction with the federal government. The international policy division of the Chamber works to facilitate investment initiatives abroad by meeting with heads of state, advocating support for business interests by U.S. embassies, and publishing guides such as its *Europe 1992.*

Another Chamber affiliate, the Center for International Private Enterprise (CIPE), is the business representative to the National Endowment for Democracy. CIPE has funded more than 160 business-oriented projects in more than 40 countries since 1983. An example of these projects is one set up in twelve countries to help business groups analyze the economic impact of proposed laws and provide information to legislators.

Communications are central to the Chamber's operations. *The Nations's Business* is its monthly magazine covering national issues of interest to small businesses. *The Business Advocate,* published bimonthly, is a legislative action magazine that includes "business ballot" polls to survey readers on policy issues. It publishes *Congressional Issues,* an annual reference book on key legislative matters affecting business; *Congressional Action,* a periodic newsletter on current legislative matters; and "Special Reports," detailed analyses of important issues. It also publishes booklets, pamphlets, and cassettes on labor issues, regulatory compliance, investments, and other topics. Chamber President Richard Lesher's column, "Voice of Business," appears in more than 670 newspapers each week; a broadcast counterpart of the column is heard on the Business Radio Network, which reaches 64 percent of U.S. households with radios. The Chamber provides press releases, op-ed pieces, and other materials that garner an average of over 500 mentions each month in print and broadcast media.

The Chamber operates BizNet, the American Business Network, a satellite broadcasting service that produces, syndicates, and broadcasts programs. Its flagship program, "It's Your Business," is a weekly debate program carried by more than 140 stations and The Learning Channel. "Nation's Business Today" is a two-hour morning news program carried on cable networks, reaching more than 60 percent of U.S. households. "Ask Washington" and "First Business" are also produced by the Chamber.

POLICY CONCERNS

The Chamber of Commerce focuses on those policy positions around which business as a whole, large and small, is able to unite. In recent years it has advocated reduction in government spending, reduction of taxes (including those on capital gains and for Social Security), deregulation, and government promotion of growth in the private sector of the economy.

Experts assembled by the Chamber have worked to dispel myths about food safety and to encourage national uniformity and consistency in food safety regulations. It works to protect small business interests in energy and environmental issues, urging caution on "greenhouse effect" responses, seeking modification of Clean Air Act provisions to protect small enterprises, and supporting development of the Arctic National Wildlife Refuge. The Americans with Disabilities Act was and is of major concern to the Chamber; it advocates keeping business compliance as simple and inexpensive as possible. Reform of product liability laws has been high on the Chamber's agenda for many years. It advocates a uniform federal law with liability limits; this would provide companies a less burdensome, more competitive operating environment.

Labor and benefits issues are ongoing Chamber concerns. It works to protect the rights of employers to set wages and use volunteer labor, recently winning an amendment to the Davis-Bacon Act that allows use of volunteer labor on construction of public housing projects. It mobilizes against federal proposals to prohibit employers from hiring permanent replacements for striking workers. Legislation requiring family or medical leave for workers was strongly opposed; the Chamber backed an alternative calling for employers to give preference in hiring to former workers who lost their jobs because of the need to take extended leave.

Extension and protection of tax benefits for business are high on the Chamber's list of interests. Among those of current concern are the research and experimentation tax credits, the educational assistance exclusion, and a request that the 25 percent health care deduction for self-employed individuals be expanded to 100 percent. The Chamber successfully fought off the funding of extended unemployment compensation through increases in payroll taxes. It advocates simplifying the tax code while protecting employers' flexibility in paying payroll taxes.

More recent among the Chamber's interests is its concern with education. Its affiliate, the Center for Workforce Preparation and Quality Education, was established in 1990 to mobilize a national grass-roots education reform campaign through state and local chambers of commerce.

TACTICS

The Chamber enjoys access to the highest level of policymakers. Cabinet members appear before its board of directors to explain and solicit support for executive branch proposals; Vice President Quayle entertained the board members and their spouses at his home.

Congressional voting records on issues important to the Chamber are carefully tabulated and widely reported to members. Voting records become the basis for candidate endorsements and campaign contributions. A Spirit of Enterprise Award is conferred on members of Congress who have at least a 70 percent pro-business voting record. Chamber members and staff are familiar on Capitol Hill, presenting testimony to committees and meeting with lawmakers and their staffs. In the 101st Congress, the Chamber submitted testimony 140 times and had more than 3,200 contacts with members of Congress or staff.

The Chamber coordinates and participates in coalitions to augment its legislative efforts. For example, it was part of a broad-spectrum coalition to include market-oriented reforms relating to food safety and the environment in the 1990 farm bill.

Grass-roots efforts are also among the Chamber's tactics. Congressional Action Network, a structured grass-roots organization, is made up of more than 3,000 local members who can be mobilized rapidly to contact members of Congress to whom they have particular access.

The National Chamber Litigation Center, the Chamber's law firm affiliate, champions the legal rights of the business community in frequent appearances before the Supreme Court. The Chamber endorsed the nomination of Clarence Thomas upon the advice of the Litigation Center. Recent important victories were handed down in *Ingersoll-Rand* v. *McClendon,* which found that companies may not be sued in state court by employees who claim their employer fired them to avoid pension obligations, and *FMC Corporation* v. *Holliday,* which ruled that self-funded or self-insured employee health care plans are not subject to state insurance regulations.

FURTHER READING

Annual Report. Washington, DC: U.S. Chamber of Commerce.

The Business Advocate. Bimonthly. Washington, DC: U.S. Chamber of Commerce.

Edsall, Thomas Byrne. 1984. *The New Politics of Inequality.* New York: W. W. Norton.

Epstein, Edwin M. 1969. *The Corporation in American Politics.* Englewood Cliffs, NJ: Prentice-Hall.

Pertschuk, Michael. 1982. *Revolt Against Regulation: The Rise and Pause of the Consumer Movement.* Berkeley: University of California Press.

Public Interest Profiles 1988–1989. Washington, DC: Congressional Quarterly, Foundation for Public Affairs.

Vogel, David. 1989. *Fluctuating Fortunes: The Political Power of Business in America.* New York: Basic Books.

Wattenberg, Daniel. 1993. "Clinton's Echo Chamber." *American Spectator,* June, pp. 18–23.

U.S. CONFERENCE OF MAYORS (USCM)

1620 Eye Street N.W.
Washington, DC 20006
(202) 293–7330

ORGANIZATION AND RESOURCES

The U.S. Conference of Mayors, founded in 1932, represents the interests of the chief executives of American cities with 30,000 or more population.

POLICY CONCERNS

Recognizing the need for a voice for America's cities, the media and Washington policymakers look to USCM for ideas on housing, health, welfare, homelessness, energy, cable television, and other issues. In the 1980s business found that hard-fought battles to deregulate energy prices, trucking, banking, and cable television sometimes meant that regulation was taken up at the state and local levels in response to consumer activism and voter unrest. Sometimes, but not always, USCM is on the same side as the other major intergovernmental lobbying organizations: those representing governors (National Governors Association), county officials (National Association of Counties), state legislators (National Conference on State Legislatures), and elected officials in smaller cities (National League of Cities*).

TACTICS

City government officials sometimes find themselves attacked in Washington public policy debates by consumer advocacy groups when a city agency (e.g., a municipal utility) produces goods and/or services for the consumer marketplace. The cities' lobby also gets drawn into public policy debates concerning cities' role as regulators of business. Examples include cable television, an issue area where national-level regulation replaced local control in the 1980s, and the rising issue of regulation of toxic substances such as lawn pesticides, where the Supreme Court has recently upheld stricter state and local regulation than that in force at the federal level.

Besides lobbying, litigation, commissioning studies, and monitoring issues under the purview of the organization's Washington-based staff, some of USCM's most important public activities and statements emanate from individual spokespersons among the ranks of the nation's mayors.

FURTHER READING

Berkman, Ronald, ed. 1992. *In the National Interest: The 1990 Urban Summit.* Washington, DC: Brookings Institution.

Gottlieb, Daniel W. 1982. "Business Mobilizes as States Begin to Move into the Regulatory Vacuum." *National Journal,* July 31, pp. 1340–1343.

U.S. PUBLIC INTEREST RESEARCH GROUP (U.S.PIRG)
215 Pennsylvania Avenue S.E.
Washington, DC 20003
(202) 546–9707

ORGANIZATION AND RESOURCES

U.S. PIRG is the national office for the college campus-based state PIRGs.* It succeeds National PIRG which was founded in 1977 at a conference of state PIRGs that voted to set up the national organization as a clearinghouse and coordinator of organizing and other multistate efforts. National PIRG was funded by small contributions from each state PIRG and by a Volunteers in Service to America grant that it used to train and place volunteers in community service jobs with PIRGs throughout the country. These community service projects ranged from organizing tenants and neighborhoods to setting up food purchasing cooperatives. National PIRG also helped organize anti-nuclear teaching materials and rallies and played a role in the "truth-in-testing" effort to reform the Educational Testing Service. However, pressure on the budgets of the state PIRGs led to a decline in their ability to support the national office, and it closed late in 1979.

U.S. PIRG was set up in 1983 at the initiative of about ten of the state PIRGs. Gene Karpinski, whose credentials include experience with Public Citizen,* Common Cause,* and People for the American Way, is executive director of a staff of eleven. The organization's budget is about $400,000, with income from the state PIRGs making up 64 percent of the revenue and membership contributions 28 percent. Individual memberships are $15 per year. There is also a U.S. PIRG Education Fund, which has 501(c)(3) status; its income is approximately $80,000 and is derived from foundation grants and individual contributions.

POLICY CONCERNS

Issues on which U.S. PIRG has been active include a Voter Bill of Rights that calls for registration by mail, registration on Election Day, more convenient poll hours, public financing for congressional campaigns, and the curbing of political action committee influence. A national campaign to help local activists establish state-level citizens' utility boards to represent telephone, natural gas, and electricity ratepayers at rate hearings before state regulatory commissions is under way with some success in Oregon and New York.

U.S. PIRG has been part of the coalition to strengthen the Superfund for hazardous waste cleanup and to strengthen federal drinking water quality standards. It was part of the National Clean Air Coalition supporting the reauthorization of the Clean Air Act. Reforming the Price-Anderson Act to make the nuclear power industry more accountable for its costs and to promote renewable energy sources has also been among its causes. It has been active on banking and credit issues, such as eliminating delays by banks in crediting depositors' checks and protecting consumers from false credit reporting.

TACTICS

U.S. PIRG serves as a resource center for the state organizations, offers assistance in organizing and fund-raising, and serves as a clearinghouse for information. It also advocates for federal action on issues that need or could benefit from attention at that level.

Tactics favored by U.S. PIRG include conducting research, releasing the results through the media, providing testimony to congressional committees, and working with both national and state and local coalitions to do direct and grass-roots lobbying.

FURTHER READING

Annual Report. Annual. Washington, DC: U.S. PIRG.

Bezold, Clement. 1987. "Beyond Technocracy: Anticipatory Democracy in Government and the Marketplace." In Jack DeSario and Stuart Langton, eds., *Citizen Participation in Public Decision Making.* Contributions in Political Science no. 158. Westport, CT: Greenwood Press.

Crenshaw, Albert B. 1993. "When a Computer Error Renders You a Deadbeat." *Washington Post,* national weekly edition, November 1–7, pp. 17–18.

Griffin, Kelley. 1987. *Ralph Nader Presents More Action for a Change.* New York: Dembner Books.

Nye, Peter. 1993. "Creative Accounting: How Audits Failed." *Public Citizen,* September/October, pp. 18–19.

U.S. PIRG. n.d. Washingtion, DC. Membership recruitment flyer.

APPENDIX: DIRECTORY OF ORGANIZATIONS

—————————— / ——————————

ACCURACY IN MEDIA (AIM)
1275 K Street N.W.
Washington, DC 20005

ACTION FOR CHILDREN'S TELEVISION (ACT)
20 University Road
Cambridge, MA 02138

ACTION ON SMOKING AND HEALTH (ASH)
2013 H Street N.W.
Washington, DC 20006

AIDS COALITION TO UNLEASH POWER (ACT-UP)
135 West 29th Street, 10th floor
New York, NY 10001

AMERICAN ACADEMY OF PEDIATRICS (AAP)
1331 Pennsylvania Avenue
Suite 721 North
Washington, DC 20004–1703

AMERICAN ASSOCIATION OF RETIRED PERSONS (AARP)
601 E Street N.W.
Washington, DC 20049

AMERICAN AUTOMOBILE ASSOCIATION (AAA)
1000 AAA Drive
Heathrow, FL 32746–5063

AMERICAN BANKERS ASSOCIATION (ABA)
1120 Connecticut Avenue N.W.
Washington, DC 20036

AMERICAN CANCER SOCIETY (ACS)
316 Pennsylvania Avenue S.E.
Suite 200
Washington, DC 20003–1146

AMERICAN COUNCIL FOR SCIENCE AND HEALTH (ACSH)
1995 Broadway, 16th floor
New York, NY 10023

AMERICAN ENTERPRISE INSTITUTE FOR PUBLIC POLICY RESEARCH (AEI)
1150 17th Street N.W.
Washington, DC 20036

AMERICAN FAMILY ASSOCIATION (AFA)
P.O. Drawer 2440
Tupelo, MS 38803

AMERICAN FEDERATION OF LABOR AND CONGRESS OF INDUSTRIAL OR-
   GANIZATIONS (AFL–CIO)
815 16th Street N.W.
Washington, DC 20006

AMERICAN HOSPITAL ASSOCIATION (AHA)
840 North Lake Shore Drive
Chicago, IL 60611

AMERICAN MEAT INSTITUTE (AMI)
P.O. Box 3556
Washington, DC 20007

AMERICAN MEDICAL ASSOCIATION (AMA)
515 North State Street   1101 Vermont Avenue N.W.
Chicago, IL 60610   Washington, DC 20005

600 Third Avenue
New York, NY 10016

AMERICAN PUBLIC POWER ASSOCIATION (APPA)
2301 M Street N.W.
Washington, D.C. 20037–1484

AMERICAN SOCIETY OF TRAVEL AGENTS (ASTA)
1101 King Street
Alexandria, VA 22314

AMERICANS FOR SAFE FOOD (ASF)
1501 Sixteenth Street N.W.
Washington, DC 20036

ASSOCIATION OF BIOTECHNOLOGY COMPANIES (ABC)
1666 Connecticut Avenue N.W.
Washington, DC 20009

ASSOCIATION OF COMMUNITY ORGANIZATIONS FOR REFORM NOW
   (ACORN)
739 8th Street S.E.
Washington, DC 20003

AUTOMOTIVE CONSUMER ACTION PROGRAM (AUTOCAP)
National Automobile Dealers Association
8400 Westpark Drive
McLean, VA 22102

AVIATION CONSUMER ACTION PROJECT (ACAP)
2000 P Street N.W., Suite 700
P.O. Box 19029
Washington, DC 20036

BANKCARD HOLDERS OF AMERICA (BHA)
560 Herndon Parkway, Suite 120
Herndon, VA 22070

THE BROOKINGS INSTITUTION
1775 Massachusetts Avenue N.W.
Washington, DC 20036

THE BUSINESS ROUNDTABLE
200 Park Avenue   1615 L Street N.W.
New York, NY 10166–0097   Washington, DC 20036–5610

BUYERS UP
c/o Public Citizen
2000 P Street
Washington, DC 20036

CENTER FOR AUTO SAFETY (CAS)
2001 S Street N.W., Suite 410
Washington, DC 20009

CENTER FOR BUDGET AND POLICY PRIORITIES (CBPP)
777 N. Capitol Street N.E., Suite 705
Washington, DC 20002

CENTER FOR COMMUNITY CHANGE (CCC)
1000 Wisconsin Avenue N.W.
Washington, DC 20007

CENTER FOR MARINE CONSERVATION (CMC)
1725 DeSales Street N.W.
Washington, DC 20036

CENTER FOR PUBLIC INTEGRITY (CPI)
1910 K Street N.W., Suite 802
Washington, DC 20006

CENTER FOR SCIENCE IN THE PUBLIC INTEREST (CSPI)
1875 Connecticut Avenue N.W., Suite 300
Washington, DC 20009–5728

CENTER FOR STUDY OF RESPONSIVE LAW
P.O. Box 19367
Washington, DC 20036

CHILDREN'S DEFENSE FUND (CDF)
122 C Street N.W.
Washington, DC 20001

CITIZEN ACTION FUND (CAF)
1406 West 6th Street   1300 Connecticut Ave. N.W.
Suite 200   Suite 401
Cleveland, OH 44113   Washington, DC 20036

CITIZENS FOR TAX JUSTICE (CTJ)
1311 L Street N.W.
Washington, DC 20005

COMMON CAUSE
2030 M Street N.W.
Washington, DC 20036

THE CONFERENCE BOARD
845 Third Avenue   1775 Massachusetts Ave. N.W.
New York, NY 10022–6601   Washington, DC 20036

CONSUMER ALERT
1024 J Street, Room 425   1555 Wilson Blvd., Suite 300
Modesto, CA 95354   Arlington, VA 22209

CONSUMER BANKERS ASSOCIATION (CBA)
1000 Wilson Boulevard, 30th floor
Arlington, VA 22209–3908

CONSUMER FEDERATION OF AMERICA (CFA)
1424 16th Street N.W., Suite 604
Washington, DC 20036

CONSUMERS FOR WORLD TRADE (CWT)
1726 M Street N.W., Suite 1101
Washington, DC 20036

CONSUMERS UNION (CU)
101 Truman Avenue   2001 S Street N.W.
Yonkers, NY 10703–1057   Washington, DC 20009

CONTINENTAL ASSOCIATION OF FUNERAL AND MEMORIAL SOCIETIES
   (CAFMS)
6900 Lost Lake Road
Egg Harbor, WI 54209–9231

CO-OP AMERICA
2100 M Street N.W., Suite 403
Washington, DC 20063

COUNCIL ON ECONOMIC PRIORITIES (CEP)
30 Irving Place   1601 Connecticut Avenue N.W.
New York, NY 10003   Washington, DC 20009

CRITICAL MASS ENERGY PROJECT
215 Pennsylvania Avenue S.E.
Washington, DC 20003

DIRECT MARKETING ASSOCIATION (DMA)
11 West 42nd Street   1101 17th Street N.W.
New York, NY 10036–8096   Washington, DC 20036–4704

EARTH ISLAND INSTITUTE (EII)
300 Broadway, Suite 28
San Francisco, CA 94133

EDISON ELECTRIC INSTITUTE (EEI)
701 Pennsylvania Avenue N.W.
Washington, DC 20004–2696

ENVIRONMENTAL DEFENSE FUND (EDF)
257 Park Avenue South   1875 Connecticut Ave. N.W.
New York, NY 10010   Washington, DC 20009

FOOD MARKETING INSTITUTE (FMI)
1750 K Street N.W., Suite 700
Washington, DC 20006

FOOD RESEARCH AND ACTION CENTER (FRAC)
1875 Connecticut Ave. N.W., Suite 540
Washington, DC 20009

FOUNDATION ON ECONOMIC TRENDS (FET)
1130 17th Street N.W., Suite 630
Washington, DC 20036

FRIENDS OF THE EARTH (FOE)
218 D Street S.E.
Washington, DC 20003

FUND FOR A FEMINIST MAJORITY (FFM)
1600 Wilson Blvd., Suite 801
Arlington, VA 22209

GREENPEACE, USA
1436 U Street N.W.
Washington, DC 20009

GROCERY MANUFACTURERS OF AMERICA (GMA)
1010 Wisconsin Avenue N.W.
Washington, DC 20007

HALT—AMERICANS FOR LEGAL REFORM (HALT)
1319 F Street N.W., Suite 300
Washington, DC 20004

HANDGUN CONTROL, INC. (HCI)
1225 Eye Street N.W., Suite 1100
Washington, DC 20005

HEALTH INSURANCE ASSOCIATION OF AMERICA (HIAA)
1025 Connecticut Avenue N.W.
Washington, DC 20036–3998

THE HERITAGE FOUNDATION
214 Massachusetts Avenue N.E.
Washington, DC 20002–4999

HUMANE SOCIETY OF THE UNITED STATES (HSUS)
2100 L Street N.W.
Washington, DC 20037

INDEPENDENT BANKERS ASSOCIATION OF AMERICA (IBAA)
One Thomas Circle N.W., Suite 950
Washington, DC 20005–5802

INFACT
256 Hanover Street
Boston, MA 02113

INSURANCE INSTITUTE FOR HIGHWAY SAFETY (IIHS)
1005 North Glebe Road
Arlington, VA 22201

INTERFAITH CENTER ON CORPORATE RESPONSIBILITY (ICCR)
475 Riverside Drive, Room 566
New York, NY 10115

LEAGUE OF WOMEN VOTERS OF THE UNITED STATES (LWVUS)
1730 M Street N.W.
Washington, DC 20036

MOTHERS AGAINST DRUNK DRIVING (MADD)
511 E. John Carpenter Freeway   1000 Vermont Avenue N.W.
Suite 700   Suite 400
Irving, TX 75062   Washington, DC 20005

NATIONAL AGRICULTURAL CHEMICALS ASSOCIATION (NACA)
1155 15th Street N.W., Suite 900
Washington, DC 20005

NATIONAL ASSOCIATION FOR THE ADVANCEMENT OF COLORED PEOPLE
    (NAACP)
4805 Mt. Hope Drive   1025 Vermont Avenue N.W.
Baltimore, MD 21215   Washington, DC 20036

NATIONAL ASSOCIATION OF ATTORNEYS GENERAL (NAAG)
444 North Capitol Street, Suite 403
Washington, DC 20001

NATIONAL ASSOCIATION OF INSURANCE COMMISSIONERS (NAIC)
120 West 12th Street   Hall of the States, Suite 636
Suite 1100   444 N. Capitol Street
Kansas City, MO 64105–1925   Washington, DC 20001–1512

NATIONAL ASSOCIATION OF MANUFACTURERS (NAM)
1331 Pennsylvania Ave. N.W., Suite 1500
Washington, DC 20004–1703

NATIONAL ASSOCIATION OF RAILROAD PASSENGERS (NARP)
900 Second Street N.E., Suite 308
Washington, DC 20002

NATIONAL ASSOCIATION OF REALTORS (NAR)

430 N. Michigan Avenue
Chicago, IL 60611–4087

777 14th Street N.W.
Washington, D.C. 20005–3271

NATIONAL ASSOCIATION OF REGULATORY UTILITY COMMISSIONERS
(NARUC)
1102 Interstate Commerce Commission Building
Constitution Avenue and 12th Street N.W.
Washington, DC 20423
Mailing Address:
P.O. Box 684
Washington, DC 20044–0684

NATIONAL ASSOCIATION OF STATE UTILITY CONSUMER ADVOCATES
(NASUCA)
1133 15th Street N.W., Suite 575
Washington, DC 20005

NATIONAL AUDUBON SOCIETY (NAS)

566 Pennsylvania Avenue N.W.
Washington, D.C. 20003

950 Third Avenue
New York, NY 10022

NATIONAL CATTLEMEN'S ASSOCIATION (NCA)

1301 Pennsylvania Avenue N.W.
Suite 300
Washington DC 20004

5420 S. Quebec Street
P.O. Box 3469
Englewood CO 80155

NATIONAL COALITION AGAINST PORNOGRAPHY (NCAP)
800 Compton Road, Suite 9224
Cincinnati, OH 45231

NATIONAL COALITION AGAINST THE MISUSE OF PESTICIDES (NCAMP)
530 7th Street S.E.
Washington, DC 20003

NATIONAL COALITION ON TELEVISION VIOLENCE (NCTV)
P.O. Box 2157
Champaign, IL 61825

NATIONAL CONSUMER LAW CENTER (NCLC)

11 Beacon Street
Boston, MA 02108

1875 Connecticut Avenue N.W.
Washington, DC 20009

NATIONAL CONSUMERS LEAGUE (NCL)
815 Fifteenth Street N.W., Suite 928
Washington, DC 20005

NATIONAL COUNCIL OF SENIOR CITIZENS (NCSC)
1331 F Street N.W.
Washington, DC 20004–1171

NATIONAL FEDERATION OF INDEPENDENT BUSINESS (NFIB)
600 Maryland Avenue S.W., Suite 700
Washington, DC 20024

NATIONAL FUNERAL DIRECTORS ASSOCIATION (NFDA)
11121 West Oklahoma Avenue
Milwaukee, WI 53227–0641

NATIONAL INSURANCE CONSUMER ORGANIZATION (NICO)
P.O. Box 15492
Alexandria, VA 22309

NATIONAL LEAGUE OF CITIES (NLC)
1301 Pennsylvania Avenue N.W.
Washington, DC 20004

NATIONAL TAXPAYERS UNION (NTU)
325 Pennsylvania Avenue S.E.
Washington, DC 20003

NATIONAL TOXICS CAMPAIGN (NTC)
1168 Commonwealth Avenue
Boston, MA 02134

NATIONAL TRAINING AND INFORMATION CENTER (NTIC)
NATIONAL PEOPLE'S ACTION (NPA)
810 North Milwaukee Avenue
Chicago, IL 60622

NATIONAL WOMEN'S HEALTH NETWORK (NWHN)
1325 G Street N.W.
Washington, DC 20005

NATURAL RESOURCES DEFENSE COUNCIL (NRDC)
40 West 20th Street
New York, NY 10011

OMB WATCH
1742 Connecticut Avenue N.W.
Washington, DC 20009–1171

OPERATION PUSH
930 East 50th Street
Chicago, IL 60615

PARENTS' MUSIC RESOURCE CENTER (PMRC)
1500 Arlington Boulevard, Suite 300
Arlington, VA 22209

PEOPLE FOR THE ETHICAL TREATMENT OF ANIMALS (PETA)
P.O. Box 42516
Washington, DC 20015

PUBLIC CITIZEN
2000 P Street N.W.
Washington, DC 20036

PUBLIC CITIZEN CONGRESS WATCH (PCCW)
215 Pennsylvania Avenue S.E.
Washington, DC 20003

PUBLIC CITIZEN HEALTH RESEARCH GROUP (PCHRG)
2000 P Street N.W., Suite 708
Washington, DC 20036

PUBLIC CITIZEN LITIGATION GROUP
2000 P Street N.W.
Washington, DC 20036

PUBLIC INTEREST RESEARCH GROUPS (PIRGs)
Addresses of state offices are listed at conclusion of the profile.

PUBLIC VOICE FOR FOOD AND HEALTH POLICY
1001 Connecticut Avenue N.W., Suite 522
Washington, DC 20036

RESOURCES FOR THE FUTURE (RFF)
1616 P Street N.W.
Washington, DC 20036

SAVINGS & COMMUNITY BANKERS OF AMERICA (SCBA)
900 19th Street N.W., Suite 400
Washington, DC 20006

SIERRA CLUB
730 Polk Street
San Francisco, CA 94109

SMALL BUSINESS LEGISLATIVE COUNCIL (SBLC)
1156 15th Street N.W., Suite 510
Washington, DC 20005

TOBACCO INSTITUTE (TI)
1875 I Street N.W., Suite 800
Washington, DC 20006

TRIAL LAWYERS FOR PUBLIC JUSTICE (TLPJ)
1625 Massachusetts Avenue N.W.
Washington, DC 20036

UNION OF CONCERNED SCIENTISTS (UCS)
26 Church Street
Cambridge, MA 02238

UNITED AUTO WORKERS (UAW)
8000 E. Jefferson
Detroit, MI 48214

U.S. CHAMBER OF COMMERCE (USCOFC)
1615 H Street N.W.
Washington, DC 20062

U.S. CONFERENCE OF MAYORS (USCM)
1620 Eye Street N.W.
Washington, DC 20006

U.S. PUBLIC INTEREST RESEARCH GROUP (U.S. PIRG)
215 Pennsylvania Avenue S.E.
Washington, DC 20003

BIBLIOGRAPHY

/

Berry, Jeffrey. 1989. *The Interest Group Society.* 2d ed. Glenview, IL: Scott, Foresman/ Little, Brown.

Bykerk, Loree. 1992. "Business Power in Washington: The Insurance Exception." *Policy Studies Review,* 11:3/4, 259–279.

Bykerk, Loree, and Ardith Maney. 1991. "Where Have All the Consumers Gone?" *Political Science Quarterly,* 106:4, 677–694.

———. 1994. "Consumer Groups and Coalition Politics on Capitol Hill." In Allan J. Cigler and Burdett A. Loomis, eds., *Interest Group Politics.* 4th ed. Washington, DC: CQ Press.

Clinard, Marshall B. 1990. *Corporate Corruption: The Abuse of Power.* New York: Praeger.

Crosby, Ned, Janet M. Kelly, and Paul Schaefer. 1986. "Citizens Panels: A New Approach to Citizen Participation." *Public Administration Review,* 46:170–178 (March/April).

Cunningham, Lynn E., et al. 1977. *Strengthening Citizen Access and Governmental Accountability.* Washington, DC: Exploratory Project for Economic Alternatives.

Derthick, Martha, and Paul J. Quirk. 1985. *The Politics of Deregulation.* Washington, DC: Brookings Institution.

DeSario, Jack, and Stuart Langton, eds. 1987. *Citizen Participation in Public Decision Making.* Contributions in Political Science no. 158. Westport, CT: Greenwood Press.

Galambos, Louis, and Joseph Pratt. 1988. *The Rise of the Corporate Commonwealth.* New York: Basic Books.

Goodman, Marshall R., and Margaret T. Wrightson. 1987. *Managing Regulatory Reform: The Reagan Strategy and Its Impact.* New York: Praeger.

Gormley, William T. 1983. *The Politics of Public Utility Regulation.* Pittsburgh: University of Pittsburgh Press.

Harris, Richard A. 1989a. "Politicized Management: The Changing Face of Business in American Politics." In Richard A. Harris and Sidney M. Milkis, eds., *Remaking American Politics*. Boulder, CO: Westview Press.

Harris, Richard A., and Sidney M. Milkis. 1989b. *The Politics of Regulatory Change*. New York: Oxford University Press.

———, eds. 1989c. *Remaking American Politics*. Boulder, CO: Westview Press.

Hawley, Ellis. 1978. "The Discovery and Study of a 'Corporate Liberalism.' " *Business and Society Review,* 52:309–320.

Katznelson, Ira. 1989. "Was the Great Society a Lost Opportunity?" In Steve Fraser and Gary Gerstle, eds., *The Rise and Fall of the New Deal Order, 1930–1980*. Princeton: Princeton University Press.

King, Anthony. 1990. "The American Polity in the 1990s." In Anthony King, ed., *The New American Political System*. 2d ed. Washington, DC: AEI Press.

Lichtenstein, Nelson. 1989. "From Corporatism to Collective Bargaining: Organized Labor and the Eclipse of Social Democracy in the Postwar Era." In Steve Fraser and Gary Gerstle, eds., *The Rise and Fall of the New Deal Order, 1930–1980*. Princeton: Princeton University Press.

Lilley, William III, and James C. Miller III. 1977. "The New Social Regulation." *The Public Interest,* no. 47 (Spring):49–61.

Lindblom, Charles E. 1977. *Politics and Markets*. New York: Basic Books.

———. 1982. "The Market as Prison." *Journal of Politics,* 44:324–336.

Loomis, Burdett A. 1986. "Coalitions of Interests: Building Bridges in the Balkanized State." In Allan J. Cigler and Burdett A. Loomis, eds., *Interest Group Politics*. 2d ed. Washington, DC: CQ Press.

McCann, Michael W. 1986. *Taking Reform Seriously: Perspectives on Public Interest Liberalism*. Ithaca, NY: Cornell University Press.

McFarland, Andrew. 1976. *Public Interest Lobbies: Decision Making on Energy*. Washington, DC: American Enterprise Institute.

———. 1984. *Common Cause*. Chatham, NJ: Chatham House.

———. 1988. "Interest Groups and Theories of Power in America." *British Journal of Political Science,* 17:129–147.

Nadel, Mark V. 1971. *The Politics of Consumer Protection*. Indianapolis: Bobbs-Merrill.

Nader, Ralph. 1973. *The Consumer and Corporate Accountability*. New York: Harcourt Brace Jovanovich.

———. 1983. "Introduction." In Mark Green, ed., *The Big Business Reader: On Corporate America*. New York: Pilgrim Press.

———. 1984. "The Consumer Movement Looks Ahead." In Alan Gartner et al., eds., *Beyond Reagan: Alternatives for the 80's*. New York: Harper & Row.

Pertschuk, Michael. 1982. *Revolt Against Regulation: The Rise and Pause of the Consumer Movement*. Berkeley: University of California Press.

———. 1986. *Giant Killers*. New York: W. W. Norton.

Salisbury, Robert H. 1991. "Putting Interests Back into Interest Groups." In Allan J. Cigler and Burdett A. Loomis, eds., *Interest Group Politics,* 3d ed. Washington, D.C.: CQ Press.

Schlozman, Kay Lehman, and John T. Tierney. 1986. *Organized Interests and American Democracy*. New York: Harper & Row.

Schmidt, David D. 1989. *Citizen Lawmakers: The Ballot Initiative Revolution*. Philadelphia: Temple University Press.

Tolchin, Susan J., and Martin Tolchin. 1983. *Dismantling America: The Rush to Deregulate.* Boston: Houghton Mifflin.

Vogel, David. 1981. "The 'New' Social Regulation in Historical and Comparative Perspective." In Thomas K. McCraw, ed., *Regulation in Perspective: Historical Essays.* Cambridge, MA: Harvard University Press.

———. 1989. *Fluctuating Fortunes: The Political Power of Business in America.* New York: Basic Books.

Walker, Jack L., Jr. 1991. *Mobilizing Interest Groups in America.* Ann Arbor: University of Michigan Press.

Weidenbaum, Murray L. 1975. "The New Wave of Government Regulation of Business." *Business and Society Review,* 15:81–86 (Fall).

Wilson, Graham K. 1981. *Interest Groups in the United States.* New York: Oxford University Press.

———. 1986. "American Business and Politics." In Allan J. Cigler and Burdett A. Loomis, eds., *Interest Group Politics.* 2d ed. Washington, D.C.: CQ Press.

———. 1990. "Corporate Political Strategies." *British Journal of Political Science,* 20: 281–288.

INDEX

/

About the Authors

LOREE BYKERK, Associate Professor in the Department of Political Science at the University of Nebraska at Omaha, coauthored *Consumer Politics: Protecting Public Interests on Capitol Hill* with Ardith Maney (Greenwood Press, 1994). She has written at length about interest groups and politics.

ARDITH MANEY, Associate Professor in the Department of Political Science at Iowa State University, has also served as Visiting Lecturer at the University of Glasgow and the University of Western Bohemia. She is the author of *Still Hungry After All These Years: Food Assistance Policy from Kennedy to Reagan* (Greenwood Press, 1989), and has worked also with officials in Central and Eastern Europe on projects associated with economic and political restructuring.

ISBN 0-313-26429-5

EAN

9 780313 264290

90000>

HARDCOVER BAR CODE